pruning
simplified

pruning simplified

A complete guide
to pruning trees, shrubs,
bushes, hedges, vines, flowers,
garden plants, houseplants, and bonsai

Lewis Hill

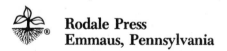

Rodale Press
Emmaus, Pennsylvania

Book design by Carol Stickles
Illustrations by Daryl Hunter

Printed in the United States of America on recycled paper,
containing a high percentage of de-inked fiber.

Library of Congress Cataloging in Publication Data

Hill, Lewis, 1924–
    Pruning simplified.

    Includes index.
    1. Pruning. I. Title.
SB125.H47   635.91'5'42   78–24372
ISBN 0-87857-248-1 hardcover
ISBN 0-87857-249-x paperback

        6 8 10 9 7 5   hardcover
    2 4 6 8 10 9 7 5 3   paperback

To Alain, Arthur, Denis, Edward, Fernand, Gerard, Jerry, Mario, Michel, Raymond, Rene, Richard, Robert, Roger, and all the other members of our 4-H club who over the years have helped in many demonstrations of pruning and organic gardening.

Contents

INTRODUCTION XIII

HOW TO USE THIS BOOK XV

CHAPTER 1
Pruning with a Clear Conscience 1

CHAPTER 2
Pruning with a Purpose 3
  Pruning while Transplanting 4
  Pruning to Train the Plant 7
  Pruning to Control Plant Size 7
  Pruning for Appearance 8
  Pruning for Production 9
  Pruning for Health 9
  Pruning for Rejuvenation 10
  Pruning for a Special Use 12

CHAPTER 3
Pruning Tools and Equipment 14
  Hand Clippers 15
  Saws 15
  Shearing Equipment 16
  Tree Sealers and Paint 18
  Better Safe Than 18
  Keep Your Tools in Shape 19

CHAPTER 4
Pruning Methods 21
  Shearing to Shape 22

Making Pruning Cuts 23
Making Large Cuts... 25
Basal Pruning 26
Pinching... 29
Disbudding... 29
Thinning Fruit.. 29
Beheading a Tree 30
Root Pruning.. 31
    The Oklahoma air-root pruning method 32
Prune According to Your Area... 36
When to Prune 36
    Are you a relocated gardener?...................................... 37
Prune According to Growth Habit 38
Pruning at Different Life Stages.. 38
The Ultimate Pruning Job 40
Beware of Overpruning.. 42

CHAPTER 5
Ornamental Trees and Shrubs.. 43
Pruning at Planting Time... 45
    Tabular list of ornamental trees 46
Pruning Flowering Trees 48
Pruning Flowering Shrubs 48
    Shrubs to be pruned after blooming 50
Restoring an Old Flowering Shrub.................................... 50
    Shrubs to be pruned before the buds show green........... 51
    Pruning old flowering shrubs 52
Pruning Lilacs 52
Pruning Roses 55
Pruning Shrubs with Colored Bark................................... 61
Fruit- and Berry-Producing Shrubs................................... 61
    Some shrubs that produce fruits or berries.................... 61
Shrubs That Need Special Care in Pruning 61

CHAPTER 6
Pruning Shade Trees 63
Pruning the Young Tree... 64
Tree Shapes.. 67
    Columnar, pyramidal, round, spreading, and weeping..... 68
Pruning the Mature Tree 69
Tree Surgery 70
Choosing the Proper Tree 72

CHAPTER 7
Pruning Evergreens.. 75
Classes of Evergreens... 75
Shearing and Pruning 76

CONTENTS

How Evergreens Grow 79
Shaping Specimen Evergreens 80
Shearing Dwarf Evergreens 81
Dwarfing Evergreens by Shearing 82
   Shear when wet 83
Pruning Narrow-Leafed Evergreens 83
Shearing Windbreaks and Screens 84
Can Older Evergreens Be Rejuvenated? 85
Pruning Broadleafed Evergreens 86

CHAPTER 8
Pruning Hedges 88
Pruning at Planting 90
Shearing a Hedge 90
   Making an arch 92
   Reviving an old hedge 92
Clipped Formal Hedges 94
Hedges for Barriers 95
Flower- and Berry-Producing Hedge Plants 96
Hedges Needing Little Care 97
   Easy-maintenance evergreen hedges 98
   Easy-maintenance deciduous hedges 98
Hedges Needing Careful Maintenance 99
Annual Hedges 99

CHAPTER 9
Artistic Pruning 100
Staking 101
Topiary 101
Espalier 103
Cordons 105
English Fences 106
Pruning a Japanese Garden 106

CHAPTER 10
Pruning Fruit Trees 108
Reasons for Pruning 109
   Central leader 114
   Modified leader 115
   Open center 116
When to Prune 123
   Lorette pruning 124
Winter Injury and Sunscald 126
   Pruning in snow country 127
Pruning Dwarf Trees 127
Dwarfing a Full-Size Tree 127
Pruning to Make Trees Bear 128

The Old Orchard 129
Pruning Sanitation 132
Cutting Grafting Wood 132
Pruning Spur-Type Fruit Trees 133
Pruning a Five-in-One Fruit Tree 133
Commercial Orchards 134
Apple 134
Apricot 139
Cherry 139
Citrus Fruit 140
Fig 140
Peach and Nectarine 141
Pear 142
Plum 144
Quince 145
Tropical and Semitropical Fruit 145

CHAPTER 11
Pruning Small Fruits 147
Grapes 147
The Bush Fruits 151
The Bramble Fruits 156
Strawberries 160

CHAPTER 12
Pruning Nut Trees 162
Pruning at Planting Time 164
Early Training 164
Pruning Mature Trees 165
Almond 165
Black Walnut and Butternut 165
Chestnut 166
Filbert 167
Hickory 167
Pecan 168
Walnut 168

CHAPTER 13
Pruning Vines and Ground Covers 170
Pruning at Planting Time 171
Early Training 172
Pruning the Mature Vine 172
Vines as blinds, vines for hedges 173
Vines for food and drink 174
The Twining Vines 174
The Clinging Vines 175
Blooming habits of clematis 176

x

CONTENTS

Annual Vines 178
Pruning Ground Covers 178

CHAPTER 14

Pruning Garden Plants and Houseplants 182
The Perennial Food Garden 185
Houseplants 186
Heavy Pruning 187
Hanging Baskets 188
Root Pruning 188
Pruning for Winter Storage 188

CHAPTER 15

Pruning Bonsai 190
Choosing Your Specimen 190
Containers 192
Equipment 192
Soil Mixture 192
Planting 193
Pruning 194
Training 194
Care 195
Repotting 196
Special Considerations 196

CHAPTER 16

Pruning Forest Trees 197
Pruning Christmas Trees 198
Pruning for Greens Production 198
Pruning for Maple Syrup Production 200

INDEX 203

Introduction

Did you ever watch an eight-year-old teach another eight-year-old how to play chess? It is a delightful experience, and in about ten minutes both can be having an enjoyable game. The teacher knows the right language to use, and the learner never has the slightest doubt that he can soon grasp the game.

But watch an adult chess expert try to teach another adult how to play, and it is nearly always painful. The expert knows far too much. He is likely to discuss all the scientific names for openings, middle game, and the closing. He dwells on all the possibilities and all the legends connected with chess. The beginner becomes far too confused, unsure, and intimidated to master such a complicated game.

Pruning is much the same. Pruning a bush or tree is not at all difficult, but sometimes the experts make it seem so. If I were showing you why and how to prune the tree in your backyard, the demonstration would be amazingly simple, and you would understand immediately. Certainly a book must be more complete, since you will want to use it as a reference for future jobs, some of which may be more involved. As you read the directions, however, learn the reasons for pruning, and begin actually making the cuts and observing the results, you will find that pruning is not the least bit complicated. Fortunately, pruning, like chess, has never been officially decreed the exclusive right of the experts.

Although you can learn pruning methods by reading a book, pruning skill, like skiing or riding a bicycle, can be learned only by actually doing it. Begin on small jobs so that you can observe carefully the consequences of each cut. You will come to know instinctively why, when, and how to prune and will then be on the way to becoming skillful — unless, of course, you are squeamish and faint at the sight of sap.

HOW TO USE THIS BOOK

Obviously you are interested in pruning, or you wouldn't have opened this book in the first place. However, people will consult these pages for a variety of reasons. Some may have a wide range of plantings that need attention, or perhaps only an overgrown hedge or a peach tree. If you want to prune only a specific evergreen in your front yard, or fruit trees, or flowering shrubs, you won't want to read an entire book on how to prune a lot of other plants in order to get the information you need; nevertheless, I suggest that you read the first four chapters before going on to the specific plant you are growing. These first chapters should help you decide whether or not your tree or plant needs pruning, help you choose the right equipment, and give you general pruning tips that are useful for all trees. For more details you then can read the chapter that deals with the specific plant or tree you want to prune.

Chapter 1

Pruning with a Clear Conscience

One fall day when I was working in the woods, I heard a noise high above me. A porcupine was sitting in the crotch of a large elm tree, skillfully cutting off large limbs and dropping them to the ground for easier nibbling. And in our back field last winter I came upon a flock of pine grosbeaks carefully nipping the buds off the Scotch pine trees.

Rabbits, mice, deer, elk, moose, and beaver also prune — not in a way that you and I would consider a horticultural achievement. They're just eating out at their favorite restaurants, but in doing so they fit into the forest's scheme of life very well.

Long before man ever thought of smithing his spear into a pruning hook, Nature was at work pruning, and she still is. High winds, snow, and ice storms help to keep trees healthy by snapping off old and weak branches. Occasionally an entire limb or top is broken off an old tree, and it grows an abundance of new branches, getting a new lease on life. In forests, the spreading tops and crowding trees shade the lower limbs of tall trees, causing them to die and fall off. Blights, hurricanes, floods, and fires set by lightning frequently thin out old trees and allow new ones to take their place.

Nature has even set up a system whereby fruit trees prune themselves by thinning their crops. We've all seen the hundreds of little apples or peaches that fall from trees in early summer if the fruit set is unusually heavy. A tree drops the extras that it hasn't the strength to develop to full maturity.

From the beginning of recorded time our early ancestors observed Nature's pruning methods and tried to improve on them. They developed the art so successfully that long before the great cities of Babylon, Jerusalem, or Athens had a stone in place, pruning was an accepted practice. It is mentioned frequently in the Bible and other ancient literature. Pruning was so well developed in those early days that it has changed amazingly little since then. Although no one is likely to use a pruning hook now, we still prune for the same reasons and in much the same way.

In spite of the long history of pruning, however, some people still question the wisdom of it. Should we interfere with the natural scheme of things? How can you improve on Nature? After all, a walk in the woods convinces that trees grow to magnificent beauty all by themselves.

The answer to these questions, I feel, is that we don't live in the wilderness anymore. We aren't able to spend all our days foraging for food. Instead we're more likely to live on tiny lots where our trees and shrubs must provide beauty, protection, food, and companionship, yet still not crowd us off our claim. We can no longer abandon our berry patch or orchard when it gets overgrown and cross the ridge to look for another homesteading plot. We can't move on just because the spruces we planted as a windbreak have begun to shut out the sun and view.

In other words, Nature is too leisurely and wasteful for our modern way of life. Although its function is to provide a healthy balance of plant and animal life, humans upset that balance long ago. These days we can't let our trees grow to full size, die, and rot peacefully for decades on the ground. We must, instead, give our plantings careful attention so that we can get the best possible use from them. We have to fertilize, prune, and protect them, and sometimes, when they have outlived their usefulness, remove them before they become a hazard. When we do these jobs we are not interfering, but rather working closely with Nature.

We frequently meet gardeners who don't feel completely comfortable about pruning and never take off quite enough wood, because they are nervous about hurting the plants. They know that plants look nicer and that fruit trees bear much better when they have been pruned, but they fear that each cut may be painful to the tree and that the whole idea is a bit sinful. The thought of keeping a tree sheared to a runty 4 feet when it might otherwise grow to 80 feet makes them feel guilty and uncomfortable. The fact is that pruning, when properly done, strengthens rather than weakens the tree.

As in all skills, certain rules must be followed, however, or pruning can be harmful. Some diseases can be spread by pruning tools, for instance. Pruning certain trees in late winter can result in a harmfully large sap loss. Cuts should be made so that the plant will grow attractively. Large cuts must be done skillfully, so there is no danger that the limb might accidentally split when it is only half cut off and tear back into the tree. What the rules amount to is that your shearing and cutting should be done for the right reason, in the right way, and at the proper time.

You can prune with a clear conscience, because it is one of the best things you can do for your trees. Liberty Hyde Bailey, the famous horticulturist, said it best many years ago: "Of all the operations connected with horticulture, pruning, shaping, and training bring the person into closest contact and sympathy with his plant."

Chapter 2

Pruning with a Purpose

One day a friend invited me into his backyard to point out a badly mutilated European highbush cranberry. "I read somewhere that all shrubs should be pruned occasionally, but I really didn't know how," he apologized. His intentions were good, but for that poor cranberry bush his little knowledge was dangerous. I felt that it would probably survive and look fine after a few more growing seasons, but his cuts could have killed a less-sturdy plant.

I feel that the basic premise of pruning should be: Always have a good reason for making each cut. Don't prune just for the sake of pruning. Pick up the clippers only to correct a faulty growing condition, to prevent a future problem, or to stimulate or redirect new growth. Very likely my friend's cranberry bush didn't need pruning at all, since European highbush cranberries grow very well on their own without pruning attention.

Since pruning should be done only for a solid reason, it's important to understand the growing habits of each of your plants, and to know exactly what you want them to do for you.

If you have a patch of raspberries, for instance, you must cut off their old canes each year, or the patch will deteriorate and disappear just as the wild ones do. Pruning is especially important if you are going to grow raspberries well, and you are not allowed much choice about it.

Yet you have a choice about how to prune some plants. A little blue spruce, for instance, might be pruned to serve in one of several ways. If you want to plant it near the front steps of your one-story house and plan to put lights on it at Christmas, you may want it to stay small for years. By shearing it closely every summer, you can keep it in a neat, tight, six-foot size almost forever.

On the other hand, if you want your spruce, along with a row of others, to grow into a thick, tight barrier between you and your noisy neighbors, you must prune it quite differently, allowing the side branches to grow thick and the top to stay low. Or, if you want it as a specimen that will grow by itself as a stately sentinel on your 50-acre estate, you probably will prune it very little or not at all.

Take a crab apple tree as another example. If you are growing it primarily to produce fruit for jellies and juice, it should be pruned as carefully as any fruit tree. You should thin the branches enough so sun can enter easily and thoroughly ripen all the fruit. Renew the old branches, and thin the fruit to encourage annual bearing. On the other hand, a crab apple grown for the beauty of its flowers and fruit may need very little pruning. Many varieties, like the Dolgo, grow into beautiful specimens with almost no training.

Crab apples also can be pruned into tight hedges that are almost impenetrable to animals and people by shearing them tightly several times during the summer, when they are growing, just as you would an evergreen hedge. They can be grown, also, as miniature trees in tubs, as espaliers on buildings, for shade, as a screen, and on and on.

Although not all plants are as versatile as the spruce and crab apple, you can still prune many of them in accordance with your needs and within the framework of their needs and growth habits.

The pages that follow will cover all sorts of reasons for pruning: transplanting successfully, training the plant, controlling size, improving appearance and health, encouraging better production, and rejuvenating an old specimen. Most pruning is done for a combination of reasons.

Pruning while Transplanting

Always get out your pruning tools at transplanting time, whether you've dug a plant yourself or you're planting a newly purchased, bare-rooted specimen. Whenever a tree or shrub is dug, and no matter how carefully, some root damage is almost certain. Even nursery trees, especially those that are dug by machine, are likely to have their roots cut and broken.

A tree or shrub planted with its top unpruned is badly off-balance. Often not enough roots are left to support the top properly, and many of the small, feeding, hair roots may be lost to the shovel. Then, as the plant leafs out, the root system will be unable to meet the increasingly heavy demands for nourishment.

You can easily remedy this undesirable situation by cutting back the top part of the tree rather severely. Fruit and shade trees planted in early spring with bare roots — that is, with the tree dormant and without a ball of soil around the roots — should be cut back about a third (either before or after planting, preferably after, as the tree is then held firmly in place).

New gardeners often hesitate to prune back an expensive, six-foot, well-branched tree to a four-foot whip. Experienced growers, however, know that, like priming an old-fashioned water pump, this is the best way to get things going. A pruned tree will quickly outgrow one that has not been pruned.

Compensatory pruning, as it is sometimes called, gives a better balance to the tree by more closely matching the top with whatever roots are left. By cutting off those buds that would have started growth earliest — those on the top of the tree and the ends of the side branches — you help prevent the new

4

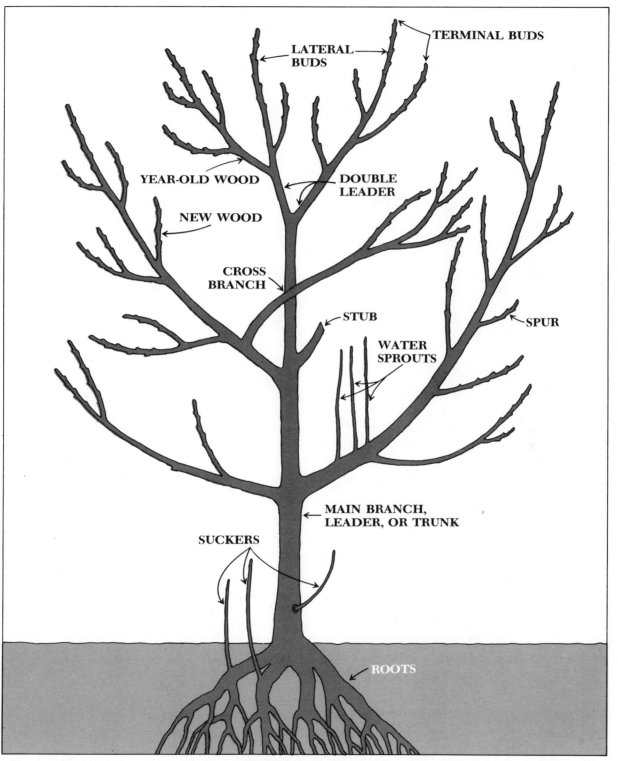

The parts of a tree.

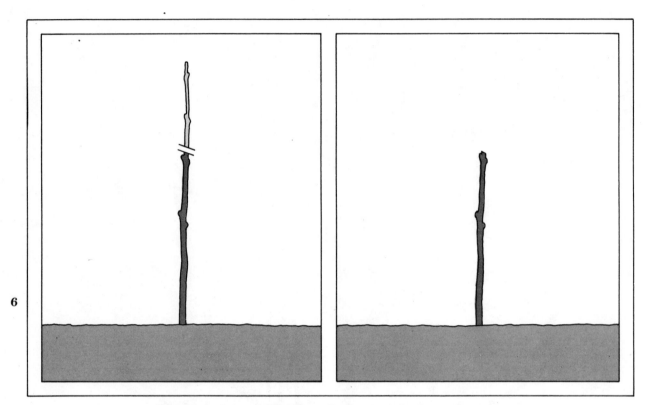

Pruning a 1-year-old unbranched tree (whip) at planting time. It is cut back one-third just above a healthy bud.

6

leaves from starting to grow as early as they otherwise would. On a pruned tree, root growth begins a bit ahead of leaf growth, and will probably always keep ahead of it, making a much stronger and better-growing tree.

Severe top pruning is needed for fruit and shade trees, flowering shrubs, roses, and hedge plants that are bought bare-rooted, even though the roots may be wrapped in a peat ball. If you dig up wild trees or plants, or if you transplant some of your own, prune them back severely. It is not only beneficial, but often essential to their survival.

Not all newly purchased trees need a drastic cutback, however. Those with a ball of soil carefully wrapped in burlap or plastic usually have most of their roots intact, as do trees that are sold growing in a large pot or tub. They need no compensatory pruning and can usually be safely planted anytime the ground isn't frozen.

Pruning to Train the Plant

Getting your newly planted tree off to a good start is one of the most important reasons for pruning. It is much better for your tree or bush to snip off undesirable branches when small, than to saw them off later.

You'll do a good job of training if you keep in mind the future use of the tree. For instance, a white pine tree that is to be kept dwarfed and bushy should have its sides and top sheared each year from its infancy. If you prefer that the pine grows into a large tree, instead of shearing it you should gradually snip off the lower limbs as the tree grows, thereby forcing its growth upward.

Although a fruit tree should be pruned only a bare minimum for the first few years after planting, so that its bearing won't be delayed, you should still prune a young tree to correct any bad crotches, to rectify any tendency the tree might have to grow lopsided, and to keep it from growing branches too close to the ground.

Most low-growing flowering shrubs, on the other hand, should be pruned when they are quite small by snipping back any skinny, tall-growing limbs; this encourages bushiness. Encourage young shade trees to grow tall and straight by correcting crotches and gradually removing the lower limbs.

In their maturity, most plants reap the benefit of some early training, just as do animals and humans, so don't neglect them in their formative years.

Pruning to Control Plant Size

If you're a gardener who works with a limited amount of land, you'd probably prefer to grow as many small plants as possible on your lot, rather than only one or two large specimens. By pruning, you can enjoy a wider variety of fruits and ornamentals than would be possible if you let the plants develop as they would in their natural state. Even most dwarf fruits, evergreens, and shrubs need some control or they will eventually get too wide.

Gardeners have discovered a great many ways to make the best use of limited space. One answer is to espalier dwarf fruit trees against a sunny wall like vines. Or, fruits or ornamentals can thrive in large tubs placed on patios and terraces. Indoor landscaping has become a popular hobby; many small trees and shrubs do well inside the house. Potted trees must be pruned carefully, since many of them are tropical and would grow to a considerable size in their native habitat.

Although dwarf varieties naturally lend themselves best to small space requirements, even large-growing trees can be kept small by severe pruning. A standard-size apple tree that might naturally reach 25 feet high and 30 feet in spread can be kept a fraction of that size. With very little trouble, hemlock or arborvitae trees that might otherwise grow 80 feet tall can be sheared into a hedge 2 feet tall by 1 foot wide.

Pruning is sometimes necessary for large trees and bushes that have begun to crowd power lines, driveways, sidewalks, or buildings. By snipping

7

back the offending branches, you can keep the plants useful, yet under control, for many years.

Pruning for Appearance

Years ago, on a visit to an eastern Ivy League college town, I was impressed with how terribly overgrown the landscaping looked around the lovely old homes. Most of the houses seemed buried behind massive clumps of yew, juniper, arborvitae, and azaleas. Possibly it was because many of the homes were rented, and people who don't own their homes don't fuss over them; or perhaps educators in those days were less interested in gardening than they are now. I don't know the reason, but I suspect that the shrubs had grown so gradually that the people who lived amongst them didn't even notice they were overgrown.

Even careful gardeners who take great pride in their homes sometimes let their plantings get away from them. New plants grow so slowly that they usually need little pruning the first few years. Suddenly they begin to grow rapidly, and soon they have become too large.

It's unfortunate that many landscapers like their work to look finished the day they put it in. To accomplish this they often use far more plants than necessary, which means that after a few years everything is too crowded. When this has happened, the extra plants should be removed, not just cut back.

Pruning for appearance involves much more than just controlling the size of the plants. It also means keeping evergreens and flowering shrubs well proportioned, removing sucker growth from the bottoms of the trees, and taking off limbs or blooms that detract from the appearance of the plant.

The entire area should be taken into consideration when you're deciding how to prune. Just as each tree and shrub should be chosen carefully and planted in the right spot, it should also be pruned so that it relates well to the rest of the planting, the house, other buildings, walks, and walls. A well-cared-for landscaping provides an attractive background for the house, just as a proper setting does for a fine jewel. Trees and shrubs should never be so showy that they detract from the house or hide it, unless you have something to hide. Plantings should look nice when viewed either from inside or outside the house.

Sometimes we are too close to our plants to see them objectively. One way to see them more clearly is to analyze your place with a fresh eye when you return home from a trip, or to compare old and new photos of your property. Are the proportions right? Do the shapes attractively compliment each other? Are you being severe enough, or are you too permissive?

A well-pruned landscape adds a great deal to the appearance and value of any property, yet can cost relatively little in time and money. In our area there are several farm homes planted with shrubs and trees mostly collected from the woods and pastures. These native plants are kept so well pruned and cared for that they produce a far more pleasing appearance than many expen-

8

sively landscaped homes that are somewhat neglected. Maintenance makes the difference.

Pruning for Production

People frequently choose to prune their plants so that they will produce larger or more attractive crops. A florist growing cut flowers for the market prunes differently than someone working in a front yard perennial border. A fruit grower prunes his apple trees differently than someone growing a decorative apple tree in the front yard for sentimental reasons. Likewise, anyone growing holly boughs for the Christmas market cares for the plants quite differently from a home gardener with a prize bush in his front yard. A berry grower wants his bushes to look nice, but his main concern is that the plants will produce large crops of attractive fruit each year for as many years as possible.

Commercial growers seldom have time to putter over their plants, and to a home gardener they sometimes seem careless and rather ruthless about their pruning. Actually they are sensible. They have learned how to prune for the greatest yield from their plants, and the vast amount of pruning they have to do makes them very efficient. Amateur gardeners can learn much from commercial pruning techniques.

Pruning for Health

Sometimes cuts are made as preventative medicine or to eliminate a disease. Even young trees and bushes occasionally have problems that pruning can solve, and aging trees, like aging people, often have numerous ones.

In spite of strict quarantine and inspections, some plants are already infected with diseases or insects when you buy them. Others, if they are newly dug and in a weakened condition or have just changed locales, may easily acquire them, because plants that are foreign to an area often do not have a built-in resistance to local troubles. Cultivated plants and landscape plants usually are subject to more disease and insect infestation than the wild, native ones.

Getting rid of the problem is the first order of business. Clip off stems, twigs, or branches that are mildewed or infested with borers, scale, or heavy infestations of other insects. Either burn them or bury them deeply so that the problem won't spread.

Dead, broken branches should be cut off smoothly to the main trunk or a limb to prevent dead stubs and jagged edges that provide an ideal situation for insect and disease invasion. Dead stubs will rot, eventually, and the rot may spread into the rest of the tree.

Animals can be a menace to the health of your tree. If you notice that mice or rabbits have chewed the bark off branches that are near the ground, snip off the branches. Any limb that has had its bark removed completely around it, will not live long no matter how narrow the girdle. It may leaf out and appear to be healthy for a while, but it will eventually die. You should

9

protect the trunks of fruit trees and other tasty plants that are susceptible to rodent nibbling with wire screening, plastic guards, or aluminum foil. Make sure the barrier extends to the height of the expected snow cover.

Large animals sometimes do their own pruning, of a sort that isn't often in the best interest of the tree. Deer and elk damage trees and shrubs by chewing off the branches and even snapping off whole limbs. Cut back ragged, chewed ends to the next undamaged limb, and smooth up and paint all wounds they've made by breaking off limbs or by rubbing the bark with their antlers. Trim off upper limbs on large trees that have been damaged by porcupines. If the chewing does not go completely around the limb, paint the wounded areas with a good tree paint such as Treekote.

Trees are damaged when branches rub buildings and other branches. Remedy these situations by snipping off the offending limbs as soon as you notice them. If you do nothing, they usually suffer bark damage that invites infection. Crossed branches are more likely to occur on deciduous trees than on shrubs or evergreens.

Remove water sprouts (the clusters of branches that grow straight upward, often from an old pruning wound) as soon as they form. These weaken the tree and cause unattractive growth that will be hard to deal with later in its life.

It's important to clip off all the suckers or little trees that sprout up either from the trunk or from the roots. These sap the tree's energy, and if you allow them to grow, they will spoil its appearance, turning it into a large bush. Furthermore, unchecked suckers growing from the wild rootstock of a grafted fruit or shade tree can crowd out the desirable part of the tree and make it useless.

Many fruit trees are especially susceptible to insects and disease, and should be pruned to prevent diseases and insect infestations. Trouble is encouraged by too-warm or too-cool temperatures and high humidity; by thinning out superfluous branches, you can admit beneficial sunlight and moving air into a tree's interior.

Pruning for Rejuvenation

Pruning often restores vitality to a shrub or tree that is beginning to show symptoms of age and is not ready to retire. There is a large, old maple in our neighborhood that, a dozen years ago, was in sad shape. A violent wind storm had broken off nearly a third of it. We expected the old tree to die, but instead thousands of new sprouts started and, with no help whatsoever from tree experts, the tree grew back all of its missing parts and more. Today it is in handsome shape and looks as if it will last for many more years.

Although you may be tempted to prune every elderly planting to stimulate new growth, this doesn't always work. Some trees and shrubs seem to enjoy being rejuvenated by severe pruning and some do not. Many kinds of roses do their best only if you cut them back nearly to the ground each year. Clematis vines, potentilla, hydrangea, lilacs, and honeysuckle all seem to benefit from occasional drastic pruning.

10

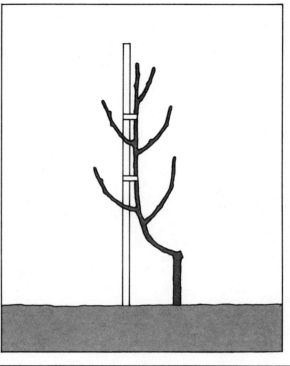

A young, forked tree can often be shaped into a strong, straight specimen by cutting off one of the forks and staking the other. In time, the crook in the stem should straighten.

Most berry-producing shrubs, on the other hand, such as cotoneaster and viburnum, need little or no pruning. And in spite of our old maple's resuscitation, drastic pruning is usually risky on old shade trees. Neither broadleafed evergreens nor conifers are likely to benefit greatly by severe dehorning (beheading) measures, either. Unless the tree is young and vigorous, a drastic slashing may prove fatal.

Rejuvenation by light and frequent pruning is usually preferable to a heavy cutback, especially on older trees and bushes. Regular pruning that begins early in a tree's life is not only less of a shock for a plant or tree, but it always looks better than a full-scale attack with shears and saw.

Orchardists prefer to renew gradually the bearing wood on their fruit trees by the annual removal of part of the older branches. This is also the best way to prune bush fruits such as blueberries, currants, and gooseberries. The bearing is uninterrupted, regrowth is moderate, and the bush or tree suffers no serious setback.

In warmer parts of the country and in tropical and semitropical climates, severe pruning is more widely practiced than in the cooler sections. Fast regrowth almost always follows a major pruning job, and in the North the soft, new growth often doesn't get completely hardened before autumn frosts begin. Winter injury results, and the tree, already weakened by abnormal pruning and regrowth, may be permanently weakened or killed outright.

Pruning for a Special Use

Tall shrubs and trees are often planted for shade, windbreaks, or sound barriers. If you live in an exposed area, a strategically placed planting of a few trees can often save a considerable amount of your heating or air-conditioning costs, or provide protection for a swimming pool, picnic spot, play area, or terrace. A tight-growing windbreak can also shield plantings of roses, berries, or fruit trees that may not be completely hardy in your area, from cold north winds. A hedge allows the soil in a vegetable or flower garden to warm up more quickly in the spring by shielding it from the wind. Evergreen hedges stop snow from drifting onto roads and paths, help to block out annoying traffic noises and fumes, and hide undesirable vistas. A hedge can provide privacy in crowded neighborhoods, also.

Pruning is frequently performed to make trees salable. A forester prunes all the lower limbs off his timber trees so that the first saw log will be completely free from knots and make fine lumber. Likewise, a Christmas tree grower prunes and shears closely so that his trees will look nice in the living room.

An old sage in our neighborhood used to say, "If you want to be happy for a weekend, get drunk. If you want to be happy for a fortnight, get married. But if you want to be happy for a lifetime, have a garden!"

Besides the benefits of fresh air, sunshine, and physical exercise, gardening offers one of the best kinds of mental therapy. It is being used successfully in the treatment of juvenile delinquents and hardened criminals. Puttering in the garden can help ease the shock that sometimes follows retirement, too.

"I work out lots of my hostility while pruning," one gardener told me. "If I am worked up over the IRS, the political situation, or my boss, I can take it out very effectively by slashing at the shrubbery. Wonderful results. I feel great." His plants look great, too.

Although there is certainly nothing wrong with being a happy pruner, we always tell our customers that if they are new at shearing evergreens and hedges, they are likely to get the best results if they are a bit "het up." A novice probably won't trim severely enough if he goes at the job singing and whistling.

You'll find it helpful to observe a skilled pruner at work. But before you take advantage of such a free lesson, be sure he is both really skillful and honestly willing to share his talents. With pruning, as with all gardening lore, a lot of misinformation gets passed around freely, often in a most convincing and knowledgeable manner.

You may prefer to keep a very natural look in your plantings, or you may feel an uncontrollable urge to create effects that will make traffic detour to drive by your place. Either way, if you follow the basic rules you can prune with a clear conscience, knowing that your trees and plants won't suffer a bit. Hopefully, it will make them, and you, feel better.

Chapter 3

Pruning Tools and Equipment

When shopping for pruning tools, you might be a bit overwhelmed by the assortment available. The home gardening boom has caused manufacturers and importers to offer as wide a range as possible. On my desk there's a mail-order catalog that features forestry and horticultural supplies. It lists 24 different kinds of hand pruning shears, 14 different long-handled pruners, and 19 hedge shears, as well as dozens of kinds of hand saws, pole pruners, power tools, and a huge assortment of sharpening tools, tree paint, and other such supplies.

Most hardware stores, garden centers, and department stores offer pruning equipment, though their assortment may be more modest than the catalog listing. If possible, you should look over the different models available, and try out how they feel in your hand before buying. Pruning tools were made in much the same way for many years, but recently manufacturers have tried to design equipment that fits the hand better and is easier and more comfortable to use. The quality of the tools varies widely. Hand pruners, for instance, range from cheap ones costing less than $5 to deluxe models that cost more than $25. For most home gardening you won't need the heavy-duty, expensive tools that commercial growers prefer, but the very lightweight, cheaply made ones are no bargain. When you're looking for equipment, the advice of your gardening friends may prove helpful.

Whether or not you choose to use power tools is a matter of personal preference. If you have lots of shearing and heavy pruning to do, you will find electric hedge shears and power saws useful. Naturally, those people who love motors and expensive gadgets will buy power equipment, while others who prefer the economy and quiet of hand tools will shy away from it.

A large assortment of tools is not at all necessary to do competent pruning. Although I've seen garden sheds that are filled with more equipment than most stores offer, there is no need to have a different tool for each plant. What follows is a list of the basic equipment you may want to consider.

Hand Clippers

Hand clippers, shears, pruners, or snips, as they are variously called, are the main tool for home use and a real necessity. Choose a quality kind. The cheap ones spring easily and don't make a smooth cut.

Hand pruners are made in two types. One works by a snap-cut method in which a sharp blade hits squarely against an anvil, and the other is a scissors type which allows a sharp blade to move past an edged one, as in scissors. Obviously some people prefer one and some the other, or both kinds wouldn't be manufactured, but I prefer the snap or anvil type for most jobs. They are less likely to need adjusting, and the blade can be easily sharpened or replaced. Most are about six inches long and can be used for everything from clipping your houseplants to pruning small twigs in the orchard.

If you have high shrubbery you'll also need pruners with long handles. These loppers are usually of the scissors type, and their increased leverage is suited also for heavier work, such as pruning fruit trees. Choose a well-made kind that won't break on the heavier jobs. Some long-handled pruners have compound levers for extra-heavy work, and these are especially good for cutting brush and thinning out excessive growths of plant material, as is done to tame an overgrown lilac bush.

The hand pruner has been developed into a pole pruner, incorporating a set of extensions that allows you to reach farther up into a tree. The blade is activated by pulling a rope that, when released, allows the blade to return to its normal position by the action of a strong spring. Pole pruners are handy for a lot of high work, especially in places where the use of a ladder would be difficult or dangerous.

Saws

Pruning saws should be used for all heavy work. Heavy-duty, long-handled pruners, even those with compound levers, tend to squeeze the limb being cut, with resulting damage to the bark. I feel that it is usually better to saw any limb measuring over 3/4-inch in diameter.

There are fine-toothed saws for smooth work and others that have coarse teeth for the faster sawing of large limbs. You may want one of each if you plan to do a lot of pruning. Otherwise you'll probably get along with a curved-blade, fine-tooth saw. I prefer the lightweight bow saw for heavier pruning jobs because it is fast, easy to use, and a handy tool in the woodlot. Carpenter's saws are not effective on live wood, and they tend to gum up and stick too much.

Pole saws give the operator extra reach, enabling him to do heavy cutting while standing securely on terra firma. However, I've found that most of them are slow and rather laborious to use.

Chain saws are useful for removing and cutting up entire trees and for sawing off large limbs, but most are designed more for cutting wood or lumber than for pruning. The cuts are usually rough, and the machine is difficult to control for precision work. Even if your chain saw is small, it is extremely easy to slash into the wrong limb, scar the trunk, or do other damage when you're pruning a tree with the limbs close together.

Shearing Equipment

Shearing, a form of pruning, involves removing soft new growth in order to get the tree to grow into a certain shape. Shearing is done primarily to dwarf trees, to shape hedges, or to develop formal or topiary shrubbery. Because shearing does not involve cutting of any heavy wood, you'll need different equipment than for regular pruning.

Long-handled hedge shears are the most common hand tools for shearing, because they are safe, durable, easy to control, and inexpensive. They are adequate for most shearing jobs, are easily sharpened, and require little muscle power. Some are available with extra-long handles, making them especially good for high work such as reaching to the top of a hedge. They're handy too, because they allow you to shear dwarf shrubs without bending over.

For extensive hedge shearing, however, electric shears are well worth the price. These shears, or clippers, vary from small, light, inexpensive models to the heavy-duty kind necessary for rugged work. Although it is generally unwise to buy the very cheap ones, most gardeners are not likely to need the costly professional models either.

When you're choosing electric clippers, inspect them carefully to be sure that they will shear the type of hedge you have. Some of the small, light models do not open wide enough for cutting heavy plant growth, although privet, ninebark, boxwood, and hemlock can usually be sheared well with lightweight clippers. If you need to cut fir, spruce, pine, arborvitae, or other coarse-twigged evergreen or deciduous plants, make certain that the shears open up wide enough to make clean cuts and don't just chew off the branches in a ragged fashion.

Hedge clippers are now available in cordless models with rechargeable batteries that eliminate the nuisance of a long electrical cord. If you use clippers with a cord, you must be careful not to let the cord get in the way. Several times I have accidentally snipped off the cord along with the shrubbery. Now I enclose the two feet of cord nearest to the clippers in a piece of 1/2-inch plastic pipe, taping the pipe to the cord so it won't slip. This makes an accidental cut less likely.

Instead of hedge shears or electric clippers, some gardeners prefer a light, fast, thin-bladed machete called a shearing knife. Christmas tree growers especially like their light weight and the fact that they are so easy and fast to use. You must be extremely careful not to shear yourself, however; professionals usually wear heavy gloves and leg guards when using them. Because the shearing knife is long, it is not the best tool to use in close work such as shearing miniature evergreens, but it is useful on hedges and windbreaks. A

16

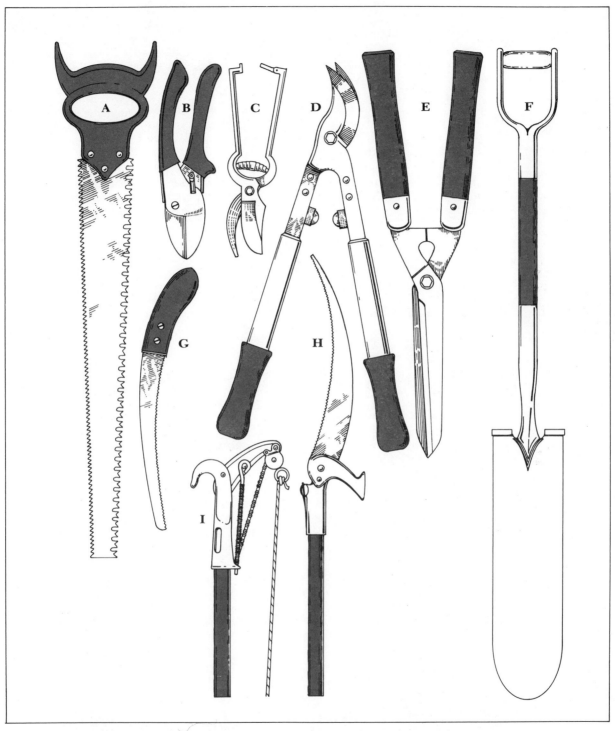

Pruning tools. (A) *Double pruning saw, with coarse teeth on one side for heavier pruning jobs.* (B) *Anvil-type hand pruner.* (C) *Scissors-type hand pruner.* (D) *Loppers, or long-handled pruners.* (E) *Hedge shears.* (F) *Long-bladed spade for root pruning.* (G) *Pruning saw.* (H) *Pole saw.* (I) *Pole pruners.*

shearing knife also has the advantage of being low-priced, durable, and extremely easy to keep sharpened.

When I'm using my machete, for safety's sake I like to keep a pair of hand clippers or a sharpening stone in my left hand as I shear with my right, avoiding the dangerous temptation to hold up a limb in front of the knife. It sounds something like preventing smashed thumbs by holding the hammer in both hands while driving nails, but it works.

You'll need one more tool to complete your pruning kit. A long-bladed nursery spade is useful for cutting off the outside roots of trees, either to check their growth or to create a compact root ball that can be safely dug up and transplanted.

Tree Sealers and Paint

Those in forestry and horticulture circles argue over the use of tree paint for sealing pruning cuts. One school of thought is that trees compartmentalize their injuries and provide their own sealing process: the tree's natural chemical and biological methods work far better than any man-made ones. Those on the opposing side are convinced that it is better to seal any wound promptly against weather, disease, and insects. Although trees may provide this protection for themselves, they don't do it quickly enough, especially if the tree is getting along in years.

Although I find neither argument totally convincing, I continue to seal up the wounds on my trees with tree paint because it makes the wound look neater and makes me feel better about it. Also, many fungi spores and bacterial diseases are always present in the air during the growing season, and an open, unsealed wound is a hearty invitation to them. It's nice to think that you've made infection a bit less likely.

There are several tree paints and dressings on the market. You can apply paints with a paint brush, or use aerosol sprays for small jobs. An easy-to-spread tree paint has been developed for use in the cold winter months.

Tree dressings are thicker than paint and are good for filling cracks in the bark as well as for sealing other small wounds. Some also can be used as a substitute for wax when grafting fruit trees. You can spread them on easily with a small paddle or putty knife.

Is tree paint any better than ordinary house paint? The question is debatable. Many people feel that paint merely seals up the wood and keeps out the weather, and therefore nearly any outdoor paint will protect the tree. Most tree paints contain an antiseptic, however, and many experts think that this helps to prevent future infections.

Large tree wounds often take many years to heal properly, and since no paint is permanent, repainting or resealing every year or two will be necessay until new growth completely covers the wound.

Better Safe Than . . .

Although pruning hardly qualifies as a hazardous hobby, it would be embarrassing to shift from performing surgery on a tree to having some performed on yourself. Keep the following safety pointers in mind.

Whenever you use a ladder, make sure it is solidly placed at the correct angle against a strong limb or the trunk of a tree. Resist the temptation to climb that extra rung or to reach out too far. And even if it's handy, a chair is never a safe substitute for a ladder.

Protective clothing is not a necessity, but a hard hat, motorcycle helmet, or snowmobile helmet can give added protection when using pole pruners or when you're sawing off limbs over your head. Heavy gloves help to prevent skin abrasions, and they're useful whenever you need to move heavy or thorny limbs or evergreen brush.

Chain saws are the most dangerous pruning equipment, and I know many expert woodsmen who have had serious accidents while using them. If you must use a power saw, either electric or gasoline, be particularly careful, especially when you're working on a ladder. Always keep your saw sharpened — a dull saw is dangerous. Avoid making the type of cuts that will pinch the saw or cause it to kick back. Keep it a safe distance from your body at all times. And finally, never use a chain saw when you are overtired.

If you do any shearing, long-handled hedge shears are probably the safest thing you can use. Shearing knives, as I mentioned, are especially high-risk tools and are best left to foresters and professionals. If you decide to use them, be sure to wear heavy gloves, leg guards, or very thick pants.

Make sure that any electric hedge clippers you use have the UL Seal of Approval, and be careful to keep them away from arms and legs when in operation. They should be kept well-oiled at all times so that they'll run smoothly and won't overheat.

Always avoid operating electric clippers or electric chain saws during or directly after a rain. Most directions recommend wearing rubber boots for insulation if you use electrical tools when the ground is at all wet. If you work on a ladder, a wooden one is safer than one made of metal when you're using electrical equipment.

You'd probably never think of using metal pole pruners or aluminum ladders anywhere near overhead power lines, but if we're to judge from the obituary column, some people do.

Keep Your Tools in Shape

Sharpening a shearing knife is easy if you know how to sharpen a kitchen knife or pocketknife. A grindstone, Carborundum stone, whetstone, or sharpening steel will do the job nicely. You can also take apart clippers and hedge shears to sharpen them with one of these stones or a file. You will have to sharpen anvil-type clippers so that the whole blade edge hits the anvil evenly and makes clean cuts.

Saws are trickier to sharpen, so unless you have been trained in this field, leave the job to an expert. You can usually find a local sharpener by looking in area newspapers or the Yellow Pages. Hardware stores sometimes offer this service.

Clippers, pruners, and electric hedge shears need an occasional drop of light motor oil on their moving parts to keep them operating well. If you use your tools on evergreens, clean off the pitch deposits periodically with kerosene. To protect metal surfaces from rust, occasionally wipe all equipment with a soft cloth dipped in light oil. Do this little chore without fail before you store the tools each winter.

Some gardeners like to hang all their tools on a pegboard or plywood sheet with a drawing or sign to indicate which goes where. This organized system makes it easy to identify missing tools and helps to ensure that they won't be left outside overnight or during a rain shower.

Sources of Pruning Tools

A.M. Leonard, Inc., 6665 Spiker Road, Piqua, OH 45356

Montgomery Ward. Mail-order offices in many cities.
Their farm catalog lists many tools and supplies.

Chapter 4

Pruning Methods

Just as an artist develops his own style of painting, each pruner develops a method of his own. However, there are certain basic rules and methods to follow that make the job neater, easier, and more beneficial to the plant.

Before you begin to prune, it helps to understand how woody shrubs and trees grow. Most of them make their spring and summer growth from buds that were set during the previous season. Although I occasionally meet people who think that a tree grows by slowly pushing itself up out of the ground like a snake coming out of a hole, most people know better. You only have to find a tree where lovers carved their initials a half-century ago to see that this isn't so! Trees and shrubs grow from the top and from the tips of their side branches. The trunk itself grows larger by the expansion of the cambium layer just under the bark, adding a new layer of wood to the outside of the trunk each year.

The new buds may start under the stem of a leaf, or they may form anywhere on the branch. Terminal buds are those at the top of a tree and at the ends of the branches, and lateral buds form along the limbs. These buds, if undisturbed, will grow into new tops, leaves, and branches during the following season.

In addition to these large and easily visible terminal and lateral buds, most plants and trees form many less obvious, tiny buds along the branches and sometimes under the bark. These are called dormant, adventuresome, or internodal buds. Unlike ordinary buds, these are reserve buds, the plant's insurance policy — they will grow only if something happens to the regular buds. Some plants produce these buds in tremendous numbers and others in lesser amounts, but most garden and forest plants and trees have them. Much of the skill in pruning involves knowing how to make good use of these buds in order to redirect growth or rejuvenate the plant.

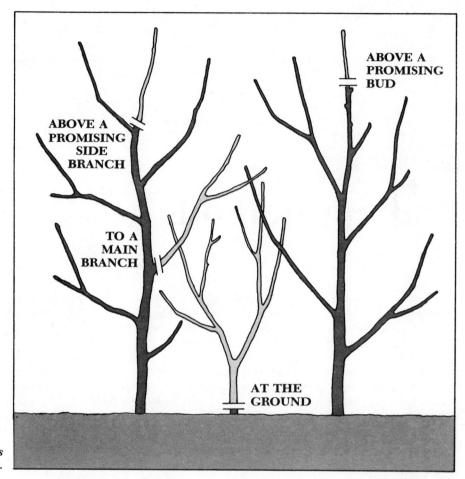

ABOVE A
PROMISING
BUD

ABOVE A
PROMISING
SIDE
BRANCH

TO A
MAIN
BRANCH

AT THE
GROUND

22

*Places where pruning cuts
can be made safely.*

Shearing to Shape

Although the term "pruning" includes any cutting or shaping of a plant, the type of pruning done entirely to shape the plant is called shearing. A plant is usually sheared when it is making its most active growth, as that growth is soft and easy to cut. Pruning, on the other hand, is essentially the cutting of older twigs and branches that have completed their growth and have hardened.

Shearing involves redirecting growth as well as removing unwanted growth. By shearing a plant that would normally grow upward and outward, you stimulate the adventuresome buds among the inner branches to wake up and grow. This results in thick, bushy growth.

For best results you should begin to shear a few days after plant growth starts in late spring, so that the redirecting of growth will begin early enough to be effective. A common mistake in shearing evergreens and hedges is to wait until the end of the growing season to cut off all the new growth to shape the plant. If a plant has its new growth neatly chopped off each year it will never get more bushy, because few of the adventuresome buds ever get a chance to grow. Furthermore, the clipped ends are likely to show throughout the year, because after the growing season no new growth will cover them.

On the other hand, when you begin shearing early, you curtail the growth of the end buds immediately. New buds will eventually grow where the cuts were made, but even before that the adventuresome buds will be stimulated to grow, resulting in a bushier plant or a tighter hedge.

Making Pruning Cuts

Since you should shear mainly the plant's soft, new growth, it is not necessary to give any special consideration to where you make your cuts. The newly cut ends will heal over, form a bud at the end, and be ready to grow the following spring.

Pruning on older wood is quite a different story. Since the plant's growth comes from its buds, carefully make the decision of where to cut.

Always cut to a bud whenever you are pruning back a branch. If you make a cut between buds, you'll leave a stub with no life in it. In addition to the fact that it looks ugly, the dead stub will rot, and the rot can spread easily

23

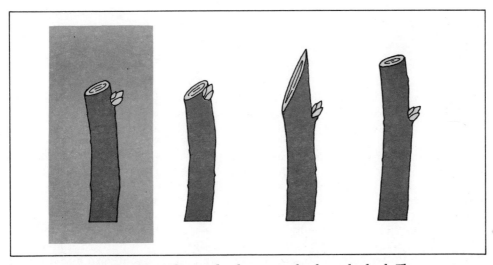

A cut should not be overly close to or far from the bud. The cut on the far left is ideal.

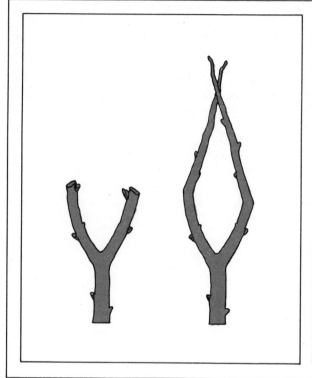 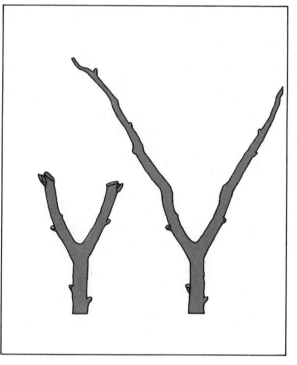

Pruning branches to inside buds will lead to ingrown limbs (left). Cutting above outside buds produces a more spreading tree (right).

24

to the rest of the tree. Likewise, when you're cutting off dead branches — for example when pruning a rose bush that has suffered winter damage — always cut back to a live bud or branch so that no dead wood will be left on the plant.

The angle of the cut is as important as its location. A slanting cut is best because it leaves less stub, and the slant dries out faster after a rain. The slant should be about 1/4-inch above the bud. If you make it closer than that, the tender part of the bud is so near to the cut end that the bud may not receive enough sap, or it may be damaged by freezing.

Now, to which bud should you cut? Trees have buds at various places on their limbs, and you should look for an outside bud and cut just above it. A limb or twig growing from an outside bud tends to grow outward and upward, whereas one from an inside bud tends to grow inward. Since you're aiming to have an increasingly spreading and upward-growing tree and want to avoid

Cut off the top of a small tree to encourage side-branching.

any crossed or inward-heading branches, make your slanting cuts above the outside buds.

Most deciduous trees and shrubs have alternate buds: when you see a bud on one side of the branch, you will find one farther along on the other side. A few trees, however, including maples and ash, grow their buds and leaves directly opposite each other. When you're pruning a branch with opposite buds, it is best to cut just above one of the double buds and snip or rub off the inside bud, leaving only the outside one intact.

Making Large Cuts

When you're pruning fruit trees and older shade trees, it is often necessary to cut off large limbs. Just as you'd cut to a live bud on small trees and shrubs, be sure to cut a large limb back to a live branch or to the main trunk

Heavy cuts should be made in three stages. First, make an undercut (1), then saw through where indicated at 2. Make a final cut to remove the stub (3).

26

of the tree so that no stub is left to rot away. The new bark cannot grow over and cover even a short stub.

When you cut off a larger, heavier limb, be careful to make the cut so that its weight doesn't cause the partly sawed-off branch to break and split back into the next branch or into the trunk of the tree. Avoid this problem by cutting in two or more steps, as illustrated.

First, make an undercut with the saw about 6 inches out from the trunk. Then, about an inch beyond that, cut off the limb. Don't bear down on the saw — let the sharp teeth of the saw do the cutting. Finally, cut off the remaining stub. The result is a smooth cut with no damage to the tree.

Even if done carefully, pruning opens up wounds on a tree. While most people are likely to be careful of their small trees and bushes, they forget that large trees need protection as well. Be careful not to make unnecessary wounds by careless use of equipment. If you use a ladder, don't let it slide along the branches and scar the bark. If you use a rope, don't let it slip, either. Gently lower pruned limbs instead of letting them crash onto other limbs.

Choose the shoes you wear with your tree in mind. Climbing in rubber or plastic soles is less harmful to the tree — and you — than leather ones that might slip. And, of course, lineman's spikes or hobnailed shoes should never be worn while climbing in a valuable tree.

Basal Pruning

Basal pruning involves cutting off limbs at the base of the tree. Sometimes trees are basal-pruned for aesthetic reasons. You can keep them the proper size for their function, or create interesting effects with evergreens or flowering trees. There are functional reasons for basal pruning as well, such as to open up living areas under large trees or to make it easier to control insects that bore into tree trunks. Highway departments and power companies sometimes practice basal pruning on shade trees to force the growth away from highway traffic or power lines. Woodsmen often basal-prune to grow long, straight logs that are knot-free. Christmas tree plantation owners do it to produce better-shaped Christmas trees, as do orchardists to aid in mechanical harvesting of fruits and nuts.

Like all pruning, basal pruning should be done when it will least damage the tree. In late summer or early fall the sap is fairly inactive, and little of it is lost by the pruning.

As in all kinds of pruning, use common sense and cut off only a few limbs during any one year so that you won't shock the tree too much. Usually a fifth of the height of a branched part of a tree can be basal-pruned at one time with no severe setback to the tree. Thus, a tree 30 feet tall with 25 feet of limb growth could be basal-pruned up about 5 feet in any one year without endangering the tree. Two or three years should elapse before you attempt the next basal pruning, however. If you're working with an older tree that has quite large lower limbs, fewer of them should be removed in any one three-year period.

27

Always cut a large limb back to a live branch or to the main trunk of the tree so that no stub is left to rot away.

28

Creating a mushroom or umbrella tree. Pruning must take place over a period of years, gradually removing both the basal and top limbs and encouraging a wide growth.

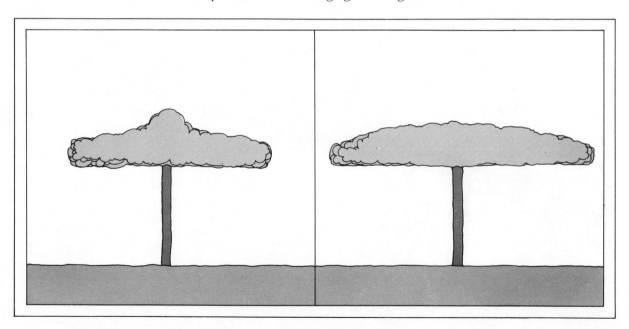

The lower limbs of evergreens are often dead or nearly so, especially if the trees are growing close together. All of these dried-out limbs can be cut off at any time of year without damaging the tree.

Pinching

Most good gardeners like to do a great deal of their pruning by pinching off any new growth that is heading in the wrong direction. With the thumb and forefinger you can remove the end tip (the growing part of the branch) to stop all growth in that area temporarily. You'll avoid a great deal of future pruning by strolling frequently through your yard and orchard during the growing season, pinching as you go.

Some gardeners like to carry a pair of hand pruners on their belt during the spring and summer, ready to draw them out at the first sign of unwanted growth. I know one grower who prefers a sharp jackknife for minor pruning of new growth that is too advanced for pinching. Dedicated, frequent pinching throughout the growing season is an efficient way to remove suckers, shorten branch growth, take off extra tops, and redirect growth with the least possible shock to the plant. It is also a useful way to disbud flowers and to thin out fruit.

Disbudding

We have several large old peony plants that produce hundreds of buds each year. If left to their own devices, they would bring forth lots of small and medium-size blooms. But peonies are such a magnificent flower that it's a shame to let them miss their full potential. So when the buds are still small we pinch off most of them, leaving only one on each stem. Now we haven't nearly as many flowers, but each one is a gorgeous giant and so heavy that the plant has to be carefully staked to support them. Florists disbud plants because sometimes one giant blossom is more desirable than a lot of smaller ones in floral arrangements.

The time to do any disbudding is just as soon as the buds form. The sooner you remove the extra little buds, the faster the plant's strength becomes concentrated on the remaining ones. Disbudding can consist of merely thinning out a few extra buds, or it can be drastic enough so that only one giant flower will bloom per branch, or even just one per plant.

The big "football game" chrysanthemums, as well as roses, dahlias, hibiscus, peonies, carnations, zinnias, asters, and begonias are a few of the large-flowering plants that respond to disbudding by producing king-size blooms. Removing the buds is practical for creating superior show flowers, but it may not always be a desirable practice in the garden or landscape.

Thinning Fruit

Thinning does for fruit what disbudding does for flowers. It is done in about the same way and for the same reason. Many fruit trees have a ten-

29

dency to set a large crop every other year, and some produce well only every third year. There's no doubt that thinning, together with proper pruning, helps your tree not only to produce larger fruit, but to produce annually as well.

During years when the tree is making a heavy set of fruit, remove a high percentage of the crop when the fruits are about the size of marbles. The remaining ones will grow much larger and will usually be in better condition. Most commercial growers thin their fruit in order to get the perfect-looking specimens you see in stores.

You too can grow fruit resembling the beauties you see in the catalogs. The best time to do it is after the natural drop in the early summer. Keep an eye on your trees, and whenever you see a lot of little fruits on the ground, give Nature a helping hand by thinning the fruit still on the tree.

If there are two or more fruits in a cluster, leave the biggest and best one and pick off all the rest. Make sure that there is a space of about six inches between each fruit you leave on the tree. Since this involves picking off 80 to 90 percent of the fruits, it's a big job. But it is worth the trouble, because two nice things happen.

First, because the remaining fruits grow so large and in such perfect shape, you'll end up with more bushels of usable fruit than if you hadn't disbudded at all. It will be the kind of fruit you'll be happy to use and proud to give to others.

You'll also be producing only a small fraction of the seeds that would grow otherwise. Since it takes far more of the tree's strength to mature seeds than to produce fruit flesh, the tree is more likely to bear a good crop every year — its energy hasn't been sapped by bearing a big crop of seeds.

Thinning is beneficial to apples, plums, peaches, apricots, nectarines, pears, and grape clusters. It is usually less practical on crab apples, cherries, and quinces. If you want to improve the size and quality of the large-fruiting varieties of strawberries, blueberries, blackberries, and gooseberries, you can thin them too. Crab apples, cherries, quinces, and raspberries are benefited more by pruning than by thinning. Remember that each variety of flower or fruit has a built-in size limit, however, and no amount of disbudding or thinning will produce a fruit or flower larger than that limit.

Beheading a Tree

Trees have the wonderful habit of growing each year, whether we pay much attention to them or not. We suddenly notice that they have grown up into utility lines or are beginning to block a choice view of the nearby mountains. Since most of us hate to cut down a good, healthy tree unless we really must, we are faced with deciding if we can safely solve the problem by cutting off the top of the tree.

As we drive around the countryside, it's obvious that this beheading — also known as tree-topping or dehorning — is often done successfully. Power companies frequently top large trees that are menacing their wires. Country dwellers sometimes behead those trees hiding lake or mountain views. Fruit

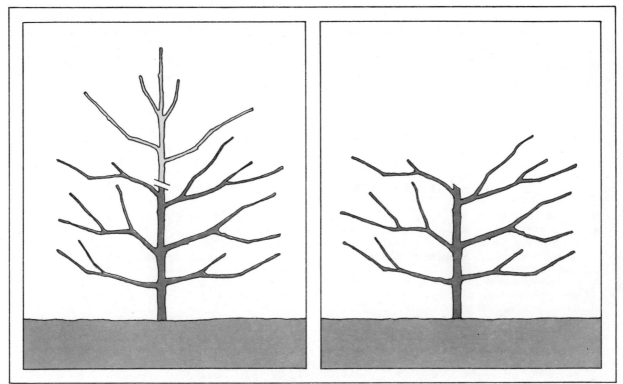

A shrub or tree that is growing too tall can be directed to spread and grow more bushlike by removing the top.

31

trees that are tall enough to hinder pest control, pruning, and harvesting are often pruned drastically to make them more accessible.

Tree-topping is not a practice I'd generally recommend, especially in the cooler climates. It usually spoils the appearance of the tree and often ruins its health. Ordinarily I top trees only as a last resort, although this can be done successfully if the tree is in good health, and if you're careful not to remove more than from a quarter to a third of the limb area.

Root Pruning

Root pruning probably is understood less, and therefore less practiced, than any other type of pruning. Many dedicated gardeners will have no part of it. They don't mind pruning trees and shearing hedges, but they consider the roots of a plant as something sacred and mysterious and not to be disturbed.

We could all take a lesson from the skilled Oriental and European gardeners who often know how to use this valuable skill as proficiently as any other garden practice. Through root pruning, they can control tree size, move large trees easily, get young trees off to a good start, and keep their houseplants to a manageable size. They can even get reluctant fruit trees to begin bearing, and flowering trees to bloom.

THE OKLAHOMA AIR-ROOT PRUNING METHOD

An interesting new method of making trees grow faster and fruit and nut trees produce sooner has been developed recently by horticulturist Carl Whitcomb of Oklahoma State University.

Whitcomb noted that a great deal of a tree's first growing season is spent in developing a long taproot that will be capable of reaching moisture even in dry weather. Only after this growth has been accomplished do the fibrous lateral roots (those that pick up the soil nutrients) start growing. Since he was aware that a tree doesn't begin to grow very well until a good root system is established, he decided to find a way to cut short the lengthy taproot development and speed up the desirable root growth.

He accomplished this by planting seeds or seedlings in milk cartons that had their tops and bottoms cut off and were filled with an artificial soil mixture of peat, perlite, and slow-release fertilizer. Rather than place the milk cartons on the ground or on benches, he set them on a wire screen that was slightly elevated off the ground, leaving an air space beneath them.

The pots were kept well watered, and soon each began to grow. However, when the taproot reached the bottom of the carton and hit the wire screen with the air beneath, the root tip promptly died, and the feeder side roots began to grow instead, soon filling the carton. The tree was then transplanted to the field where it continued its speedy lateral root development.

Mr. Whitcomb noted that not only was the growth rate of the air-pruned trees greatly increased, but that the survival rate of those trees, when transplanted into the field, was a surprising 100 percent, even when planted out in the heat of summer. He has successfully transplanted trees that are usually so difficult to move that nurseries seldom carry them — the black gum and the Kentucky coffee tree, for instance.

Air pruning can also speed up the growth rate of all seedling plants, even those that produce short taproots. It is of less value to rooted cuttings, because most plants grown from cuttings naturally develop a heavy fibrous root system.

Organic gardeners may want to experiment with this innovative method by thoroughly mixing one cubic foot of perlite or vermiculite with one cubic foot of peat moss, and a quart of dried cow or sheep manure. This mixture should be sufficient to fill 25 to 30 milk bottles. After planting the seeds or setting in the seedlings, treat them as any potted plant, although it may be necessary to water them more frequently, since they will dry out quickly on the elevated wire screen. Transplant them into the field or to larger pots before the roots overcrowd their small milk cartons.

32

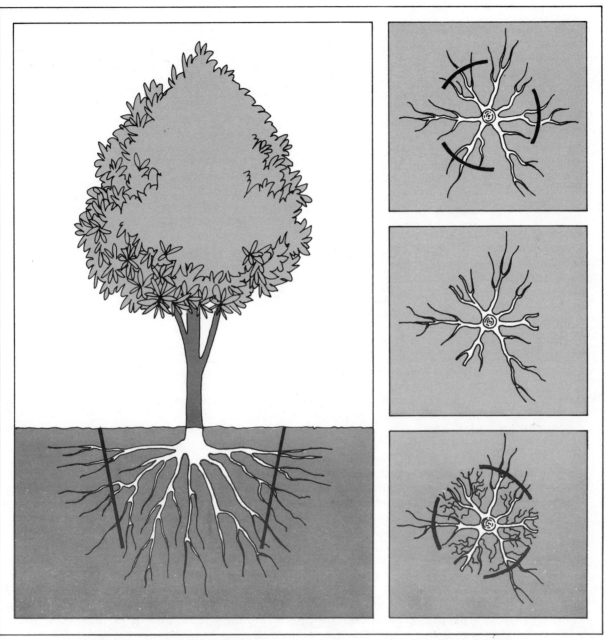

Prepare a tree for transplanting by removing from one-third to one-half of the roots. Use a sharp, long-bladed spade to cut the roots at intervals, as indicated by the lines intersecting the roots. Carry out the first pruning in early spring (top right). A second, midsummer pruning should take care of the remaining uncut roots (bottom right), and the tree will be ready for transplanting early the following spring. Cut the ring to the diameter of the ball of soil you intend the tree to have.

Root pruning sometimes means digging up the plant and cutting back its exposed roots. It also is practiced without moving the plant from its spot in the ground; you don't see the roots in this process, but simply cut all around the tree with a spade that has a long, sharp blade. There's no need to feel guilty or uncertain about either practice. As with regular top pruning, the plant doesn't seem to mind a bit, and usually thrives as a result.

Root pruning at planting time. Many gardeners ignore the nursery's directions for root-pruning their newly purchased stock. Cutting back the tops is understandable, but why would anyone want to cut off roots? Don't new plants need all the roots they can get?

Sometimes it isn't necessary to touch the roots, but more often than not, a newly dug, bare-rooted plant has received some ugly wounds caused by the digging. Broken, ragged ends should be cut off cleanly so that they will heal over quickly and begin to send out the hair roots that supply food for the plant.

Roots need to be shortened occasionally to make the plant more convenient to handle. Strawberry plants, for example, should have their long, stringy roots clipped back a few inches at planting time, both to make them easier to plant and to stimulate fast, new root growth.

Root pruning before transplanting. Trees and shrubs are often root-pruned before they are moved to minimize the damage to them at digging time. Nurseries will cut a small circle around each growing tree every year or two to encourage a compact, yet full, root system so that the tree can be transplanted with little shock or setback. If you wish to move some of your trees or to dig up wild ones, you can use the same method. Simply root-prune them at least one growing season before you move them. The process is simple and practically insures planting success.

Suppose you want to dig up the 15-foot maple on Uncle Harry's farm. Or perhaps your neighbor has offered you the beautiful 8-foot spruce he planted by mistake in front of his picture window. You can move either one with ease, as long as your donor will give you at least a year to do it.

Using a sharp, long-bladed shovel, make a circle around the tree, cutting straight down with each thrust. Don't skip any spots. Make sure that you cut each bit of root all the way around the circle. Some of the larger roots may be rather tough, and a firm thrust will be necessary to sever them. When digging an evergreen, cut the circle just at the outer reach of the branches. For a deciduous tree, cut just inside the branch spread but at least two feet from the trunk, even if the tree has no branches.

You can root-prune any time of the year the ground isn't frozen, but all root pruning is best done in early spring. Trees need a larger root system to supply their required moisture during the winter, and by pruning them in the spring you allow time for additional roots to grow.

After the long roots have been severed, most root growth will take place within the circle. The small roots develop into a tight ball that will come up with a clump of soil for easy transplanting in the early spring.

Even large trees can be moved safely when they have been root-pruned in this manner. Space out the pruning over several years to avoid cutting off

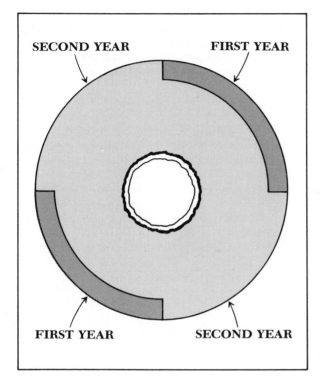

SECOND YEAR   FIRST YEAR

FIRST YEAR   SECOND YEAR

To transplant a large tree, the root pruning should be done over a period of two years to avoid cutting off too many roots at once.

too much of the root system at any one time. But for huge trees, cutting the roots and digging would be a major job best left to the experts and their special equipment, unless you're willing to take a chance.

Root pruning to check top growth. An established tree is sometimes root-pruned, even if it will never be transplanted, in order to slow down its growth. Although you might think it more logical to check tree growth by cutting back the branches, this isn't always the best way: pruned trees usually try to grow back branches to replace those they've lost as soon as possible, so the tree may grow faster than ever. Root pruning, on the other hand, cuts off part of the supply of nutrients and slows down growth without a stimulating effect.

In addition to controlling tree size, you may want to slow down top growth for other reasons. Fruit trees in rich soil often grow so well that they go right on growing for many years before producing any fruit. Sometimes flowering trees will also make lush growth for a long time, but won't bloom. Root pruning can slow down a tree's growth activity and thereby force it to bloom and bear.

Root pruning is also useful to control houseplant growth. Most small houses don't have room enough for indoor gardeners to keep repotting their plants indefinitely into larger containers. If you have plants that are becoming overgrown, you can carefully remove the plant from its pot, cut back all the outside roots, and replant it with some new soil in the same pot. (See page 188.) Bonsai growers rely heavily on root pruning to keep their plants small yet ancient-looking.

Prune According to Your Area

Because there is a tremendous difference in weather conditions throughout the country, it is difficult to give good, precise directions on how much or when to prune. However, you can follow these general guidelines.

If you live where summers are humid, good air ventilation is necessary to prevent disease, so prune sufficiently to let in sun and air. On the other hand, where summers are hot and dry, trees — as well as their owners — benefit if the leaves and branches are thick. The limbs can grow close together with no harm to the tree and should not be pruned heavily.

If you live where snows drift deeply and icy crusts form, prune deciduous trees so they will branch above the snow line and thus avoid breakage of the lower branches. Also, in snow regions, evergreens should be pruned into a pointed or rounded shape so that heavy ice and snow loads won't collect on top and crush them.

36

When to Prune

When is the proper time to prune? If you were to ask this question at a gathering of gardeners, whether professional nurserymen or weekend green thumb gardeners, you'd be assured a stimulating conversation. Each person has a definite idea on the subject. Some even maintain that the best time to prune is whenever you feel like it.

The best time, in my opinion, depends on several variables — the condition of the plant, the length of its growing season, when it blooms, and whether its buds form on new growth or only on older wood.

Late-winter pruning. Most gardeners like to prune many of their trees and shrubs in late winter. Fruit trees are often pruned then, as are roses, broadleafed evergreens, vines, and some flowering trees. Since "late winter" means a different time in each locale, take it to mean whenever the days have begun to lengthen and warm up noticeably, with no sign of swelling buds or new growth. The gardener and orchardist aren't so busy at this time of year, and the first breaths of spring stimulate the feeling of wanting to get busy in the garden. The branches are bare then too, so it's easier to see what you're doing.

Although most pruning is done in late winter, this can encourage a fast regrowth of wood, often at the expense of fruit and flowers. It's true that if you prune annually, the pruning is usually moderate and regrowth therefore is seldom excessive. However, if you're a year or two behind with your pruning and must do a heavy amount at once, winter may not be the best time.

Most experts don't like to prune when the wood is frozen. Not only is a warm, sunny day more comfortable for working, but there is also a general

ARE YOU A RELOCATED GARDENER?

Southerners who move to the North and northerners who move to the South usually both realize that a large part of all necessary pruning should be done when the tree is dormant. The problem is that, in their new location, they aren't always sure when dormancy takes place and how long it lasts. Newcomers to the South often prune too early in the season, before the tree or plant has become completely dormant. Southerners who move north often prune tender plants such as roses, grapes, peaches, and cherries heavily in late fall or early winter. In both cases severe winter injury is likely. Before you begin any major pruning, better check with your extension service or a local garden expert if you are gardening in unfamiliar territory.

feeling that cutting on cold days damages the cells in the frozen wood and that cut areas don't heal properly.

Spring pruning. Inspect your plants each spring, and remove any branches damaged by ice, snow, or wind. Repair any wounds that may have been inflicted by roving animals or winter sportsmen.

A few gardeners hold out for regular spring pruning for some plants, but since the greatest sap movement takes place in spring, it seems to me that this is a poor time to do almost any pruning except for repair work.

Spring is the time to pinch off buds that may be starting branches or tops in the wrong places, and to remove new suckers, water sprouts, or any other branches that are beginning to grow in the wrong direction.

Early summer pruning. This is the season when every plant is making its greatest growth. For this reason it is a good time to shear evergreens and hedges. It is also the best season for pruning shrubs that bloomed in the spring, such as lilac, bridal wreath, honeysuckle, and spring-blossoming spireas. These plants should be pruned just after they finish blooming so that they will have time to start developing a new set of buds which will bloom the following spring.

Early summer is also the best time to continue corrective pruning on young trees, such as pinching or cutting off any limbs that might form extra tops, bad crotches, or suckers.

Late summer pruning. Late summer, when all growth has stopped but the leaves have not yet fallen, is a good time to prune certain trees. The birches and maples that bleed so badly when pruned in late winter and spring can be safely trimmed then, as can most other shade trees.

This is a good time to do basal pruning on evergreens. The small amount of pitch that oozes out of cut limbs is sufficient to seal the wound, but not enough to distress the tree.

37

Many people think that late summer is the best time to prune fruit trees. The tree will be stimulated to set more flower and fruit buds and fewer branch and leaf buds the following year. By removing branches in late summer, you will cause far less regrowth than you would in late winter.

Fall pruning. Some growers prefer to do all their pruning just before winter sets in. The leaves having fallen off, they can see what they are doing; there's no sap running, and the weather is still pleasant.

It sounds like the perfect time to prune, but the feeling isn't unanimous. Some people think that fall pruning encourages winter injury that must be corrected with additional spring pruning which in turn encourages more regrowth.

In all but the most northern areas, autumn is an excellent time to cut back roses, especially tea roses. It's also a good time to cut back clematis, hydrangea, buddleia, crape myrtle, potentilla, *Tamarix parviflora*, hibiscus, and many other shrubs. Woody vines should be pruned at this time, as well as the small fruits and grape vines.

Prune According to Growth Habit

38

Each tree and plant has its own natural growth habit. A Lombardy poplar, for example, grows straight up, and it would be difficult to prune it into a low hedge or to expand it into a spreading shade tree. An American elm, on the other hand, is slender, tall, and spreading at the top, and a spruce is cone shaped.

Even varieties within each species have distinctive growth patterns. Within the apple family, for example, the McIntosh is a broad, spreading tree, but the Yellow Transparent prefers to grow upward, forming lots of tops and crotches that need corrective pruning so that the tree won't split when loaded with fruit. Certain varieties of birch and willow "weep" and should be pruned to emphasize that pattern of growth. Creeping hemlocks, junipers, and globular or pyramidal arborvitae also have distinctive shapes that can be encouraged.

Pruning can alter a plant's natural habits to some degree, but you should try to compliment these habits as much as possible. All species look best when they are pruned to conform with their natural growth habits.

Pruning at Different Life Stages

Just as pruning should differ according to the growth habit of various plants, it should also be done in different ways depending on the age of the plant. We sometimes forget that they, like animals and humans, go through various life stages, from infancy to old age.

When a tree or shrub is small, much of the pruning you need to do is corrective, such as pinching buds and redirecting branches to get the plant to grow in a strong, attractive shape.

During the prime of its life, the plant may benefit if you give it some

39

A clump tree. The forked trunk on the right should be sawed off.

additional help, including more corrective pruning, and pruning for rejuvenation, production, beauty, or usefulness.

In a tree's old age, pruning is usually done to keep it healthy and to prolong its useful life. The life expectancy of the individual tree must be taken into account. No amount of pruning will prolong the life of a Lombardy poplar much beyond its anticipated 20 or 30 years, but a bristlecone pine may live for thousands of years without ever having a branch removed. Find out the approximate life span of each of your plants in order to prune properly.

The vitality of the tree is a factor as well. Extremely vigorous trees and shrubs can be pruned more severely than those with tired sap. Vitality not only varies with each species, but it can also vary from year to year, depending on soil and weather, and can change considerably as the plant grows older. You should adjust your pruning to the plant's present state of vitality. Just because a flowering crab thrived from a severe cutback when it was 6 years old doesn't mean that it could stand the same treatment at age 40.

Each tree will sooner or later reach a stage when it is impractical to spend vast amounts of time and money on it, and you must consider replacing it. Often it's difficult to make the decision to recycle an old tree as firewood and mulch, but this process is also a part of good gardening and conservation.

40

Dense growth can be thinned out to expose the trunk and to encourage blooming.

Old derelict trees are not only unsightly; they are also dangerous and harbor insects and disease.

The Ultimate Pruning Job

After we have made the unhappy decision to get rid of a dying tree or shrub, we are faced with another problem — how to remove it.

It is no great difficulty to dig out a small tree or shrub and haul it to the dump. But should you have a large, dying tree located between your house and the neighbor's garage, with a power line in back and a busy street in front, you must be more cautious. If you own a shiny, new chain saw, this isn't the best occasion to show it off. Large trees in tight areas must be taken down in sections, and a professional should be hired to do the job.

If your cuts will pose no risk to buildings, wires, or other trees, you may still want to have a skillful lumberjack help you with the job. It is comforting to know that someone else is standing by with a spare saw in case your own fails or if you have guessed wrong and the tree has fallen across Main Street.

If conditions are favorable and you decide to do your own cutting, choose a day with no wind, or when a light wind is in your favor. A tall tree catches a lot of air, and even a light breeze can push it considerably. If your tree's center of gravity makes it difficult to fell, sometimes you can shift its balance in your favor by cutting off a heavy limb or two. When there is room, it's possible to hitch a very long rope to the upper branches and have someone pull it by hand or by vehicle while you are cutting. Plan the move extremely carefully so that your helper won't be caught by the falling tree.

If you do your own cutting, make sure that you have an absolutely clear space in which to fell the tree. You may want to lay down a few limbs or planks to keep the tree from smashing into the ground. If it falls on them, it will be easier to saw without cutting into the dirt.

With an axe or saw, cut a V-shaped notch three or more inches deep in the side of the tree, in the direction you want it to fall. The bigger the tree, the deeper the notch should be. On the opposite side, start to saw at a level just above the notch. As you saw, slant downward toward the notch, making sure that you won't be sawing above or below the notch. Check occasionally to make sure that you are cutting through the tree evenly. If one side gets cut

41

A double tree. It is weak and will eventually split. Train young trees to a single stem for the first few years.

through first, the tree may twist and fall in the wrong direction. Check continually to see that the cut being made by the saw is open and isn't tightening up because the tree leans in the wrong direction. If the cut begins to get tight, remove the saw immediately, and be prepared to run for help. Often you can push the tree so it will fall in the right direction by using long poles or by pounding a wedge.

If all goes well, your tree will soon be lying in the right spot, ready to cut up. Usually it is better and easier to saw from the top end, working gradually toward the heavy trunk. Make sure the log doesn't lie in such a way that it pinches the saw as you cut. You can use a wedge on a large log, if necessary, to keep the slit open.

In deep, shady, moist woods, a stump rots quickly, so your best bet is to emulate the natural condition of a forest and speed up the rotting process by cutting off the stump as close to the ground as possible and by covering it with something to keep it moist. Since wood needs both moisture and nitrogen for the decay bacteria to work, keep the stump covered with a mixture of manure, leaf mold (rotten leaves), and soil to a depth of three or four inches. Pile several inches of old hay on top of that to retain the moisture, and water the heap now and then in dry weather. As a rule, hardwood stumps, such as maple and birch, rot much quicker than the pitchy softwoods like pine, spruce, and cedar.

If you plant a new tree near the old stump, feed it generous amounts of manure or cottonseed meal each year to compensate for all the nitrogen that the decaying roots constantly take from the soil.

Beware of Overpruning

With pruning, just as with fertilizer and medicine, more is not necessarily better, and sometimes it is disastrous. So keep your pruning urge carefully under control.

Whenever you pick up your tools, bear in mind that plants live and grow because of photosynthesis. Living plant tissue is produced in leaves or needles when light combines the minerals and water taken up by the roots from the soil with the carbon dioxide from the air. Whenever too many leaves or needles are removed, the tree or plant can no longer manufacture enough of the organic compounds that maintain growth and develop flowers and seeds.

At the risk of being repetitive, I again remind you always to have a good reason for making each cut. All pruning should be done with an eye toward preventing future problems, rather than to correct past mistakes.

When you prune skillfully, it is not obvious. Yet, like weeding your garden, it becomes quite noticeable when you haven't done it.

42

Chapter 5

Ornamental Trees and Shrubs

A popular song of the sixties, "Little Boxes," protested the thousands of little modern houses that all looked alike. " . . . little boxes on the hillside, little boxes all the same." The song didn't mention that much of the landscaping was similarly dull, consisting of a tall evergreen in each corner, groups of spreading evergreens around the house, one green shade tree, and a green lawn.

Fortunately, during the last decade that picture has been changing. Flowering trees and shrubs have become popular in the United States. Many tourists came home from Europe with the conclusion that most American landscapes have far too much greenery in them. Consequently, each spring we see more and more beautiful flowering crab apples, dogwoods, azaleas, hawthorns, redbuds, and lilacs adorning the countryside. Throughout the summer, roses and other colorful flowering shrubs compete with perennial borders, and in the fall there are more blooms, berries, fruits, and colored foliage than ever before. Some shrubs and trees are planted just because their colored bark brightens a barren landscape during the winter.

You can get your landscaping off to the best possible start by choosing your shrubbery carefully. Don't choose a shrub or tree just because you like it or because it grew on Grandpa's farm. Consider first whether it is suitable for your own area. Although you naturally want to surround yourself with plants that you enjoy, it is equally important to choose the ones that are suited for your growing conditions and climate. Rhododendrons and azaleas need an extremely acid soil, for instance, while lilacs and hydrangeas need soil containing generous amounts of lime. Some plants are extremely hardy and can thrive in northern Minnesota, but others do well only in places with long growing seasons and mild winters.

44

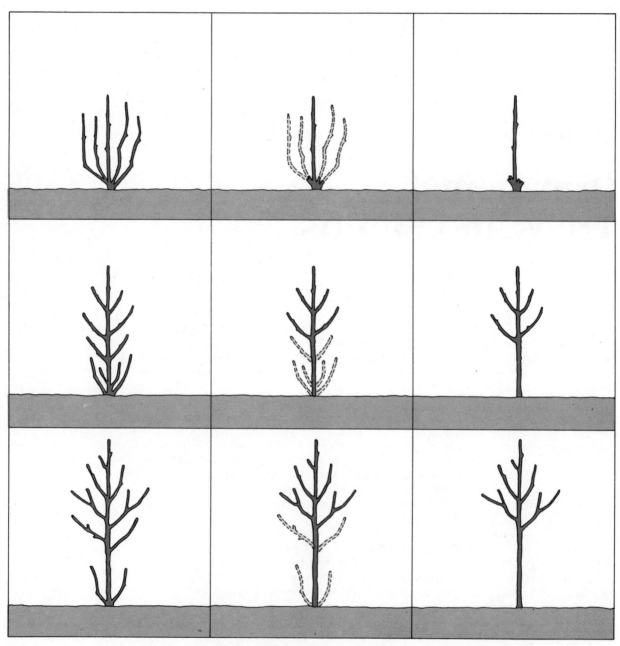

Turning a shrub into a tree. In the first year, prune to a single stem (top row). Cut off the lower branches in the second year (middle row). Continue to prune off bottom branches as the tree grows taller until the desired treelike form is reached (bottom row).

The plant must be suited for the conditions in the spot you have in mind, as well as for the general area. Some viburnums do best in light shade, but others need plenty of sun. A hemlock hedge might be ideal for a sheltered valley location, but don't subject it to cold, drying north winds in winter, or it will look beat up all summer.

Choose a flowering tree or shrub not only for its own appearance, but also for the way it fits into the surroundings. Many plants that would grace a large, old country home would be too large and coarse to compliment a ranch house. Before you choose a plant, research its growth habits and its ultimate size.

A plant should fit into your lifestyle, too. If you don't like to putter in the garden, or if you are away for most of the summer, your plants should be the kind that need very little pruning or other care. Likewise, if you garden only at a summer home and return to a city apartment in September, you won't want plants that require winter pruning. If you choose the right plant for the right place, you'll find that most flowering shrubs and trees don't need much pruning.

Pruning at Planting Time

When you buy a tree or shrub, often its roots are bare, wrapped only in peat moss or some other material to keep them moist. Or you may buy a plant growing in a large pot, or one with its roots enclosed in a ball of soil wrapped in burlap or plastic.

If it is growing in a pot or a ball of soil, you don't have to prune it. The roots are safe and undisturbed, so no compensatory pruning is necessary. If the roots are wrapped up without soil, however, you must prune unless the directions state that it has already been done.

Begin by inspecting the roots to determine how badly they were damaged when the plant was dug up. Be sure to keep the roots in a tub of water when you inspect them because they will suffer badly if they are exposed to the air for more than a few minutes. (Newly acquired, bare-rooted nursery stock should always be soaked for five or six hours after you get it home.) If any roots are broken, use hand pruners to cut them smooth so there will be a minimum amount of exposed wound to heal over. Prune only the broken roots, leaving all others intact.

The top can be pruned either before or after planting, although it is easier to do it after, since the plant is then held firmly upright by the soil. Prune back a third to a half of the tree, depending on how badly the roots were broken. If the root system looks small and has been damaged, you should take off half the top to compensate for the loss, but never more, because the plant will need enough leaves to sustain the roots that are left. If the roots aren't badly damaged, reduce the total limb surface by a third, cutting back the top and the limbs to two-thirds of their former length. Some gardeners do prefer to cut off some limbs entirely, leaving others undisturbed, but either way seems to work well as long as you remove approximately a third to a half of the top. Always remember to cut on a slant above an outside bud. (See page 23.)

Flowering shrubs that will eventually grow six feet tall or more, such as lilacs and viburnums, should be treated as trees when you plant them. Prune them back from a third to a half, cutting out any weak branches. Leave a few

46

TABULAR LIST OF ORNAMENTAL TREES

Scientific Name	Common Name	Special Remarks
Amelanchier	shadbush	Prune only to shape, as either bush or tree
Carpinus Betulus	European hornbeam	Prune to tree form
Carpinus orientalis	Oriental hornbeam	Prune to tree form
Cassia fistula	golden-shower, senna	Cut back season's growth to short spurs after blooming
Cercis	redbud	Prune after blooming if necessary
Cornus florida	flowering dogwood	Prune as little as possible, heals slowly
Cornus Kousa	Kousa dogwood	See *Cornus florida*
Cotinus obovatus	American smoke tree	Prune to grow as bush or small tree, cut off fading flowers
Crataegus	hawthorn	Prune to shape in late winter, renew branches if necessary
Elaeagnus	Russian olive	Prune only to control size if necessary, in late winter
Euonymus atropurpurea	burning bush	Prune in late winter, only if necessary
Franklinia Alatamaha	Franklin tree	Prune to tree form
Halesia monticola	silver-bell	Needs pruning rarely
Hydrangea paniculata 'Grandiflora'	peegee hydrangea	Prune in late winter

of the tall, stronger branches intact to encourage upward growth and earlier blooming.

Smaller-growing flowering shrubs, including roses, potentilla, spirea, and

Scientific Name	Common Name	Special Remarks
Koelreuteria paniculata	golden rain tree	Prune to shape when young
Laburnum anagyroides	golden-chain	Prune after blooming
Magnolia	magnolia	Prune just after blooming
Malus	flowering crab apple	Prune to shape, renew old wood if necessary
Myrica cerifera	wax myrtle	Prune to remove winter injury, or to shape, in late winter
Myrica pensylvanica	bayberry	Prune to remove suckers, winter injury
Oxydendrum arboreum	sourwood	Needs pruning rarely
Prunus	flowering almond, apricot, cherry, peach, plum	Prune to shape in late winter
Rhamnus davurica	buckthorn	Prune to shape in late winter
Sorbus	mountain ash	Prune to tree form, in late winter
Symplocos paniculata	sweetleaf	Prune to shape, renew old branches
Syringa reticulata	Japanese tree lilac	Prune right after blooming, if necessary
Viburnum	cranberry bush, nannyberry, black haw	Prune in late winter only as necessary

weigela, should have all of their branches cut back by half when they are planted, to encourage bushy growth.

Pruning Flowering Trees

A flowering tree will be stronger, longer-lived, and less likely to break in ice and wind storms if you train it to grow with a central leader for the first ten feet at least. (See page 114.) Some plants, such as tree lilacs and mountain ash, form a lot of lower limbs, so prune frequently for a treelike effect, especially until the tree is mature. The branches on most ornamental flowering trees are not heavy as a rule, and their berries and fruit seldom add much weight, so careful training of the limb structure is not as necessary as it is on fruit trees.

Keep the tree trunk as a single stem, and don't allow groups of heavy branches to grow from the lower part of the tree. You should train flowering trees as trees rather than as large bushes. Cut off all suckers that sprout from their roots. Grafted trees, like the flowering crabs and hawthorns, tend to send up a lot of suckers at the base. These should be cut off immediately because they grow so fast that they can quickly overtake and crowd out the good part of the tree.

In most cases, early training and sucker control are all the pruning your flowering tree will need for many years. As with any tree, prune off the branches that upset the symmetry and appearance of the tree, and remove all branches that are growing so close to the ground that they interfere with lawn mowing. As the tree gets older, thin out any branches that are growing too dense so that it will continue to bloom well. Thinning will also help prevent the tree from aging too fast.

The time to prune most trees is just after the blooms fade. However, prune in late winter any trees that produce berries or fruit so that you won't interfere with the production.

When they receive proper care, many flowering trees live to be quite old. Flowering crabs sometimes live for over a century and tree lilacs for even longer. An enormous tree lilac in our neighborhood is far over a hundred years old. It has outlasted many of the apple trees planted around it and is still in fine shape.

Pruning Flowering Shrubs

Like the flowering trees, most deciduous flowering shrubs need pruning rarely, although sometimes you must remove old wood to rejuvenate them, thin out wood that is growing too thickly, or keep them from growing all over the place. Some shrubs, such as the honeysuckles, viburnums, and lilacs, may grow too tall and will need to be cut back. Remove broken, dead, or diseased branches whenever you notice them.

Before you prune a flowering shrub, check to see whether it blooms on wood produced the same year or on wood that grew during the previous season.

48

A young flowering crab, ready for a light thinning of the branches, removing any crossed limbs.

Late winter is the best time to prune the shrubs that are grown mostly for their fall foliage, like Amur maple and euonymus. Those shrubs that are grown primarily for the beauty of their bark in winter should also be pruned in late winter. The bright, red-twigged dogwood is one of these. Most berry-producing shrubs, such as the cotoneaster, pyracantha, and viburnum, usually need very little pruning. If necessary, prune these shrubs in late fall after the berries have either been eaten by birds or have passed their prime.

SHRUBS TO BE PRUNED AFTER BLOOMING

The best time to prune shrubs that bloom on year-old wood is just after the blossoms have faded. You should then allow the shrub to grow new branches and to form the buds that will bloom the following year. The following shrubs bloom only on year-old wood.

Berberis (barberry)
Buddleia alternifolia (butterfly bush)
Cotinus Coggygria (smoke tree)
Daphne
Deutzia
Forsythia
Jasminum (jasmine)
Kerria japonica (Japanese rose)
Kolkwitzia (beautybush)

Lonicera (honeysuckle)
Philadelphus (mock orange)
Physocarpus (ninebark)
Pieris
Spiraea (spring-blooming varieties, including bridal wreath, Thunberg, and Veitch)
Syringa (lilac)
Weigela

50

Cranberries, viburnum, and others often produce an extra-heavy crop of berries only every other year. Although you can encourage annual bearing by pruning, a better and easier way is to cut off part of the flowers in the summer during years when the shrubs are blooming heavily. This pruning will prevent overbearing and encourage the bush to bear a good crop the following year.

My wife likes to cut branches of cotoneaster, red viburnum, or other berries for interior decoration in the fall, and she sometimes worries that this is detrimental to the ornamental plants. It's true that when the plant is small it isn't a good idea to cut off the branches, although a few berries can be snitched with no harm. As the bush gets older, however, you do no damage if you gather a moderate amount of the colorful berries to use for bouquets or holiday decorations. Naturally, it is better to cut off the branches with clippers rather than to break them off in jagged tears. Since most of next year's fruit buds are near the ends of the limbs, don't sacrifice too many of them.

Restoring an Old Flowering Shrub

Often the question of how to prune an old, deciduous flowering shrub comes up. Is it possible? Is it worth the trouble? How can it be done?

It depends on the variety of plant, its vigor, the care with which you prune, and the climate. You can slash back some tropical and semitropical plants mercilessly, and they will quickly grow back into youthful, thrifty plants. Shrubs in northern climates need to be treated more carefully, and in most cases it's best to spread major pruning jobs over several years. Cut back only a few limbs at a time, and as they regrow you can remove a few more. In this way you can revitalize your shrub or tree. A gradual renewal is better for the shrub's health, and its appearance is less drastically altered during the process. Early spring is usually the best time for restorative pruning.

Keep in mind that shrubs and flowering trees have definite life spans, and, if they are nearing the end of their days, pruning often won't help them revive. Just as when fruit and shade trees reach this stage, it is better to cut them down and plant new ones nearby.

SHRUBS TO BE PRUNED BEFORE THE BUDS SHOW GREEN

Shrubs that form flowers on wood grown the same season should be pruned when the plant is dormant. For example, you can keep *Hydrangea arborescens* 'Grandiflora' and *H. paniculata* 'Grandiflora' low by pruning them nearly to the ground in late fall or late winter, and they will still bloom heavily the following summer. Prune these shrubs before the buds show green:

Abelia x *grandiflora*
Abelia Schumannii
Amorpha canescens (lead plant)
Aralia elata (Japanese angelica)
Artemisia (sagebush, southernwood, wormwood)
Buddleia (butterfly bush) Exception: *Buddleia alternifolia*
Callicarpa japonica (beautyberry)
Calluna vulgaris (heather)
Caryopteris (bluebeard)
Cephalanthus occidentalis (buttonbush)
Cytisus nigricans (broom)
Diervilla sessilifolia (bush honeysuckle)
Euonymus kiautschovica (spreading euonymus)
Fatsia japonica (Japanese fatsia)
Franklinia Alatamaha (Franklin tree)
Garrya (silk-tassel)
Hamamelis virginiana (witch hazel)
Hibiscus syriacus (althaea)
Holodiscus discolor (ocean-spray)

Hydrangea arborescens 'Grandiflora' (hills-of-snow)
Hydrangea paniculata 'Grandiflora' (peegee hydrangea)
Hypericum (St.-John's-wort)
Indigofera incarnata (indigo)
Lagerstroemia indica (crape myrtle)
Lespedeza (bush clover)
Nandina domestica (sacred bamboo)
Potentilla (cinquefoil)
Rhamnus Frangula (alder buckthorn)
Rubus odoratus (flowering raspberry)
Salvia Greggii (autumn sage)
Sambucus canadensis (American elder)
Sorbaria (false spirea)
Spiraea (all spirea species that bloom in summer, including Billiard, Japanese, and hardhack)
Symphoricarpos (coralberry, snowberry)
Tamarix odessana (tamarisk)
Vitex agnus-castus (chaste tree)

PRUNING OLD FLOWERING SHRUBS

Here are some ways to restore an old flowering shrub when heavy pruning is in order.

Too large. When a shrub gets overgrown, cut a few of the older stems completely to the ground and shorten the remaining ones to just a bit lower than the height you want the shrub to be. Then allow it to grow back enough to cover the pruning wounds. In future years, prune to keep it at the size you want.

Too tight. Many low-growing shrubs, such as potentilla, hydrangea, and moss roses, become too dense after a few years of unregulated growth. You can thin these out by pruning at least half the stems to the ground the first year, and the remaining half the second year. Or, if the bush is vigorous, cut it completely to the ground and allow it to grow back.

Too loose. Flowering quince, some shrub roses, and many other shrubs tend to grow tall, loose, and floppy. When plants begin to droop over and touch the ground, it is time to shorten them. Cut back all the leggy branches, and remove a few of the older ones entirely.

Too twiggy. Honeysuckle, ornamental blueberries, dogwood, and some viburnums are among the shrubs that are likely to grow many small branches at the ends of their limbs as they get older. As a result, the blooms are fewer and the berries smaller. In addition to thinning the old wood, clip off this dense outer growth to renew the plant and revive its earlier blooming and bearing vigor.

(See facing page.)

52

Pruning Lilacs

Lilacs *(Syringa)* are one of the most widely planted and most beloved flowering shrubs in the country. They also are one of the shrubs that will need pruning eventually. Because they were introduced into the colonies so long ago and are such long-lived plants, many of the bushes now growing in American yards are over two hundred years old. Obviously, some of them are long overdue for a bit of attention.

A neglected, elderly lilac bush will need care in two areas. First, too many branches are probably growing out of the roots. These stems crowd both the main bush and each other. Second, there are likely to be some old, overgrown trunks that have lost most of their vitality. You'll need to take your saw and clippers to both.

Begin by cutting away all the small, thick sucker growth at the base of the plant. This will allow you to see which of the remaining larger stems need to be cut. Select several of the strong, younger trunks to remain as your new bush, and cut off all the rest, especially those that are old and decrepit. The exact number you leave will depend on the area your bush covers, and whether or not you want to shrink the size of that area. Make all cuts close to the ground, and cut carefully so that you don't slash into any adjoining stems.

Pruning a mature shrub.

After the pruning, help the bush recover and thrive by feeding it a mixture of dried manure (about 20 pounds for the average-size bush), and two or three cups of garden lime. Scatter this in a circle a foot away from the bush, just before a light spring rain can wash it into the soil.

Major pruning of this sort is necessary only once a decade or so. Usually you only need to prune a lilac by cutting off the fading blooms. Like many flowering shrubs, if allowed to go to seed the energy drain on the lilac bush is so great that it may bloom sparingly the following year. By pruning off the old blossoms, you help to insure regular blooming. Cut off the fading blooms only, and don't touch the stems and leaves. The farther you cut back, the more likely you are picking off next year's blooms. Of course, if you have a long hedge of tall-growing bushes, this snipping may be an impractical task, and you'll have to settle for heavy blooms whenever the lilac wants to provide them.

Some lilacs are grafted on ash or privet roots that may send up some shoots that look quite different from lilac plants. Prune or pull out any foreign-looking sprouts before they can threaten the real lilac.

54

Pruning the suckers and old stems from a lilac.

Old lilac blooms are cut just above the forming buds for next year's blooms.

Many of us take lilacs inside to enjoy their blooms and fragrance. When you're picking flowers for bouquets, cut the stems to another branch without leaving a dead stub. Never tear them off. Although heavy picking isn't likely to disturb an older, well-established plant, cut sparingly, if at all, from young bushes during the first years they bloom.

Pruning Roses

If you were to ask anyone, young or old, to name the perfect flower, the answer would most likely be the rose. For centuries, in both legends and in backyard gardens, the rose has been one of the world's most popular flowers. Modern horticultural science has developed roses in a wide range of colors, and there are varieties that bloom on bushes, vines, hedges, or even trees. The petals and hips are popular in teas, jellies, and numerous other culinary and aromatic concoctions. It's only right that the rose gets special mention when it comes to pruning. Each of us wants our rose bushes to live up to their full, beautiful potential.

Unless your rose is growing in a pot when you receive it, cut it back drastically as soon as you plant it. This cutting has almost always been done by the nursery for ease of shipping and for the convenience of the gardener. But if your bush is more than eight inches high and has never been cut back or has been only partially cut back, you should prune it. Cut it down to about six or eight inches above the dark line that shows where the ground level was when it was dug. Be sure to cut to a live bud or branch each time so that you leave no dead stubs.

Most roses are bud-grafted, and the big, burllike spot just above the roots is the graft. Plant the rose so that the graft is just slightly below ground level.

Although some polyanthus, florabunda, and tea roses are quite vigorous, many have been weakened by hybridization, and they need special care, especially the first year. Fading blooms should always be snipped off, but don't cut any blooms with long stems from hybrid roses during the first year. In future years, as soon as the plant has developed several strong, tall canes, moderate cutting of blooms will be perfectly safe. Cutting roses in full bloom, with long stems and some leaves, is actually summer pruning, so be sure that you don't scalp the plant. Leave at least two well-developed leaves between your cut and the place where the branch joins the main stem.

Most roses are thorny critters, and you'll appreciate a pair of heavy gloves when you're pruning and carrying away the clippings. Always cart away the clippings from the rose garden, because they'll be a breeding place for diseases and insects if left on the ground. Be especially careful to use sharp clippers so that you don't crush the stems and cause cell damage.

The kind of pruning you do, and when you do it, vary according to the

56

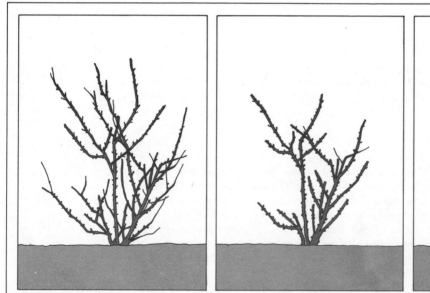

A rose with new spring growth just beginning (left), pruned high (center), and pruned moderately (right).

classification of rose and your climatic conditions.

Tea roses are the most common roses in the United States. Hundreds of named varieties are offered in catalogs, garden centers, and supermarkets every spring. You can choose from recently introduced, patented varieties, or the old, reliable favorites such as Peace and Red Radiance.

You must prune roses each year to keep them blooming well. The flowers bloom on new shoots sprouting from canes that grew the previous year. You must cut out all older, unproductive wood, and remove the weak, broken, and diseased branches as well. Thin out any canes that are growing too close together so that the remaining ones will be sturdier and more prolific.

If you live in the South, you can safely prune tea roses in the fall or even during the winter, if temperatures don't drop too low. Although these are the traditional times to prune in warm areas, many gardeners feel that the plant suffers less winter injury if it is pruned in very early spring instead, just as the buds are beginning to swell. Hard frosts are usually over by this time, and the sap isn't yet flowing enough to cause a heavy loss from the cut ends.

If you prefer tall-growing roses, thin out the old and weak canes and those that are crossed, winter-damaged, or growing too thick. You may not want to shorten them at all except to make the drooping canes a bit more stiff. If short, bushy plants fit into your garden scene better, cut all the ends of the canes farther back. Always cut on a slant just above a bud or to a live branch, and retain enough leaves and stem to feed the plant. For cutting heavy branches, you may need a saw or loppers.

You can prune heavily those roses that grow vigorously, but cut wood sparingly from the slower-growing, weaker kinds. Heavy pruning doesn't always stimulate a weak plant to grow faster. In fact, depriving it of necessary leaf area may make it grow less lively and with fewer blooms.

Tea roses can in no way be described as northern plants, although with careful attention you can grow these beauties even if you live where winters are rough. Not only are tea roses easily killed at low temperatures, but the cool, short growing season makes it difficult for them to make a good heavy growth and harden it up before the first frosts. Under these conditions, northern gardeners should not attempt any fall pruning. A few weeks before winter arrives, lay the tall canes down on the ground carefully, and cover the entire bush with several inches of soil, evergreen boughs, fiberglass insulation, or rose-covering material. This should be done before the temperature drops below 15 degrees F. Don't worry if all the leaves haven't yet fallen off.

In the spring you may find a lot of winter injury in spite of the covering. By the time you have pruned it off, you may not have much bush left, so allow floppy branches or weak canes to stay: the bush will need all the leaf area it can get.

Whether you are a northern or southern gardener, seal all your large pruning cuts with tree paint or rose paste, to help them heal over faster.

You can effectively disbud tea roses to grow large exhibition flowers. Pick off all the smaller buds, and leave only the large, fat bud at the top of each branch.

Hybrid perpetuals are a form of tea rose. Although hardier, they are otherwise similar, and you can treat them in the same manner.

57

58

Pruning roses. Tea roses (left) should be pruned of their tall growth to avoid damage from winter weather. The polyanth-us (center) is pruned of both weak, young twigs and old stems, leaving young wood. Prune shrub roses (right) to keep them looking like shrubs.

Florabundas resemble tea roses; however, they often grow taller, and they have several large flowers in a cluster, so they are seldom disbudded. Prune them in the same way. When they are dormant, cut out nearly all the wood that is over one year old. Cut back slightly any younger wood and remove all weak branches.

Polyanthus roses produce clusters of small and medium-size blooms, and these, also, are seldom disbudded. The bush needs very little pruning. Treat it much like a flowering shrub. The canes tend to stay small and may need some thinning out eventually. Remove any wood that no longer produces blooms.

Shrub roses greatly resemble old-fashioned roses and have a half-wild appearance. They can grow for years with no care at all but look their best with at least a little attention. Shrub roses are usually allowed to grow tall for a hedge effect, but if you like shorter, heavier-blooming plants, you can cut the bush back to a foot from the ground early each spring before any growth starts.

Moss roses, sweetbriers, cabbage roses, and rugosa roses are all pruned in nearly the same way. All are quite vigorous, so if you don't prune them annually, cutting back heavily may be necessary to keep them in their place and to remove old, rotten wood.

Some shrub roses, especially rugosa, produce large numbers of red seed pods called hips. These are a rich source of vitamin C. Although it is better to cut off the fading blooms of most roses so that the bush won't produce energy-draining seeds, these roses are so vigorous that it doesn't harm them a bit if you let the hips develop. Pick them off after a light frost, before they freeze hard and turn mushy.

Rambler roses are usually not grafted. All the new canes coming from the roots are part of the main plant, so you don't need to worry about wild suckers crowding out the good canes. As the shoots appear, prune or cut out all the weak ones, and leave only three to five strong, husky ones to grow.

Ramblers bloom best on year-old wood, so allow the shoots to grow freely the first year. Secure them to a fence or trellis the following year, and they will bloom. In the meantime, select three to five of the young shoots, and allow them to grow for blooming the following year. In late fall, or the following spring if you live in the North, cut out all the canes that have produced blooms. Tie the new canes to the fence or trellis, and they will bloom that summer. Repeat this process every year.

Climbing roses differ from rambling roses by having a more upward habit of growth that enables them to better climb a trellis. Many of the best hybrid

59

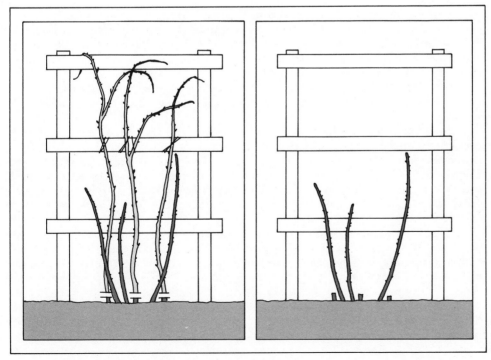

Pruning climbing roses. The 3 new canes shown here aren't trimmed.

tea roses are now available in climbing form. Their flowers are large, and they bloom for most of the summer, unlike the short blooming season of the ramblers.

In areas of the country where winters are mild, pruning can be done in late summer after the blossoming season is over. Where temperatures fall so low that it is necessary to lay the vines on the ground and protect them with a cover of soil and boughs, wait until spring to do the pruning.

Each year, cut back close to the ground all the canes that have bloomed recently. Snip off any weak growth on the new canes, too. If the remaining new, strong canes still seem to be too numerous, cut out a few of these also. Your plant should have a balance of current year's growth, year-old, and two-year-old wood. Climbing roses bloom mostly on wood that is two years old.

Tree roses are usually either tea, grandiflora, or floribunda roses that are grafted or budded on top of a brier or rugosa rose that is three feet high or more. Although they have a beautiful, formal look, they are much more difficult to grow and maintain than bush roses, and usually need staking. In the North, the whole plant must be bent over and buried during the winter in order to survive.

Remove all suckers growing on the main stem or from the roots as soon as they appear, or they will crowd out the grafted rose in a short time. Keep a close check to see that none of the wild rose suckers are growing in among the regular rose branches. Although the foliage is similar, the wild invaders can be spotted by careful observation.

Lightly prune the top of the rose tree by thinning out any weak branches and cutting out old branches that are no longer blooming well. Cut back the rest to five to ten inches from the graft. Do this in early spring before the green buds appear. In cold areas where the trees are buried for the winter, don't dig them up until all the hard frosts of 25 degrees F or less are over. Even though some sprouts may have already started, you should do any needed pruning at that time. You can snip during the growing season for shaping.

Rose hedges need heavier pruning at planting time than those grown as specimens in the garden. Set the plants two feet apart or slightly closer, and prune them to within four or five inches of the ground when you plant them. Each year, in late fall or very early spring, cut back enough of each plant to produce a bushy, hedgelike effect. Then, during the summer when the bushes grow too tall or wide, snip back the ends to keep the hedge looking nice and even.

Thorny multiflora roses are still planted for living fences in some areas; however, this type of hedge has many disadvantages. They are very wide and sprawling plants, which makes it difficult to get near enough to trim them, and it is nearly impossible to keep out the grass and weeds that spring up among them. In my opinion, the flowers are not attractive, and the birds scatter the seeds all over so that the plant sometimes becomes a pesky weed. If you decide to use them in spite of their drawbacks, prune them as tightly as possible from their youngest days, and carefully restrain them in their rows.

60

Pruning Shrubs with Colored Bark

Many maples, beeches, birches, roses, euonymus, brooms, and viburnums have distinctive bark color that can add beauty to an otherwise bare winter landscape. Although most of these are grown primarily for their summer beauty, a few are planted mainly for the color of their winter bark.

You should prune these plants in late spring to keep the wilder-growing varieties within bounds and to thin out growth so that the remaining stems will be larger, showing the colored bark better. Every six or seven years you may need to cut some of the larger stems to the ground to renew the plant.

Varieties having red bark are *Cornus alba* (Tartarian dogwood), *C. siberica* (Siberian dogwood), and *C. sericea* or *stolonifera* (red-osier dogwood). Try *Kerria japonica* (Japanese rose) for green stems. *Cornus sericea* 'Flaviramea' (golden- or yellow-twig dogwood) has yellow bark.

Fruit- and Berry-Producing Shrubs

If you consider the fruit important, prune these shrubs lightly to keep them in shape and to correct any damage caused by animals, weather, disease, or insects. Prune in early spring before any growth starts, although you can pick the fruit and berries in moderation in the fall. Some berry-producing shrubs are unisexual, including bayberry and winterberry. Only the female plants produce fruit, so if you want berries you must plant both male and female shrubs.

SOME SHRUBS THAT PRODUCE FRUITS OR BERRIES

Berberis (barberry)
Chaenomeles (flowering quince)
Cornus (dogwood)
Cotinus (smoke tree)
Cotoneaster
Crataegus (hawthorn) Best with a minimum of pruning.
Elaeagnus (Russian olive)

Euonymus atropurpurea (burning bush)
Ilex verticillata (winterberry)
Lonicera (honeysuckle)
Myrica pensylvanica (bayberry)
Pyracantha (fire thorn)
Rosa rugosa (rugosa rose)
Viburnum (cranberry bush, nannyberry, black haw)

Shrubs That Need Special Care in Pruning

Cornus florida (flowering dogwood) is one of the large shrubs, and in the areas with cold temperatures it's not a good idea to prune off its lower branches to make it into a tree. The tender bark sunscalds easily, and it will crack and split in the winter sun.

Cotoneaster requires little pruning except to shape. Some make excellent espaliers if properly pruned.

Deutzia should be pruned before all the flowers are completely gone so that new growth will start faster. Prune heavily for bushy growth. Prune off the suckers that come from the roots.

Hydrangea arborescens 'Grandiflora' (hills-of-snow), *H. quercifolia* (oak-leaf hydrangea), and *H. paniculata* 'Grandiflora' (peegee hydrangea) should be pruned in late winter. On the other hand, you should prune *H. macrophylla* (big leaf hydrangea) just as the flowers are fading, because it blooms on the tip of year-old wood.

Jasminum (jasmine) need constant heavy pruning, pinching, and shearing to keep them looking good. You can train most as a bush, or they can be espaliered as vines. Prune them anytime needed.

Lavandula (lavender) should be pruned heavily right after blooming. Plants pruned in late summer or early fall will likely suffer heavy winter injury. If you plan to dry the flowers, pick them just as they begin to open.

Liquidambar plants branch from the ground, so pinching terminal buds won't induce bushy side branching. Allow them to grow into their natural shape, but prune to space branches.

Morus alba (mulberry) tends to be brittle. Prune to shorten branches and to encourage a smaller, bushier tree that can better resist wind and other weather damage. Staking is usually beneficial to a young tree. Do not overfertilize mulberries.

Symphoricarpos (coralberry, snowberry) may grow leggy as it gets older. Prune the branches in very early spring, if necessary.

Tamarix parviflora (small-flowered tamarisk) blooms on the previous season's wood, so, unlike other tamarisk, this one should be pruned immediately after flowering.

Vaccinium (blueberry), when grown as an ornamental, needs pruning to remove old wood and to shorten branches that are bending over. For fruit, thin the branches and cut back twig growth at the ends of the branches, as described in Chapter 11.

Weigela needs heavy pruning to get rid of dead wood and winter injury which is often considerable.

Chapter 6

Pruning Shade Trees

Years ago there were about a dozen large maple and elm trees growing around one of the older houses in our neighborhood. The family members could tell you during which year each was planted, because each tree recalled a certain event.

"This is Effie's tree," they would say, "planted in 1887, the year she was born." One tree was Sarah's, and the other was George's, and so on. Trees commemorated the time Grandma and Grandpa got married, and the year Grandpa died. One even marked the time that a younger son had taken over the farm. Long after the farm was sold, family members returned for picnics under their trees.

Trees are still used as living reminders, just as they were then. Each year our small nursery sells a large number of commemorative trees. People plant them for births and marriages, as tributes to admired teachers, to commemorate special conventions, as memorials for a beloved friend or relative who has died, and as gifts from a graduating class.

It isn't necessary to plant a tree as a memorial for you to establish a personal relationship with it. A large shade tree is especially solid, strong, and dignified. It is a place where youthful secrets can be shared in a tree house and where everyone can cool off on a hot day as a breeze rustles the leaves above. I know one delightful lady who likes to hug the huge trunks of shade trees! In short, trees are special, and like everything else we treasure, they are worth our care and protection.

The term "shade tree" usually connotes a deciduous tree, although evergreens can also be shade trees. Evergreens will be covered in detail in the next chapter, however, so here I'll discuss only the trees that shed their leaves each autumn.

Don't take the term "shade tree" too literally. It also embraces trees like the Lombardy poplar that offer little in the way of shade. Shade trees also serve to define borders, to shield houses from noisy highways, to provide a protected living or playing area, and to offer autumn color, among many other purposes.

Since large trees are the kings and queens of the landscape, you should plan their locations with care. The rest of the landscape should relate to them as well as to the buildings.

Pruning the Young Tree

Shade trees are usually sold with their roots enclosed in a large ball of soil, so you will seldom need to prune them at planting time. Just don't disturb the root ball when you plant it.

However, if you purchase a small tree with no root ball or dig up a wild tree and transplant it, you should prune when you plant. (See Chapter 5.) Severe pruning is often necessary when you're planting a bare-rooted tree, because often a lot of root damage has been inflicted when it was dug up. Prune any broken roots with a smooth cut. Cut back the top, or leader, to two-thirds of its original length, and cut back all branches to about half their length. Always make your cuts on a slant, just above a bud, and cut to an outside bud on the side branches.

64

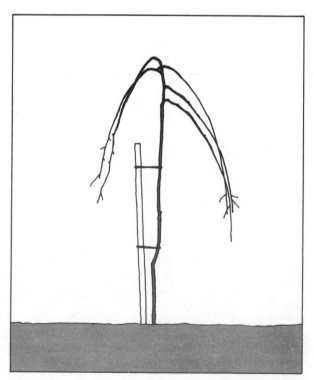

This weeping flowering crab apple needs a taller stake to hold up the weeping central leader if it is to develop into a well-shaped tree.

This young maple tree is making abundant sucker growth. All these suckers, as well as the weaker lower limbs, should be cut off close to the trunk in late summer.

Some trees that have been growing for several years in a large container before being sold will develop a circular habit of root growth. If this pattern continues after the tree is planted, the increasing size of the encircling roots can strangle the tree in later years. When you buy a container-grown tree, check the outside roots to see if this strangulation is occurring. If it is, prune off or spread out the offending root, and plant the tree in a good mixture of soil and compost to encourage quick growth of new, outward-reaching roots.

If the tree grows well, no additional pruning may be needed for many years, although occasionally a tree develops weak crotches that collect dirt and water. The wood in these crotches eventually begins to rot, and the rot may spread to the rest of the tree. You can do some snipping and pinching during the growing season to prevent the formation of a crooked top or crossed branches. Wait until the dormant season, however, to do any heavier pruning. Often you can help the tree to grow straight with a strong central leader by tying it to a tall stake.

Basal pruning. When the tree is 12 to 16 feet tall, decide whether or not you want to cut off its lower branches. If the tree is growing as part of a screen you probably will not, but if it is to grow into a large specimen shade tree — one you'll be able to picnic, play, and mow under easily when it is fully grown — you must begin some basal pruning.

Deciduous trees shade a house in summer, while admitting winter's lower rays.

The ideal way to shape a shade tree is to clip off all limbs that start too close to the ground as soon as they start, thereby directing more of the tree's growth upward. If you have neglected to do this early shaping, and large limbs are growing too low on your young tree, be sure that the tree has developed a good top before you cut off any of the bottom branches. The old rule is a good one: Never cut off more than a quarter to a third of a tree's branch area. A certain amount of leaf area is always necessary to feed the tree. If several good-size limbs must be cut off, spread the basal pruning over several years by cutting off only one or two each fall. By not being too hasty, you will allow the tree time to grow additional leaf area at the top to compensate for the loss of basal limbs, and you'll avoid shocking the tree.

Don't procrastinate when it comes to basal pruning, however. It's not only easier to cut off the bottom limbs of the tree when they are still small, but also you leave a smaller pruning wound to heal over. Basal limbs tend to grow upright on most trees when they are young, so it often seems unnecessary to cut them off. However, as the tree grows larger and wider these limbs spread outward and downward. Unless they are removed, they will become a nuisance by the time the tree is 15 or 20 years old. A distance of 8 feet from the ground to the first branches should be the bare minimum for most lawn trees. Prune street trees to 12 to 15 feet so they won't interfere with traffic.

Basal pruning not only makes a tree look more treelike, but it also lets in additional light and air to make your lawn, flowers, and other plants grow better. And your house will be more comfortable and energy-efficient year-round — large deciduous trees are Nature's air conditioners. They provide cooling shade in summer, and after their leaves have fallen in autumn, they allow sunlight through to warm your house when you need it most.

Take advantage of large, deciduous shade trees by proper basal pruning. To develop a high umbrella effect, cut off the lower limbs of your tree to the most beneficial height. A few seasons of noting how the sun enters the house at different times of the year will help you to ascertain what that height should be. Like a wide overhang or a window awning, the high shade trees let in the sun during the winter months, and block out the hot summer sunlight as well.

67

Tree Shapes

To avoid making major pruning mistakes when you're training a young tree, keep in mind what its mature shape would be naturally. As a rule, allow trees that grow in a pyramidal and columnar form to keep their lower

Basic tree shapes. From left to right: columnar, pyramidal, spreading (mounded), and weeping.

COLUMNAR

Acer platanoides 'Columnare' (columnar maple)
Betula pendula 'Fastigiata' (pyramid birch)
Carpinus Betulus 'Fastigiata' (pyramid hornbeam)
Fagus sylvatica 'Fastigiata' (upright beech)
Malus x *robusta* 'Erecta' (flowering crab)
Pinus Cembra (Swiss stone pine, especially *P. Cembra* 'Columnare')
Pinus Strobus 'Fastigiata' (upright white pine)
Pinus sylvestris 'Fastigiata' (upright Scotch pine)
Populus (poplar) Particularly upright is *P. nigra* 'Italica' (Lombardy poplar)
Prunus Sargentii 'Columnaris' (Sargent cherry)
Quercus robur 'Fastigiata' (pyramid English oak)
Sorbus Aucuparia 'Fastigiata' (upright mountain ash)
Thuja occidentalis 'Pyramidalis' (pyramid arborvitae)

PYRAMIDAL

Abies (fir)
Alnus oregona (red alder)
Cedrus (true cedar)
Corylus Colurna (Turkish filbert)
Fagus (beech)
Ilex Aquifolium (English holly)
Ilex opaca (American holly)
Larix (larch)
Magnolia (magnolia)
Nyssa sylvatica (black gum)
Picea (spruce)
Pinus nigra 'Pyramidalis' (pyramid Austrian pine)
Quercus palustris (pin oak)
Taxodium distichum (bald cypress)
Taxus cuspidata (upright yew)
Thuja occidentalis (American arborvitae)

ROUND

Acer palmatum (Japanese maple)
Acer platanoides (Norway maple)
Catalpa bignonioides 'Nana' (umbrella catalpa)
Fraxinus (ash)
Magnolia x *Soulangiana* (saucer magnolia)
Malus Sargentii (Sargent's crab apple)
Tsuga diversifolia (Japanese hemlock)

SPREADING

Acer (maple)
Betula (birch)
Fagus (beech)
Gleditsia (honey locust)
Phellodendron amurense (cork tree)
Pinus (pine)
Platanus (plane tree)
Populus x *gileadensis* (Balm of Gilead)
Quercus (oak)
Tilia (basswood)
Ulmus (elm)

WEEPING

Betula populifolia 'Pendula' (white birch)
Fagus sylvatica 'Pendula' (beech)
Larix decidua 'Pendula' (larch)
Picea Abies 'Acrocona' (Norway spruce)
Pinus Strobus 'Pendula' (white pine)
Prunus Persica (peach)
Salix babylonica (willow)
Sorbus Aucuparia (mountain ash)
Tsuga canadensis 'Pendula' (Canada hemlock)

branches. Spreading and ball-shaped trees look better and are more useful as shade trees if you remove their bottom branches. Trees with weeping habits, except possibly evergreens, need to be pruned enough so that the lower limbs do not flop on the ground. Light conditions and whether or not it has plenty of room to grow are also factors affecting the tree's mature form.

Most catalogs list the botanical and horticultural names of a plant as well as its common name. Many of the horticultural names describe the growth habit. When you see 'Fastigiata,' 'Columnare,' or 'Erecta' you can be sure the tree will take on an erect, upright form. 'Pyramidalis' indicates a cone shape. 'Globosa,' like globe, naturally indicates a round shape. 'Nana' means dwarf, and 'Pendula' refers to a hanging or weeping growth habit.

Pruning the Mature Tree

Even if you gave your trees the best training and pruning care when they were young, they will probably continue to need pruning even after they've matured. Weather, disease, and other unknowns will take their toll, no matter how carefully you planned the tree's location or performed its initial shaping. Or you may acquire a full-grown tree, having had no choice about its early training or choice of location. There are special factors to consider when you need to prune a mature tree.

69

The large limb on the left should be cut off close to the main trunk.

You must cut off a large branch carefully, so that you will do as little damage as possible to the tree, and to the surrounding plants and structures. Remove large limbs in sections, rather than all at once, to avoid having too much weight drop at one time. Tie a rope around the limb before cutting it, make any large cuts as directed in Chapter 4, and then ease it gently to the ground. Finally, paint over the cut end to seal out the weather and to facilitate healing.

Some older trees deteriorate ahead of their time because highway paving limits their growing area, or because erosion washes the good topsoil away from their roots. If environmental conditions have caused a loss of good root-growing area, the tree may need additional fertilizer to compensate for it. Premature aging of a tree can also be caused by road salt washing onto the root system, drainage from a nearby septic field, air pollution, or damage to the bark from lawn mowers, animals, insects, or disease. So, in addition to pruning, good tree care includes regular feeding with a good organic fertilizer containing nitrogen, and protection from the many hazards to which trees are vulnerable.

Tree Surgery

Tree surgery is the removal of major parts of a tree and the healing of bad wounds. It is a specialized job that usually requires extensive training and equipment. Even so, you can take care of minor tree surgery by yourself and save a considerable amount of money.

If you own a tree that has become decrepit, or if you have acquired a sad specimen along with your new property, you should first consider if the tree is worth saving. Life span varies greatly according to species. Some of the giant redwoods are estimated to be three or four thousand years old, and trees of many other species in this country are older than the Republic. However, some members of the poplar family are over the hill by the time they have reached the age of 30.

Natural and man-created environmental hazards may shorten a tree's life considerably. If it is near the end of its days, the best tree surgery in the world won't add many months to its life, and you'd be better off cutting it into firewood and replacing it with a young, healthy tree.

However, a tree that looks bad is not always ready to die, and taking down an old tree is a difficult and often expensive operation, especially if buildings, streets, or power lines are nearby. A tree that is only a little battered can benefit greatly from surgical care.

First, cut out all dead or rotten wood, as well as any wood that has been damaged by woodpeckers, ants, or other creatures. Saw off smooth, to the nearest live juncture, any limbs that are broken or partially broken, and seal all the cuts with a good tree paint or dressing. If you use a chain saw, be extremely careful not to cut into any healthy limbs accidentally, including your own.

You should brace a limb that is beginning to split to another solid, strong one by drilling a hole through both limbs and running a strong bar with a

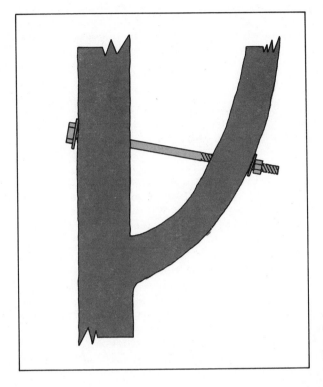

A heavy, weak limb can be secured by drilling holes through trunk and limb and joining them with a threaded bolt, nut, and large washers.

threaded end through them. A large washer at each end will prevent damage to the tree. You can also attach a cable to bolts through both limbs for bracing. Sometimes a large chain or wire rope is wrapped around both limbs to prevent splitting, but these could cut into the bark of the tree and make ugly wounds, so I don't recommend this method.

As I mentioned before, trees of any age may develop openings or cavities as a result of a wound. If the opening is not covered, it can develop into a canker or accumulate dirt and grime, and begin to rot. That rot will gradually spread into the rest of the tree, making it a place where insects and disease will proliferate.

The first step in filling a cavity is to clean it out carefully. Remove all dirt, old bark, insects, and rotten wood right down to solid wood, much as a dentist cleans out a tooth prior to filling it. If possible, flush out the area with clean water. Then smooth out the rough edges and fill the hole with a good tree-cavity sealer. Asphalt compounds, such as those used in patching driveways and roofs, are suitable, but avoid any compound containing creosote, since it is poisonous to trees. The commercial tree sealers made by Treekote are good because they usually include an antiseptic that discourages reinfection of wounds.

Check any tree-cavity jobs now and then to see that the material hasn't slipped out during hot weather, and to make sure that the filler hasn't shrunk and ceased to fill the opening. Add more material whenever necessary so that new wood can eventually grow neatly over the whole filling.

Choosing the Proper Tree

It is important to choose the type of tree you like and one that is suitable for the location you've chosen. For example, many small-growing trees are suitable for tiny lots, whereas a large-growing tulip tree or an enormous Balm of Gilead needs a more spacious area. Pick varieties that grow well in your climate and do not require more time than you have to give them.

The following shade trees succeed well in many locations and are widely planted across the country. There are also hundreds of others that are popular in more limited areas. Often there are many varieties within the same species, so your choice is wide and almost endless. Prune them according to the rules for all shade trees, unless exceptions are noted.

Acer (maple). There are many varieties of this beautiful tree. They branch well, and produce an abundance of large, heavy leaves that have excellent fall color. They are also excellent shade trees. Sizes range from the small-leaved and dwarf-growing maples, such as Chinese, to the giant sugar maple and red maple that may grow over a hundred feet tall.

The Norway maple is a nice tree for planting along streets, and varieties of it have been introduced with red and variegated foliage. The silver maple grows fast, but it requires considerable pruning. Its shallow roots sometimes present a problem in lawns and under sidewalks.

Prune all maples in late summer, since they bleed badly if pruned in late winter or spring.

Aesculus (horse chestnut). The horse chestnuts and buckeyes have been long planted as street trees, although I feel there are certainly many better choices. The trees eventually grow too large for most street plantings and city lots, and they are dirty trees. Throughout the year they drop flowers, inedible nuts, leaves, and twigs, and as if these drawbacks weren't enough, they are quite susceptible to disease.

Betula (birch). Although there are many kinds of birch with white, yellow, or gray bark, the paper white (canoe) birch is most people's favorite. Their leaves are small, so grass and flowers can grow well in its dappled shade. The leaves of some varieties suffer badly from leaf miner attack, and as they grow older these trees become unattractive unless often sprayed. Paper white and gray white birch are often grown in clumps or groupings. In addition to early training, you should prune them to show the white bark at its best advantage. Do this in late summer or early fall to avoid bleeding. Never pull the papery bark from the tree because it will permanently disfigure the trunk.

72

Carpinus (hornbeam). There are several kinds of this long-lived tree, such as the European, American, and Japanese. All are small-to-medium size, bushy trees with attractive foliage. They are difficult to transplant, grow very slowly, and are sometimes clumpy. Prune them only to keep them in a tree form, and just leave their rugged, natural appearance undisturbed for as long as possible.

Fagus (beech). The smooth, gray bark of the American beech and the interesting foliage of the European beech make both of these trees valuable in a landscape planting. The American variety should be basal-pruned to show off its attractive bark in the northern winter landscape. Beech limbs are heavy, so it's best to train the tree early to grow with a central leader. However, eventually the limbs will probably grow into a crotch.

Fraxinus (ash). There are numerous kinds of ash, but the green ash is one of the most popular. It is attractive and tall and is a good street tree that needs little care. The leaves are fernlike, and the tree produces an abundance of keys (seeds) similar to those of the maples. It is inclined to leaf out late in the spring and drop its foliage early, showing very little fall color. Much of the fall clean-up is eliminated because the leaves don't accumulate on the ground. By pruning the lower limbs you help to force the growth upward and enhance the natural upright growth of the ash family. Other pruning is minimal.

Ginkgo biloba (ginkgo). This is a good street tree because of its resistance to disease, insects, and pollution. It grows tall and reaches well above wires and street lights. Individual trees produce either male or female flowers. Only male trees should be planted if they can be identified, as the female blooms produce fruits with a strong, unpleasant smell. Basal pruning can help emphasize its height, but prune it as little as possible. It becomes more attractive as it matures.

Gleditsia triacanthos (honey locust). This tree provides only light shade, so grass grows well beneath it. There's only minor leaf accumulation in the fall. Some of the newer varieties add color and don't produce the messy pods formed by the regular variety. High basal pruning makes it a good substitute for the American elm that, alas, has fallen victim to Dutch elm disease all over the country. Prune in late summer to correct the bad crotches that tend to develop. Keep it growing to a central leader as long as possible.

Liriodendron Tulipifera (tulip tree). A huge tree that needs lots of room, the attractive tulip tree has large flowers hidden among its leaves each spring and sports golden fall color. It is disease-resistant, which makes it an ideal shade tree wherever room and climate permit. Pruning is seldom necessary.

Phellodendron amurense (cork tree). The cork gives a filtered shade effect. It has a broad, spreading top, beautiful foliage, attractive bark, and grows well under city conditions. There are few insects and diseases that bother it. Since it is not a tall tree, it should be allowed to branch close to the ground. The wide-spreading branches and furrowed bark add to its charm. It needs pruning only to keep a straight central leader.

Platanus (plane tree, sycamore). Both trees need careful basal pruning when they are young in order to develop a strong central leader. Large limbs are likely to develop, but since it is such a strong grower, this creates no problem.

Populus (poplar). As most of the poplars are short-lived, they are useful wherever you need temporary, fast-growing trees. The most commonly planted is the tall, slim Lombardy. The large-leafed Balm of Gilead is probably the largest and longest-lived of them all. Prune poplars in late summer.

Quercus (oak). Members of this large family of majestic trees typically grow more slowly than the maples, but, like them, oaks are best suited only for the larger lots because of their size. In certain areas they are somewhat susceptible to disease and insect damage, but live for decades nevertheless. They have excellent, long-lasting fall foliage. Pruning should be limited to removing dead, diseased, or broken wood, and to training when young.

Salix (weeping willow). This widely planted tree has little besides its graceful beauty to recommend it. The wood is very brittle and breaks easily, and the leaves are small. Being susceptible to insects and disease, it is short-lived as well. It grows very fast, however, and leafs out early in the spring. Some varieties are suitable for planting only on wet ground, and others do well only in dry areas.

Both pruning and staking are necessary early in the tree's life. This is to prevent it from "weeping" when it is too young, which would cause it to become a misshapen bush instead of a graceful tree. Later in the tree's life, constant pruning is necessary to prevent the long branches from dragging on the ground and becoming a nuisance. Because they grow very fast and are short-lived, they should ordinarily never be fertilized. Remove dead wood as soon as you discover it, of course, but avoid overpruning whenever possible, or you will stimulate too much regrowth. Prune in late summer, since weeping willows bleed badly if pruned in late winter or spring.

Tilia (linden, basswood). Some of the numerous varieties of this family are suited for one part of the country and some for another. They are tall trees with beautiful foliage and bark, and produce fragrant flowers that are attractive to bees. Some have large leaves. High basal pruning should be practiced to emphasize their tall growth and distinctive bark as they grow to their majestic size.

Chapter 7

Pruning Evergreens

When I first became interested in home landscaping some thirty years ago, I was impressed by the hundreds of beautiful, bushy balsam firs and white spruce that dotted the pastures of many northern New England dairy farms. These evergreens were obviously quite old, but the cows had kept them trimmed to a neat, compact size, and many looked strikingly better than the conifers that graced the manicured lawns in the village.

Since they were free, I moved a few of them from our cow pasture to our front yard. I watered them often, and sheared them carefully, but they soon grew out of shape, got too big, and lost their beauty.

So I began to watch more closely as our hungry herd of Holsteins did their shearing. Obviously they were doing something right! I noticed that they began eating the pale green, soft, new growth as soon as it started in the spring, and they always chewed the trees on dewy mornings or during a rain. As soon as the short growing season was over, the cows stopping snacking on the evergreens and went on to other fodder, allowing the cut ends to heal rapidly.

As soon as I began to imitate the shearing techniques of our bovine botanists, my landscaping efforts began to improve. In fact, it wasn't long before one of the town's best gardeners stopped by to ask what my pruning secret was, and where I had learned it.

By following the example of the cows and experimenting on my own, I discovered that with proper pruning I could keep an evergreen at a certain size, or I could allow it to grow so slowly that it hardly seemed to be growing at all. If the pruning is done correctly, the tree will look as if it grew that way naturally.

Classes of Evergreens

Trees in general are usually divided into the deciduous or evergreen categories. Deciduous trees lose their foliage during the winter, while ever-

An evergreen sheared to pointed form. This natural-looking shape is suited to locations where heavy snowfalls might crush trees trimmed to a flat or rounded shape.

76

greens keep theirs year-round. Although we tend to think that all evergreens are conifers, some members of this large family do not bear cones. Yews and junipers, for example, produce berries instead. To add to the confusion, some conifers are not evergreens. Larch (tamarack) and taxodium both look as if they should belong to the evergreen family, but they always shed their needles for the winter. There are also a considerable number of shrubs that are deciduous in the North and yet evergreen in the South.

It is difficult to try to classify evergreens because there are thousands of varieties, from the mosslike ground covers to the giant redwoods. The most convenient way to divide them is into the broadleafed and narrow-leafed kinds. In this text, the term *narrow-leafed evergreen* will refer to fir, hemlock, juniper, pine, spruce, yew, cedar, and arborvitae. Although some of these do not have needles, I am including them in that category because they have most of the other characteristics of the narrow-leafed group. The broadleafed evergreens include azalea, boxwood, camellia, holly, laurel, pieris, rhododendron, and the like.

Shearing and Pruning

As I noted before, cutting off the soft, new growth of a tree or plant during the summer months is called shearing. This is done to confine the growth of the plant, while ordinary pruning is essentially the removal of woody limbs when the tree is not making an active growth. Evergreens are more likely to be sheared than pruned, although you should cut away dead, diseased, or broken branches — sometimes basal branches or even the entire top may be removed for one reason or another. If you have to prune limbs, do it in late summer, fall, or winter when the tree is dormant. If you cut into the limbs during the growing season, they are likely to bleed badly.

I like to think of shearing as giving the tree a haircut. You cut off the ends of all the branches on the outside of the tree, much as you would shear a sheep or a dog. Each type of evergreen makes a different growth: the new growth on hemlocks tends to be droopy, while that on spruce or fir is stiff.

When pines are growing, they send out numerous little upright shoots called candles. If you want the tree to grow a little, wait until the candles are two to four inches long, and then pinch or clip off just the very tips. If the tree is as large as you want it ever to get, let the candles grow to about an inch and then shear them off.

Long-handled hedge shears are the best tools for shearing, because they are easy to control and safe to use. Thin-bladed shearing knives are good for fast work and are widely used in Christmas tree plantations, but they are

77

The spruce on the left has been allowed to grow naturally, while its civilized cousin on the right has been sheared each year in early summer.

78

*The candles on top and sides
are trimmed on red, white,
and Scotch pines to maintain
a compact appearance.*

difficult to use for the precision work required in home landscaping, and they can be dangerous, too. Electric clippers can be a big help when you're doing a lot of shearing that must be completed early in the growing season, because they are so much faster than hand shears. We've found them especially good for shearing hedges. If you have only a few small evergreens, you can give them a light pruning by simply pinching off the ends of the soft, new growth with your fingers. This pinching is especially effective on the stiff, upright candles of the dwarf pines.

If you start shearing the tree when it is still small, you'll get the best results. I often hear people say, "When that tree gets to the height I want it, I'm going to start shearing it." This is a mistake. It is difficult and usually impossible to get a tall, loose-growing tree to tighten up and look nice if you start shearing too late in its life.

Your shearing, even when the tree is tiny, should conform to the shape you want it to be when it finally reaches the desired height. It is difficult to change the shape of a tree once it is well established. If you allow it to grow too wide at the base, for instance, it will be very difficult to decrease the width later on without spoiling the look of the tree.

How Evergreens Grow

Many people think that trees grow just as children do, throughout the year without a pause. Unless you've observed them carefully, you may never have noticed that narrow-leafed evergreens have a faster growing season than do the deciduous trees and shrubs that grow throughout most of the summer. The entire growing season for most evergreens lasts only about three weeks, although some varieties such as hemlocks and junipers do have a longer season, and yews make a small additional growth in late summer wherever the climate permits.

Be aware of the growing season of evergreens, because that is the best time to shear them. Pines, most spruces, firs, and yews begin to grow about the time that freezing nights are over and the ground is warming up. This may vary from April or even earlier in the South to mid-June in the colder sections of the country. Arborvitae, cypress, hemlock, and juniper start their growth a little later in the season. Fortunately, because evergreens have a built-in dormancy that is well adjusted to their locality, they seldom start to sprout much ahead of schedule each season. Even during an unusually early warm spell in winter, they are likely to wait until the proper time to start growing.

Evergreens make their new growth from buds that were formed the preceding year. These buds are brown, and you can spot them at the end of each twig from midsummer to the next spring. In addition to these fat, obvious terminal buds, the tree produces thousands of smaller buds that ordinarily do not grow. Proper shearing temporarily stops the active growth of the large, fat buds, and stimulates the sprouting and growth of many of the smaller ones tha lie dormant all over the branches. Thus, when you shear off the new growth, the tree's energy that normally would cause a few limbs to make active growth upward and outward is redirected into these thousands of smaller twigs, and you force the tree to grow bushier.

To get the best results, begin the first shearing soon after growth starts in the spring. Don't allow the tree to make a lot of growth before you shear it, or the smaller buds will remain dormant. By shearing when the new sprouts are still short, the small interior buds will start growing at once.

There is another reason for shearing during the early part of the growing season. The cuts you make on the new growth will heal quickly, and new buds will form where the cut was made. These new buds will grow the following spring. They completely hide any shearing wounds, and the tree looks for all the world as if growing that way was its own idea. If you shear too late in the season, you will cut off these newly formed buds, and the unsightly cut stubs will show all year.

Whether you shear your evergreens more than once during their growing season will depend on the amount they grow that year and on the size and shape you want them to be. Shearing only once gives a more natural look to the tree, since the new growth is uneven. Many gardeners prefer this unshorn appearance, although eventually the tree may grow too large. Two or three shearings may be necessary if you want to keep your plant growing in the tightest, most compact form.

79

It is important that shearing be an annual event. We warn our customers not to take their vacations during the evergreen-growing season because if even one year's clipping is missed, it is difficult to get some trees back into shape. A good shearing takes only a few minutes per tree, and it is time well spent. I'd recommend that you look over your plantings every day or two when they are making their most active growth. By observing the beautiful spring-green growth you'll not only keep abreast of how they're doing, but I've a hunch that the plants will respond to your presence too, and thrive because of it.

Shaping Specimen Evergreens

Chances are that the beautiful, tight blue spruce you admire in your neighbor's yard was sheared last spring and several springs before that, as was the bushy hemlock in the public garden, and the globe arborvitae on the church lawn. Specimen trees attain a special beauty through proper shearing.

If you're planning to plant a specimen tree, it is important that you choose the right variety of tree, and then after it is established you must shear it to compliment its natural growth habit. A pine, for example, is not ordinarily a good choice for a sheared specimen tree because it grows too fast and also tends to lose its lower branches. Pines look best when allowed to grow into magnificent, full-size trees. Firs also lose their lower branches after a few years, although they make attractive temporary plantings. If you want a medium-size, stately specimen that will last a long time, choose an arborvitae, hemlock, or spruce. These hold their branches to the ground very well, especially if you shear them regularly.

When you buy a young tree for a specimen, choose a bushy, well-shaped one so that you get your project off to a good start. If the tree is thin and ill-shaped, or was dug from the wild, you must prune it severely at planting time to get it into a more compact shape.

Specimen trees should be allowed to grow a little each year in their early life, so one or two shearings each growing season are enough, unless you are trying to achieve a very formal look. A week after the first shearing you may need to give the tree another light clipping if it is growing out of shape or if you need to remove any extra tops.

Hemlock and American arborvitae grow as cone-shaped, narrow pyramids and look best when they are sheared to this form. Spruce trees tend to develop a cone shape too, but are a bit more spreading at the base.

Keep the top of each tree sheared to a point, or at least rounded off. Not only does this shaping make a natural-looking tree, but a pointed tree is less likely to be damaged by ice storms or heavy loads of snow than a flat-topped one. All parts of evergreen trees need sunlight, so it is important that the upper branches never get any wider than the bottom ones. Shaded twigs will die.

After the tree has reached the desired size, severe shearing will probably be necessary to keep it from growing any larger, and several shearings may be necessary during the growing weeks. Although these will in no way hurt the

80

tree, it's better to give it several light clippings than to take off too much at once.

Ordinarily an evergreen grows about one foot each year. By shearing you can shorten this growth to no more than a few inches per year, which appreciably lengthens the time you can enjoy your tree before it gets too big and has to be replaced. If you prefer not to shear severely, you can shear lightly and let your tree gradually increase in size throughout its life. However, if you choose to practice severe pruning, the tree can be kept small for a lifetime, getting thicker and more beautiful all the time. The branches will become so dense that you can even lay your ladder against the strong, thick branches of a larger tree when you're pruning the top.

These tight trees make a favorite nesting place for birds, as they like the protection of the dense branches for raising their young. More than once we've had to refuse to sell a tree that a mother robin has claimed for her nursery, and occasionally we've been thrilled to find a nest among the boughs of our sheared Christmas tree; according to tradition, this is an omen of good luck for the next 12 months.

Shearing Dwarf Evergreens

With the popularity of the one-story ranch house and the necessity for small lots in crowded areas, there is an increasing demand for small landscape

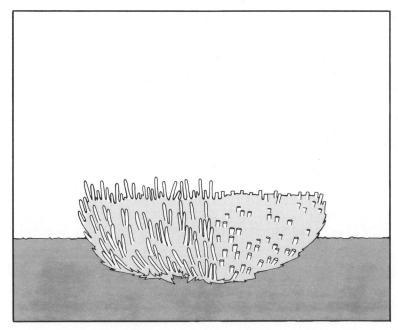

This dwarf pine is sheared to keep it from spreading too wide.

plants. Many species grow short and shrubby naturally, like the spreading yew, some mugho pines, and trailing juniper. Other dwarf evergreens are freaks of nature — that is, runts that failed to grow into large trees. A dwarf tree can be propagated by grafting or by cuttings, and many new varieties of conifers have been introduced this way. We now have named varieties of dwarf white pine, dwarf Scotch pine, dwarf Norway spruce, dwarf balsam fir, and many more. These undersized trees are so popular that horticulturists tramp through woods and pastures looking for even more interesting mutations of nature to propagate.

In addition to the natural dwarf evergreens and the freaks of nature, we have a new source of small evergreens. A whole new industry is at work crossing the various dwarf plants now in existence, thereby creating even more varieties. Botanists are busy trying to classify and name thousands of diminutive evergreens.

Although miniatures range from rock garden-type trees that grow only a few inches high to varieties that may grow several feet tall, most of them will likely need some shearing. Nearly all will need to be clipped around the sides occasionally if they are to retain their compact shape. A spreading yew that's two feet tall and ten feet across may be an interesting sight on an open hillside, but it looks out of place beside the front steps.

Each type of dwarf evergreen should be sheared only enough to keep it within bounds and looking good. Creeping junipers need only to have their outer ends snipped and dead branches removed. You should allow an upright Scotch pine (*Pinus sylvestris* 'Fastigiata') to grow to its natural tall, skinny shape, usually without any pruning. Weeping pines or hemlocks should be permitted to droop. Spreading, creeping, globe, and vaselike evergreens should each be clipped according to their natural growth habit. Shear them only when the plant starts to grow out of shape or out of bounds, only during its active growing season so that the cut ends will heal over quickly.

Dwarfing Evergreens by Shearing

If you want to grow dwarf evergreens, it is much better to buy and plant the varieties that are true dwarfs whenever possible, rather than to shear taller-growing specimens. Not only do the dwarfs look more natural, but they are easier to care for, and there is less danger that they will outgrow the spot you've given them.

If you live in the country, however, you might like to experiment and create your own dwarf evergreens from wild trees. Native wild trees have the advantage of being both dependably hardy and free. If you're careful to shear them severely each year, wild trees personally dwarfed by you can make excellent low-cost landscaping.

If you want to keep a spruce, fir, pine, hemlock, or arborvitae to a height of one or two feet for a lifetime, simply follow the instructions for shearing specimen trees. Instead of one or two light shearings each year, however, you will probably need to give the tree more. Sometimes you may need to shear four or five times, which will mean giving the tree a tight clipping every four or five days during the growing season. Your shearing must be especially severe once the tree reaches the height you want it to be so that it will never get any larger. Root pruning every few years is one way to slow down the top growth and make shearing easier and more effective. (See page 35.)

I advise customers to do their shearing when they are angry. If you go into the front yard singing or whistling, you won't cut off enough. The secret of good shearing is to snarl as you slash, at least until you get the hang of it.

By intensive shearing, you can keep a tall-growing species of evergreen small practically forever. We have a native white spruce in our backyard that is more than 50 years old. If we had allowed it to grow, it would probably now be over 50 feet in height. But I've sheared it to stay 3 feet tall and can keep it that size for another 50 years if I tend to business.

SHEAR WHEN WET

If possible, shear all the narrow-leafed evergreens when they are wet, just as the cattle do. An ideal time to trim is after a rain or when the trees are covered with early morning dew. When they are damp, the sheared ends will not turn pinky brown right after they are cut. Don't worry if you must shear the needle evergreens when they are dry, however. The browning is only a temporary discoloration, and will soon disappear. Only the evergreens with needles seem to have this browning problem, so wet-shearing isn't necessary with cedars, cypress, junipers, or arborvitae, or the broadleafed evergreens.

Pruning Narrow-Leafed Evergreens

When spruce trees and some other evergreens are young, they have beautiful lush branches that grow to the ground. As a spruce grows larger, some people like to cut out a few of these lower branches so that the handsome trunk can be seen. In some cases they may even prune off all of the lower limbs to feature the trunk. Consider this decision carefully before you cut, because once the branches are off, you can't put them back!

Do any heavy pruning of this type in late summer or fall. If you prune in early summer, the tree will bleed badly, and in very cold weather the frozen, brittle wood may break in the wrong places, injuring the trunk.

If you need to shorten limbs only slightly, do it in the very early spring, so the new growth will cover your cuts within a few weeks. The amount you cut should be *very* small, however, because at this time of year it is dangerous for the tree.

Annual pruning of a spruce. The cut on the pruned tree (right) shows where to prune to reduce its size.

If you are basal-pruning a very large evergreen, you may find that sometimes a lower limb has a large, fat, burllike growth where it joins the trunk. If so, cut the limb just outside the burl rather than close to the trunk as you ordinarily would. Cutting too close makes an unnecessarily large wound.

Owners of forest trees who want to grow fine lumber sometimes basal-prune to make the bottom log free of knots. This type of pruning is also used to force wild Christmas trees to grow bushier and in better shapes. (See Chapter 16.)

Shearing Windbreaks and Screens

Spruces, arborvitae, and hemlocks make ideal screens or windbreaks, because they grow slowly and tightly, and they hold their lower branches to the ground, even late in life. Pines and firs grow faster, but because they tend to lose their bottom limbs eventually, they are less desirable for this purpose.

Evergreens used as tall windbreaks need pruning and shearing mainly early in their life to help them grow in a tight pattern and close to the ground. To accomplish this, clip the tops and sides each year for the first two or three years. If you decide to keep your windbreak cut back to a reasonable height, you'll also want to keep the sides sheared so that the width will be manageable. Make sure that the top part of the tree is never wider than the lower. The bottom branches of all evergreens need all the light they can get.

Can Older Evergreens Be Rejuvenated?

People often ask me if they can renew an evergreen tree or hedge that has grown too large and out of shape by cutting it back nearly to the ground. Although you can do this to a lilac bush with good results, it is not overly successful unless the evergreen is young and vigorous. Yews are an exception, however, and often you can cut back even an older plant heavily, and it will recover and begin to grow again.

The common rule for pruning an evergreen is that you should never take off more than a third of its total green material. If you are planning to top

85

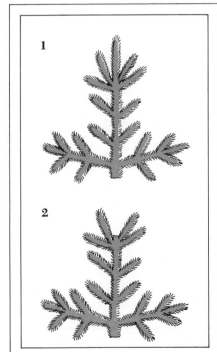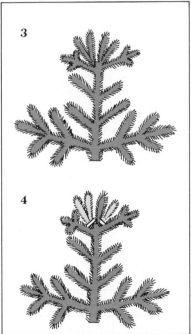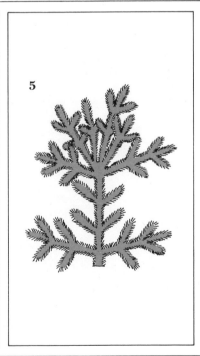

Steps in restoring a broken top.

trees, basal-prune them, or cut off greens for Christmas, remember that removing more than a third is likely to cause a severe shock to the tree.

Pruning Broadleafed Evergreens

The list of broadleafed evergreens is so long that I'll make no attempt to cover them individually, with the exception of those that are most common. Compared to the narrow-leafed evergreens, the broadleafs generally need very little pruning, and the pruning they do need is similar for all of them.

Azalea, holly, mountain laurel, and rhododendron are grown over much of the United States, while bamboo, bay laurel, hollygrape, jasmine, leucothoe, oleander, olive, and many others are grown in the warm South and along the Pacific Coast. In addition to these, there are many shrubs that are deciduous in the North and evergreen in the South, such as certain varieties of abelia, andromeda, azalea, barberry, cotoneaster, daphne, euonymus, pyracantha, privet, and many viburnums.

86

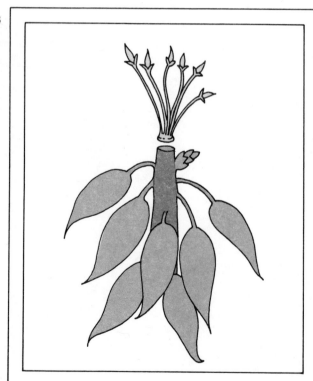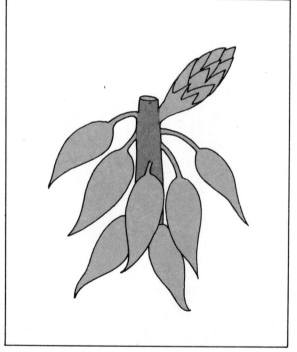

Be careful in removing old flower clusters from azaleas so that the newly forming buds are not damaged.

Most broadleafed evergreens are sold potted or with their roots in a ball of soil, so no pruning at planting time is necessary. Early pruning to train the plant is important, however. Azaleas, mountain laurel, and rhododendrons are closely related, so their early training is much the same. Many varieties of these plants tend to have a loose habit of growth. Therefore, some pinching or cutting back of the new growth is necessary if you want a tight, compact bush. Simply snip off the terminal, or end, buds of the new sprouts during the early summer, forcing the latent buds to develop and grow along the sides of the branches.

If you want your bush to stay compact, continue this type of pruning for the life of the plant. After the plant reaches blooming size, you should distinguish between the small end buds — the ones to be pinched off if the branches are growing too long — and the big, fat blossom buds that will be next spring's blooms. The blossom buds are the ones to leave on the plant.

Camellias and hibiscus also need some pinching of the end buds in the early summer if you want the plants to grow bushy. If you prefer a tall, vinelike growth, or choose to espalier them, cut out the shoots that are growing in the wrong direction. Train the longer shoots by carefully bending them and tying them to the lattice or trellis in the way you want them to grow.

Holly needs very little pinching when it is young, since it tends to grow tight naturally. You may need to shear Japanese holly for shaping. All hollies will need annual clipping during the growing period if they are being grown as hedges. If you want your holly to grow tall, however, prune it as little as possible until it starts its upward growth. It may take a few years before it decides to get growing, so be patient.

Maintenance pruning. Limit your maintenance pruning of the broadleafed evergreens to removing fading flowers immediately after they have bloomed so that the plants won't waste any energy in producing seeds. Any branches that are too long can be shortened at the same time. Cut off winter injury and broken branches anytime. Go easy on picking flowers for bouquets from small plants during the first few years, but you can cut them safely from mature plants in moderate amounts with no damage to the plant. Holly branches can also be cut from a mature bush at Christmas time for decoration. In fact, this time of year seems to be about as good a time as any to prune holly.

Renewal pruning. As broadleafed evergreen shrubs grow older, they occasionally need rejuvenation. In the South, rhododendrons, azaleas, mountain laurel, and others are often cut back completely to the ground to renew them. Usually they are fertilized heavily with cottonseed meal and manure a year or two before this operation to help them to withstand it.

It works best, however, to spread any heavy cutback over two or more years, especially if below-freezing temperatures are common where you live. Do heavy pruning of this type in late winter or very early spring, because growth can start soon after.

You can prune hibiscus severely in early spring also. Cut out any winter damage and all branches that are broken or out of shape. Thin out growth that is too thick, and cut back all the remaining branches. Hibiscus blooms on new wood, so even if a bush is cut back to a foot or so from the ground, it will still bloom well during the following season.

Where there is no frost, you can grow a poinsettia into a large shrub. To get it and similar plants to bloom well, cut back all the branches in early spring. You can renew the whole bush at the same time if it needs it, by cutting it down to about a foot from the ground.

Broadleafed evergreen trees, such as camellias, magnolias, and gardenias, seldom need pruning. Some shaping in early life is practically all that is ever necessary. Avoid making any large cuts unless conditions absolutely require it, because the cut ends seldom heal well.

Though most of the broadleafs are grown for their blooms, some of the smaller-leafed ones are widely planted for green hedges and topiary. Japanese holly, boxwood, and evergreen privet are some of these. Shear these during the summer to the shape you want. I will discuss their care in the following chapters.

88

Chapter 8

Pruning Hedges

Recently a friend of ours sold his home. An avid gardener, he had added a few dollar's worth of plants to his property each spring, and since he always bought small- and medium-size plants, his entire investment over a ten-year period wasn't more than $300. As soon as he got home from work each day, he would putter away in his garden, pruning and shearing his flowering plants and fruit trees. His particular pride and joy was a beautifully sheared hemlock hedge.

"I'm sure that the landscaping sold my place," he told us. "And I'm pretty sure I got $10,000 more for it because of the landscaping." His neighbor's identical house on the same street was still unsold, even though he was asking $8,000 less for it. He had only a few anemic-looking bushes growing around his place.

Our friend was delighted about the monetary success of his investment, but more important, his gardening hobby had given him pleasure and relaxation over the years. As soon as he moved, he started to landscape the grounds around his new house, and the first thing he planted was a long hedge of tiny hemlocks. He already has begun to shear it.

Although a hedge makes an attractive border or backdrop, many are planted for reasons other than beauty. A hedge can mark property lines, shield out traffic noise and fumes, hide unattractive views, discourage trespassing, insure privacy, form windbreaks or snow traps, and even shelter nesting birds.

The way you shear a hedge varies according to its purpose. You can trim it into a tight and formal shape or allow it to grow loose and natural. You can make it tall, medium, or short, or if you want, you can sculpt the top into towers and castle walls. You can have an evergreen or deciduous hedge, and one that produces fruit or flowers.

Caring for a hedge is not difficult, yet as you drive around it's obvious that many gardeners are not too skilled in the art. Perhaps the old English expression, "homely as a hedge fence," refers to one of these unkempt rows of bushes.

Just as barbers probably did during the long-hair era, real gardeners sometimes feel an almost uncontrollable urge to stop their cars, grab their shears, and start clipping whenever they see an untidy hedge.

We get more questions about how to prune a hedge than about any other type of pruning, except possibly that of fruit trees. People seem to realize that they should trim their hedges, but they hesitate to prune as severely as they should.

Pruning at Planting

It is particularly important to get each hedge plant off to a good start. Each one should grow in a bushy form at about the same speed as all of its companions. Start with healthy, compact, small plants if possible.

How much cutting back does a new hedge plant need? If you set out well-shaped, bushy, nursery-grown specimens with their root balls intact, or if they are pot-grown, you probably won't need to do any pruning at planting time.

Those plants that you dig from the wild, however, need to be cut back heavily, as do bare-rooted, nursery-grown hedge plants (see page 4). Cut back about half of the top, just before or just after planting to compensate for the roots that were lost or damaged when the plant was dug up. Another reason for trimming back spindly or tall hedge plants is so that you will have a dense, symmetrical hedge.

To get a tight, low-growing, sheared hedge, set out the plants two feet apart, measuring from the center of each plant. You can plant tall-growing hedges, such as a lilac hedge, several feet apart, but the exact distance depends on how quickly you want a tight hedge. The farther apart you plant them, the longer it will take for the plants to intermingle.

You can dig a hole for each individual plant, but if they each have a large root ball, it is easier to plant your hedge in one long trench. Either way, if you are planting a straight hedge, use a string stretched taut to mark the line, just as if you were getting ready to plant your peas in a garden row.

Unless you're having a mass planting, you should never plant a hedge more than one plant wide. Set the plants in a single rather than a staggered line unless you plan to use your hedge only as a high windbreak or a snow trap.

Shearing a Hedge

The best time to shear any hedge is when it is making its fastest growth. Most needle evergreens make their growth early, so you won't need to shear them after midsummer. (See Chapter 7.) However, most deciduous plants, like the privet, ninebark, and barberry, grow for a longer period, so you must trim them off and on throughout most of the summer. Broadleafed evergreens such as the boxwood and Japanese holly also grow over a long period, so they will need some shearing throughout the season. You should prune flowering

90

A hedge placed along the windward edge of a yard will make an effective snow fence, keeping snow from driveways and paths.

plants only after the blooms have faded so that new buds can set for the following year. Rose hedges are the exception, and are best pruned in early spring or late fall. Shear them in summer only if they are growing either too tall or too wide.

Begin to shear your young plants just as soon as they start to grow noticeably — sometimes the first year and certainly by the second. Even if you want your hedge to grow to four feet, don't wait until it gets to that height before you start to shape it. In order to have a tall, tight hedge, you should first develop a small, tight hedge and let it grow larger gradually. Just as it is difficult to make a single, tall, loose-growing tree compact and bushy, it's no easy job to tighten up a large, loose-growing hedge.

You'll need to trim an informal hedge only once or twice a year, although the more vigorous varieties, such as privet or ninebark, may need additional clippings. Formal hedges need more attention with a cutting every few days during their growing season to look their best.

The best guideline to use for most hedges, I've found, is to trim them whenever they look as if they need it. Just as you wouldn't wait for your lawn to become a field before mowing it, you should trim your hedge throughout the growing season. It will be thicker and better looking if you cut frequently, removing only small amounts at a time. The hedge will be healthier too, because it will expend less of its energy on useless growth.

One common mistake that gardeners make is to shear off the top of the hedge while ignoring the sides. Soon the hedge is irregular and too wide, and sags under the weight of heavy rains, ice, or snow. And if anything happens to an individual plant, you can replace it much more easily if the hedge is slender.

You should always shear a hedge so that the bottom is wider than the top. The difference may be barely noticeable, but it is extremely important. Hedges that are even slightly wider at the top always look top-heavy, and the lower branches, lacking their full share of sunlight, become thin and soon die.

Unless you have an excellent eye for such things, you may want to put up posts and a string as a guide when you're shearing long, straight, formal hedges, so that you don't end up with a lopsided row.

I've found that the easiest way to trim the half-mile of arborvitae hedge surrounding our grounds is with electric hedge shears, since the job has to be done quickly and often, while the plants are making their fastest growth. Electric shears are fast, easy to handle, precise, and less tiring to use than hand shears. Shears with long handles and blades are excellent if you don't have to prune a great deal of hedge. A shearing knife is handy for informal shearing, but it isn't easy to do accurate work with it.

92

MAKING AN ARCH

Frequently we are asked how we trained the archway in our hedge. Probably the easiest way to make an archway is to plant two tall trees four to six feet apart to act as sides of the arch. Bend them over carefully to the desired height, and tie them together to form the arch. (Spring is the best time to bend them.) Within a few years they will grow together in a natural graft.

You can also make an arch by grafting the two trees together initially. Hemlock, arborvitae, and most other tall-growing evergreens, as well as some deciduous plants, will fuse together well. You can also build a wooden trellis in the proper shape, and plant a vine to cover it. If you choose the proper vine, it will look very much like a part of the hedge.

Plant the trees far enough apart so that by the time they have grown thick and full you will still have enough room to push your lawn mower and other equipment through the opening.

Whether you choose a hedge archway or one made of vines, you should shear it every year to keep it thick and bushy. If you keep the sides of the arch narrow enough to allow light to enter, the branches on the underside of the arch will stay green and growing.

REVIVING AN OLD HEDGE

You may be faced with an overgrown hedge, with plants that are too tall, too wide, or growing out of kilter with each other. If the plants are thrifty and healthy you may be able to cut them back nearly to the ground and allow them to start over. Your chances for success are best with a deciduous hedge. Overgrown privet, ninebark, pyracantha, potentilla, lilac, barberry, bayberry, spirea, buckthorn, and many others will quickly regrow in a healthy condition if you cut them back to a foot or more from the ground.

You can also cut back and renew a few evergreens. Yew (*Taxus*), boxwood, and holly, for example, will often respond well to a severe pruning. Spruce, pine, fir, and hemlock can seldom be rejuvenated in this manner, however, and arborvitae will survive a hard pruning job only if the plants are young. You usually have a choice of either shaping overgrown evergreens into a tall, informal hedge, or taking them out and starting over with new plants.

93

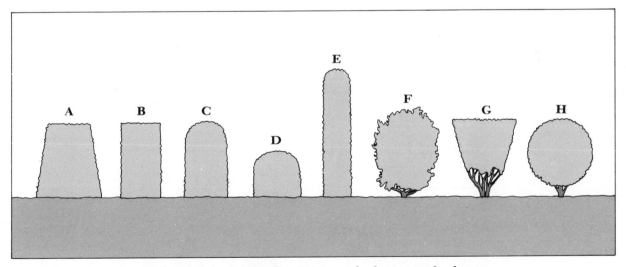

Hedge shapes. A box effect (A) is good where snow loads are not too heavy. The sides of B are too straight, and lower branches may not get enough sunlight. Shapes C, D, and E are suited to areas with heavy snows. F is an untrimmed hedge. The top of hedge G is too wide, making this shape undesirable—the sun can't reach lower limbs and snow will crush the top. The canopy hedge (H) is best-suited to sunny climates without heavy snowfall.

Canopy trees and hedges can be grown like umbrella trees. While interesting to look at, these are difficult to prune and maintain.

Clipped Formal Hedges

Although the formal, English-garden style of landscaping is seldom used around homes these days, tightly clipped hedges are still popular. Those that are used most frequently are listed here.

Buxus (**boxwood**). For much of the United States, boxwood is synonymous with hedge. The tightly sheared hedges and formal topiary gardens of Long Island and the area surrounding Washington, D.C. are usually boxwood, a shrub that was introduced from Europe during colonial settlement. It shears beautifully, and it is healthy and long-lived.

Ilex (**holly**). Wherever it grows well, holly (particularly Japanese holly) makes a beautiful, tight evergreen hedge. It's important to choose the best variety for your region, because hardiness is often a problem in some areas. It needs just enough shearing to keep it well shaped.

Ligustrum (**privet**). Members of the privet family are among the most popular hedge plants. The plants are inexpensive, or you can easily grow your own from cuttings. They grow densely, have small leaves, and you can shear them by hand or with light electric hedge clippers. Varieties are available for every region except the coldest parts of the country. Shear the plant in summer, while it is making its rapid growth. Numerous shearings are necessary to keep it looking tidy.

Physocarpus (**ninebark**). Ninebark is not usually hailed as a great hedge plant, but in northern New England, the upper Midwest, and Canada, it is a most satisfactory one. You can shear its very dense foliage into a beautiful shape. It has attractive white flowers in early spring and reddish foliage in the fall. If you want a low-growing hedge, plant a dwarf variety to save yourself considerable shearing.

Picea (**spruce**). Spruce comes in many varieties of dwarf and full-size trees. All can be grown into sheared hedges, but those with the shorter needles look best. Choose a variety that is suitable for your area as well as one that will grow to the height you want.

Taxus (**yew**). There are many varieties of yews available, and you'll find one suitable for your region unless you live in the coldest and most exposed sections of the country. The upright-growing ones are best for hedges. If your nursery sells them, choose plants that are grown from cuttings, since they are likely to be more uniform in color and growth habit than those grown from seeds. The red berries on the female plants add attractive fall color to the landscape.

Thuja (**American arborvitae**). The Eastern white cedar makes an ideal, fast-growing, tall hedge. It's a good windbreak and snow barrier, and an excellent choice for mass planting. You may find it too coarse for short, small hedges. If your soil is acidic, you must add additional lime for the best color and good growth. Choose the pyramidal variety for tall, narrow hedges that need shearing only on the top.

Tsuga (**hemlock**). The lacy-looking Canada hemlock can be sheared into one of the most beautiful hedges. Young seedlings and transplants are inexpensive, and although the trees are not fast growers, they grow into a long-lasting hedge. The Carolina hemlock is a good choice in the areas where it grows well.

Ulmus parvifolia (**Chinese elm**). A few years ago the Chinese elm was widely planted, but because it has so many faults, it is not as popular today. It grows fast, but the wood is weak and breaks easily. It is also short-lived, and the foliage tends to attract insects that breed there and spread to other plants.

Hedges for Barriers

We once planted a row of Colorado blue spruce for a customer who wanted to stop trespassers from using her private yard as a shortcut to the public beach. The prickly trees were perfect for the purpose. No one in a bathing suit has yet been known to push through those sharp-needled plants.

Sometimes hedges are planted solely to keep out unwanted visitors, human or animal. These living fences are often cheaper to establish and maintain than real fences, and they appear less hostile.

In time, and with careful pruning, most plants can be grown into a barrier hedge, but thorny, rugged plants are best if you have a choice. Shear your plants in the summer when they are making their growth. You have a choice of doing it once over lightly — just enough to produce a thick, informal hedge — or frequently and severely to achieve a neater, more symmetrical, and more formal appearance. In either case, follow the general rules for shearing, and never allow the plant to grow wider at the top than at the bottom. Use the following plants in barrier hedges.

Berberis (**barberry**). Barberries have long been used for this purpose, and you know why if you've ever tried to grasp a sprig. The thorns are inescapable. In areas where they do well, they are ideal barriers. In places where they are short-lived or suffer winter injury or insect trouble, choose another plant. When they begin to deteriorate, cut them to the ground and they'll renew themselves.

Crataegus (**hawthorn**). Hawthorns make very effective barriers. Choose varieties that are especially thorny and those that will grow to the height you want. Shear them tightly whenever necessary.

Gleditsia (**thorny honey locust**). Use a thorny variety when planting a barrier, since the thornless kinds aren't as effective. Plant them three feet apart and shear them heavily.

Malus (**crab apple**). You can treat these like hawthorns. The wild varieties make the best hedges — Robusta is a good prickly one in the North. Plant them two or three feet apart, and shear them heavily in early summer for thick bottom growth.

Picea (**spruce**). When spruce is used as a barrier hedge, the pricklier the plant, the better. Colorado spruce is one of the best choices, since it is fast-growing and will grow in a wide range of soils and climates. Tight shearing is necessary to make it impenetrable. Colorado spruce varies from bright green to blue white in color, so if the hedge is to be grown for beauty as well as for a barrier, choose colors that are uniform or else you'll have a mottled effect.

Prunus (**plum**). Native plums make a good barrier fence if they're sheared tightly. Treat them like hawthorns and crab apples. Plant them two or three feet apart.

Rosa (**rose**). Shrub roses are most common for this use. Keeping them in a uniform shape may be difficult because of their informal growth habit, although their flowers will be beautiful. Unfortunately, if weeds and weedy shrubs seed and grow among them, they'll be a problem to remove.

Flower- and Berry-Producing Hedge Plants

Ordinarily, plants don't produce flowers or fruit well when they are sheared into a tight hedge pattern. Allow them to grow naturally, pruning rather than shearing them. The following plants produce well when grown as an informal, lightly pruned hedge. Prune all of them directly after flowering when necessary, unless exceptions are noted.

Berberis (**barberry**). Choose a variety that will grow to the size you want.

Prune or shear it to keep it from growing too wide. The upright-growing kinds are best.

Cotoneaster. Most varieties need little shearing. Prune it in early spring if it's necessary to control the size. Choose the upright-growing varieties.

Hydrangea. Cut back the tops severely in early spring. You may cut nearly to the ground or cut it according to how much you want it to grow the following summer. The fall-blooming peegees are best for tall, informal hedges. Cut off the dead flowers right after they have bloomed.

Hypericum. The bright yellow flowers of this low-growing hedge are a gay spot of color in the summer. Prune it in late summer to remove the seed pods and, if necessary, to renew old wood.

Lonicera (honeysuckle). These are excellent for attracting flocks of birds to your yard. Prune the hedge to remove old wood and any dead branches. Shear it to keep it in shape.

Philadelphus (mock orange). The white, fragrant blooms make this a worthy consideration if you're looking for a tall, beautiful hedge plant.

Prunus (flowering plum). If necessary, prune this right after blooming, and shear it as needed during the summer to keep it in shape. Most of these don't bear any fruit.

Pyracantha (fire thorn). Cut off the old wood in late fall to promote heavier crops of berries. You can shape many varieties into espalier and other unusual forms.

Rhamnus (buckthorn). The tall, upright variety is often used as a hedge. The plants are attractive and produce berries over a long season for the birds. Sometimes they get thin at the base of the plant, so prune them closely when they're young to insure bushiness at the bottom of the hedge. In some areas, birds cause a problem by dropping buckthorn seeds all over, and they grow up as weedy plants.

Rosa (rose). Cut out dead flowers and older canes right after blooming. Rugosa varieties produce excellent hips. (See "Pruning Roses," Chapter 5.)

Syringa (lilac). Prune it to remove fading flowers and suckers right after blooming. For any major pruning, see "Pruning Lilacs," Chapter 5.

Viburnum. Prune it lightly right after blooming to keep it in shape. When you need to prune heavily, do it in fall or late winter.

Hedges Needing Little Care

Those gardeners who have limited time, or those who don't especially like to putter around the garden, may prefer to have low-maintenance hedges. "Low maintenance" means that a hedge needs only a few clippings per season, or else that you can clip it quickly and easily.

Ordinarily, upright-growing shrubs with fine twigs and small needles or leaves are easier to care for than the coarser-limbed, spreading varieties or those with larger leaves or longer needles.

A young, growing hedge will need less attention than it will when it has reached the size and shape you want. Often one annual pruning is enough for

97

EASY-MAINTENANCE EVERGREEN HEDGES

Ilex (holly). Upright-growing varieties need two or three relatively easy shearings each season.

Picea (spruce). Dwarf-growing varieties of Norway spruce, such as birdsnest, need only one easy shearing on the sides each year.

Taxus cuspidata 'Capitata' (upright yew). This variety and other upright-growing yews need one to three easy shearings each year.

Thuja occidentalis (American arborvitae, white cedar). One or two easy shearings will control this favorite in northern gardens.

Tsuga canadensis (Canada hemlock). One or two easy shearings will keep this beauty looking nice for years.

EASY-MAINTENANCE DECIDUOUS HEDGES

Acanthopanax (five-leaf aralia). The two-to-four clippings necessary each year are easily accomplished.

Acer campestre (hedge maple). Even though the foliage on this plant is large, it is attractive and easy to grow where climate permits.

Berberis (barberry). Choose the upright-growing kinds for the easiest maintenance — mentor, truehedge, and box barberry, for example.

Buxus microphylla var. *koreana* (Korean boxwood). This low-growing plant with fine foliage shears easily. With power clippers, large plantings can be beautifully maintained.

Carpinus (hornbeam). Both the native and European kinds make a tight, slow-growing, easy-to-maintain hedge that will grow fairly tall, if you wish.

Euonymus alata 'Compacta' (winged spindle tree). The dwarf size of this plant makes it easy to care for.

Euonymus Fortunei (wintercreeper). A fast-growing, easy-care hedge plant. Many different kinds offer a variety of foliage.

Forsythia. The dwarf varieties make an easy-to-care-for, informal, blooming hedge.

Ligustrum (privet). Upright-growing kinds such as dwarf border privet are easy to care for, even though several prunings are needed during the summer.

Malus (crab apple). The various crab apples can be sheared into tight hedges that are easily maintained, although some additional care is needed initially to shape them. It is better not to use grafted varieties, because suckers are difficult to control.

Rhamnus Frangula (buckthorn). The columnar varieties such as tallhedge are best, but careful early shearing is sometimes necessary to keep the plants tight at the bottom.

Viburnum. Sheared or unsheared, many of the viburnums make neat hedges. Some are dwarf naturally, so choosing the mature height you want will insure the least care and make berry production more certain.

evergreens in their formative years, but after the hedge is mature, one heavy pruning and an additional three or four light ones may be necessary to keep it looking good.

Hedges Needing Careful Maintenance

There are some plants that demand extra care to keep them looking nice. This doesn't mean that they require full-time professional care, but you'll need to spend a little more conscientious time to maintain them.

All evergreens, such as pines, firs, spreading yews, and blue spruce, require heavy, meticulous pruning. The mugho pine, a low shrub with coarse limbs, may need an occasional clipping with hand pruners.

Throughout the growing season, give extra attention to many of the spreading deciduous shrubs, such as spreading barberry *(Berberis)*, flowering quince *(Chaenomeles)*, winterberry *(Ilex verticillata)*, beautybush *(Kolkwitzia)*, and honeysuckle *(Lonicera)*. Large, coarse trees like the larch *(Larix)* and oak *(Quercus)*, fast-growing trees like poplars *(Populus)* and willows *(Salix)*, and prolific growers like ninebark *(Physocarpus)* need more attention because of their growth habits.

Annual Hedges

I'm often asked for the name of the beautiful little evergreen that turns a bright red in late summer. It's sometimes difficult to convince gardeners that the Mexican firebush *(Kochia)* isn't a formally sheared evergreen at all, and that it is easily grown each year from seed. Although this plant seldom needs pruning if it is well spaced and gets plenty of sunlight, many annuals do need a bit of pinching and shaping to get them to grow as a tight, informal border. You can grow dahlias, marigolds, petunias, geraniums, ageratum, impatiens, and zinnias as low summer hedges. You should remove their fading blooms regularly to encourage continuous blossoming.

99

Chapter 9

Artistic Pruning

When I was very young, my family occasionally shopped in a neighboring town. Although there were several routes we could take to get there, I always begged them to drive by the "umbrella tree." On a small patch of land in his neat pasture, a local chicken farmer had sheared a dozen or so native spruce and white cedar (eastern arborvitae) into balls, umbrellas, cones, eggs, and other exciting shapes. Many people still speak fondly of those trees, and I wonder if he ever realized how much his work was appreciated by the young and old who passed by his farm. It was a novel sight in the North Woods, and many people went out of their way to look at his topiary. I'm sorry that I never met the famer to tell him how much I enjoyed them — long before I grew up he had either died or moved away — and the exciting shapes I admired so much had grown up into ordinary large trees.

His creations inspired me because I learned that one doesn't have to be an English gardener working with yew or boxwood to grow fancy shrubbery. I also learned that a planting doesn't have to be two hundred years old to look good, and that artistic pruning is possible even in the North where snow sometimes gets eight feet deep or more.

Visitors to Disneyland, Williamsburg, and Longwood Gardens in Pennsylvania love to photograph the topiary, the pleached walkways, and the mazes of clipped hedges. A few are even inspired to attempt such artistry in their own home gardens. It's a great delight when a little bush or tree that you have been clipping at for years suddenly turns into a handsome specimen. The process is slow, much as a bushy mess of whiskers turning into a svelte beard.

Many of the artistic forms of pruning were developed in Europe or Japan where small lots made the *multum in parvo* concept necessary. In this country, espaliers, topiary, and the like are usually created more for aesthetic reasons than because of space limitations.

Although fancy topiary and other artistic prunings demand patience and skill, the simple shearing of evergreens and the shaping of flowering shrubs and fruit trees is so easy that anyone can have fun doing it. Many varieties of dwarf plants developed recently are ideal for artistic shaping, because they grow so slowly. Often they are practical, too. Some commercial fruit orchardists are growing their trees as sheared hedges, cordons, fences, and other forms that were once considered more ornamental than useful.

Artistic pruning requires time during the growing season. Most of the shearing must be done in early summer when the trees are growing rapidly, so if you count on scuba diving in Aruba or fishing in Alaska in May or June, this hobby isn't for you. You'll need to be in your garden several times a week when the plants are growing, even if only for a few minutes each time.

The pruning of an artistic form must go on throughout the life of the plant, and frequent snipping and shearing will be part of your summer chores, just as you have to mow the lawn and pull the weeds in the vegetable garden. If you have spent years creating a beautiful espalier, topiary, or other horticultural masterpiece, and then forget it as you go on to other projects, you'll find, a year or so later, that it has become overgrown and is probably past help. But such is the life of a gardener — a thing of beauty is a job forever.

Staking

Staking is often necessary when you're doing artistic pruning. Put in sturdy wood or metal stakes *before* they are needed, if possible, because driving stakes into the soil around large plants will damage their roots. Use the proper tying material when you tie a plant to a stake. Plastic ribbon, cloth or nylon strips, and rawhide cord are all fine because they don't cut into the bark; do not use plastic tape, wire, string, or rope.

Topiary

Shearing reaches its zenith in topiary — trimming trees and shrubs into geometric forms, arches, animals, or other shapes. Two centuries ago this art form became so popular that it was overdone in many European gardens. It has never been common in America, except in some formal or exhibition gardens, probably because most Americans prefer an informal and unstudied look — and because they don't have hired gardeners to do the work.

Boxwood, holly, and yew are varieties most often planted for evergreen topiary, but arborvitae, cypress, hemlock, and spruce also may be used. Pines, Colorado spruce, and most of the firs are a bit coarse for this purpose.

Best suited for deciduous topiary are the Chinese elm, cotoneaster, ninebark, privet, pyracantha, Japanese and Amur maple, and similar trees and shrubs. Sometimes even the coarser-growing trees such as maples, birches, and hornbeam can be sculpted into bowers, arches, unusual shapes, and twisted-forest forms.

English ivy is trained to grow over wire shapes into giraffes, camels, and others, as can be seen in the topiary garden of the New York Botanical Garden Conservatory. The potential shapes of topiary are limited only by the

Examples of topiary.

patience, care, and imagination of the gardener, and sometimes by climate.

Simple topiary consists of shearing a plant into the form you want, beginning when it is still small. More complicated forms, for instance four trees that form the legs and finally the body of an elephant, require some careful planning and usually a framework of wood or metal. My wife saw such an elephant in Thailand — it formed a massive arch over a driveway, tall enough for a car to drive beneath.

If you decide to take on a topiary project for your own backyard, start with small, tight-growing plants, and plant them in an area where they are surrounded by full light. Shear them often when they are growing, to create a closely grown, tiny-leaf (or needle) effect. You can't expect to take a large tree and sculpt it into an artistic shape like an artist chiseling away at a block of marble. Instead, shear the basic cone, pyramid, or whatever shape you wish, and gradually allow bulges to appear, then shape the bulges into a head, or leg, or other form.

Whether for the initial shaping or maintenance, shearing should begin as soon as growth starts and continue as long as necessary throughout the summer. Evergreens usually need only two or three shearings each year; deciduous plants have the advantage of growing faster and producing quicker results, but they need more shearing. Creating a large topiary may take years or even decades of careful pruning, and once completed, it still will need to be pruned forever.

Most topiary is grown in the warmer zones where snow can't crush it. Northern experimenters should use only the hardiest plants (native specimens are usually best), and topiary shapes should be pointed or rounded on top and narrow in width so that they won't collect heavy loads of snow and ice. Build a wooden tepee around more fragile pieces, or simply shovel the snow off after each big storm.

Espalier

The espalier is one of the most familiar artistic pruning forms and is just the thing if you want to grow trees or shrubs in an extremely small space. An espalier is a plant grown flat, like a vine, against a wall, fence, building, or trellis. Fruit trees are often chosen as espaliers, because they are both productive and pretty, in leaf and flower. Dwarf apples, pears, quinces, citrus fruits, and figs are most commonly used. Plums, cherries, peaches, and apricots are more difficult to train, as are the bush fruits and nut trees.

In warm climates, an espalier will do best in a spot that will not get direct sun all day: the wall reflects heat that will make the leaves and fruit suffer on hot days. In cool climates, however, the more sun your espalier gets, the better. Sheltered espaliered fruits ripen earlier than those grown in the open and subjected to cooling winds.

A white wall is preferable as a growing background in the South, since it absorbs little heat; a dark-colored wall attracts heat and is better in the North. Grapes can often be grown in cool northern areas by espaliering them against a dark, south-facing building, even where it would be impossible to grow them only a few feet away from the building.

In planning an espalier, you'll want to keep in mind that some sort of support is necessary. Although nails can be driven into a wooden surface and the branches tied to them, this is not a good practice: pruning is difficult when the branches lie flat, and repainting the building is nearly impossible. Instead, build a support structure for the plant at least six inches away from the wall. For this you can use a lattice, trellis, or wire fence. The last-named is easiest and usually the most practical for fruit trees.

Set two sturdy posts, seven or eight feet tall, at the expected outside spread of the espalier, and staple smooth wire from one to the other like a wire fence. Place the first wire about three feet from the ground and the others about a foot apart. Brace the posts to prevent the wires from sagging. Plant the tree or shrub just in front of the fence, roughly midway between the posts.

If possible, select trees that branch in a way that fits into your espalier plan. Should you be unable to find a well-shaped tree, it's better to start with a whip, or you can prune all the limbs off a small branched tree, and start training each new branch as it grows.

Shrubs, on the other hand, can usually be trained to grow on a trellis or lattice more easily than on a wire fence.

When growth begins on your new plant, allow to remain only those branches growing in the right direction. Clip or pinch off all the others throughout the growing season. Bend the branches as they grow, while they are still pliable, and secure them with twine or vine clamps to the supporting wire or trellis in the pattern you want.

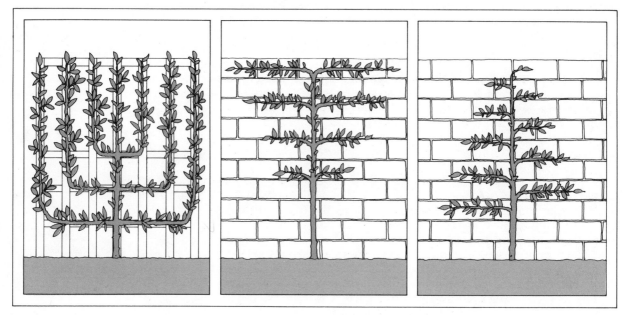

Varieties of espalier.

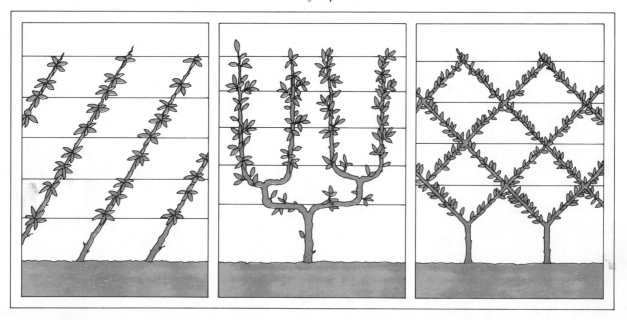

There are a number of designs you might wish to consider: fan shapes, candelabras, fountains, diamonds, and triangles are only a few of the possibilities.

It may take several years of growing and shaping to "finish" a complicated pattern. Even after your tree has become an artistic triumph, you must continue to prune through the summer to keep it looking attractive. Be careful not to prune away the short, stubby spurs that bear the fruit. Flowering crabs and hawthorns need to have their older spurs thinned out occasionally, as they get too numerous, but always leave enough to bear the crop.

Many shrubs can be trained as beautiful espaliered forms, especially in the areas of the country that don't get severe winters. Camellia, cotoneaster, flowering crab, flowering quince, forsythia, fuchsia, hawthorn, laurel, magnolia, pyracantha, taxus, and viburnum are among the shrubs or small trees that are commonly grown in this manner. Those plants that grow in a vigorous manner, such as lilac or hydrangea, are unsuitable for espalier planting because you'd be frustrated trying to keep them pruned.

A few nurseries sell small espaliered trees and shrubs that have already had their training started. Although a headstart would probably make training easier for you, there are benefits from starting your own. You can use the kind of plant you want, choose your own design, and save money, as well.

Cordons

Cordon is the French word for cord or rope, and refers to a planting (usually of a dwarf fruit tree) that extends in ropelike fashion, either vertically or horizontally. A tree or shrub is trimmed to grow in a tall, slender shape in what is often called the beanpole method. Europeans have used this method of growing plants for centuries, but it's only now becoming popular in America.

To grow a cordon, choose an upright-growing tree or shrub that will not grow too tall or too fast. Dwarf apples and pears are good fruit trees to grow in this fashion, while the stone fruits — the peaches, plums, and cherries — and the citrus fruits are more difficult to train as cordons.

Start with a branchless tree. Plant it as usual, and prune back the top from a third to a half, cutting to a good fat bud. If you choose to start working on a tree that is already branched, cut all the side branches off close to the trunk, leaving a single, straight whip. Then place a sturdy stake close to the newly planted tree. Tied to the stake, the tree will be trained to support a heavy load of fruit. As the tree grows, clip or pinch all the new growth coming from the sides to four or five inches in length, allowing the main trunk to grow to a height of six feet for easy reach. Continue to prune just as you would an espalier, always snipping off any growth beyond the four- or five-inch limit on the side branches.

Cordons must be kept to a manageable size, but as the roots grow, this may become more difficult. Prune the roots by cutting around the tree (see page 35) to slow down the growth of the tree.

In addition to the regular pruning of a fruit tree, you may need to prune off some of the fruit buds in late winter to prevent overbearing. If too many

105

fruits set anyway, thin them out in early summer when they are still small so that the tree will produce a crop annually.

To grow a cordon horizontally or obliquely — angles even more contrary to the plant's normal growth habits — you'll have to prune heavily to keep the plant attractive.

Cordons were formerly grown mostly as ornamental trees, and the style was not widely used by fruit growers. However, some commercial orchardists are now experimenting with growing fruit trees as upright cordons. Apple growers are planting as many as six hundred dwarf cordons to the acre versus 35 full-size trees. The initial cost of buying, planting, and training is high, but subsequent pruning, insect and disease control, and harvesting costs are less, and the planting comes into full production many years sooner than a regular orchard.

English Fences

Small trees, especially dwarf fruit trees, are sometimes grown in rows about eight or nine feet apart as freestanding espaliers — that is, without the aid of a wall or building. To create this English fence, you allow four to six branches to grow on each tree in a method that resembles the Kniffen system of growing grapes (see page 149), except that the branch ends of each tree are grafted to the branch ends of the neighboring tree.

You can put in wires, pipes, or boards, secured to heavy posts, to train the young trees and hold up the heavy fruit on fruit trees until the limbs are sturdy enough to do the job. English fences are part espalier and part horizontal cordon. Like both, they need frequent pruning and pinching all summer, and throughout their life to keep them looking like a fence. They will probably need a root-pruning job every three or four years as well, to keep them from growing too fast.

Grafting the limbs together is a simple operation. When the tree is big enough so that the branches grow past those of the neighboring tree, make a slanted cut at the ends of both branches and join the cut ends together, lining up the inner bark layers so that the sap can flow freely between them. Then wrap the juncture with freezer tape or rubber (not plastic) electrical tape. In a year or two the ends will grow together into one long branch.

Dwarf fruit trees, especially apples and pears, grow well in this fashion, as do flowering crabs and similar flowering trees. Like the espaliers, the process is demanding and time-consuming, so you should attempt it only if you can devote enough time to keep it looking finished and manicured.

Pruning a Japanese Garden

A Japanese garden is almost always built on uneven land. It usually features running water and distinctive, small trees greatly resembling very old, full-sized trees.

The skillful pruning process that makes possible this kind of landscaping is similar to that used on bonsai plants grown in shallow dishes. If you were to shear a 5-foot Colorado blue spruce in the usual manner, it would be an attractive, stiff, formal specimen. However, a similar 5-foot tree grown and pruned in the Japanese method would resemble a 100-foot spruce that had been growing for a century or more on a windswept Colorado mountaintop.

Almost any tree can be dwarfed in the Japanese manner, but some are more attractive and easier to prune in this fashion than others. The slow-growing conifers and dwarf trees or shrubs make the best choices for this kind of landscaping. Even with these, occasional root pruning and frequent top pruning are necessary to get a bonsai effect. (See Chapter 15.)

No long, large limbs should be allowed to develop. Restrain the size by careful pruning and by thinning out the branches, rather than by shearing the ends. Cut back branches to another branch or joint, and thin the limb area by cutting off some of the branches at the trunk. Part of the charm of an ancient-looking specimen is being able to see its trunk. During the growing season you'll need to snip and pinch frequently, and an annual heavier pruning is usually necessary during the dormant season in late fall.

To add to the ancient, weathered look, you can grow the tree in soil that is covered with several inches of moss. A few years later, remove the moss and let the gnarled roots become a part of the tree's trunk.

By positioning a few carefully selected rocks that have interesting shapes, you'll nearly complete the picture. If you can manage to get a brook to wend its way through the landscape, or construct a natural-looking fountain, all you'll need is a kimono and a bottle of sake as you relax in your masterpiece.

Chapter 10

Pruning Fruit Trees

I'm always surprised at the modest yields gardeners expect from their orchards. I have a friend who always has a superb vegetable garden, a wonderful bed of roses, and the best strawberry patch in town. Each tomato is a jewel. Every stalk of corn produces two large ears, and every flower in his perennial bed looks as if it is posing for the cover of a garden magazine. Yet, in spite of his gardening skill, he seems to be perfectly satisfied to take whatever his fruit trees hand him.

And often this isn't very much. He has good fruit during the rare years when conditions are perfect, but his fruits usually are small, misshapen, poorly colored, and infested with insects. Furthermore, he typically gets a crop only every other year.

I'm sure that when his trees were young they were full of vigor and produced excellent fruit. Young trees almost always bear large, colorful fruit because they still have very few limbs so that the fruit gets lots of sunlight. However, as the trees mature and grow more branches, you must prune to keep them producing well. Most trees naturally produce a large crop of fruit every other year, so if you want your trees to grow an annual crop you must give them some special attention. Pruning is a neglected art, however, and one that novice fruit growers don't completely understand.

Pruning fruit trees doesn't need to be confusing. As I mentioned before, it is like learning to play chess. If you follow the simple, basic rules, you can leave the scientific jargon to those who are intrigued by it.

First of all, an orchardist must be aware that his tree consists of two parts — most fruit trees are grafted. The roots usually belong to a type of tree that produces low-quality fruit, whereas the top is a good-bearing variety that has been transplanted on the rootstock. The two have been grafted together because this is the most efficient way to produce large numbers of quality fruit trees. Fruit trees grown from seed seldom resemble the parent tree even slightly, and growing trees from cuttings or layers is slow and extremely difficult.

Grafted trees, although they are convenient for the propagator, sometimes pose problems for growers. If rodents happen to chew in a circle around a tree below the graft, new shoots will grow from the roots of the inferior tree, and you will lose the good variety of fruit above the graft. This is because the sap will not flow above the girdled area of the tree. The little suckers or small trees that grow up around the base of grafted fruit trees spring from this semiwild understock as well, and even if you transplant them, they probably will produce poor fruit.

Reasons for Pruning

Some gardeners enjoy pruning their fruit trees and consequently do a good job. However, no one should prune simply for the fun of it — you should know the reasons for pruning. All of the following are equally important to the health and maintenance of your trees.

Prune to get the tree off to a good start. Although it isn't easy, you should cut back any bare-rooted young tree at planting time. When we prune trees for customers at the nursery, they wince and say that it looks as if we are slaughtering the poor things, but we assure them that it is one of the best

Poor training in its first years has allowed this tree to develop a weak, U-shaped, crotched top. Cutting out the fork on the right will result in a crooked leader, but that is nevertheless a big improvement, and the crook will later straighten out considerably.

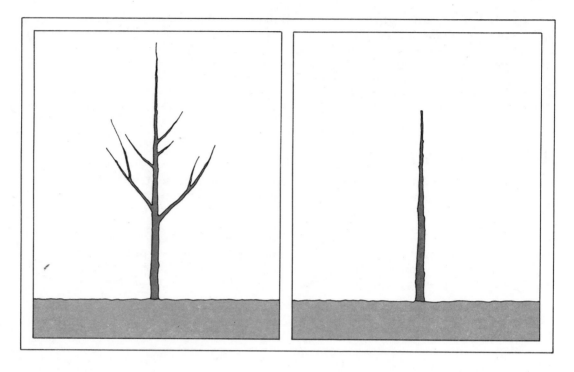

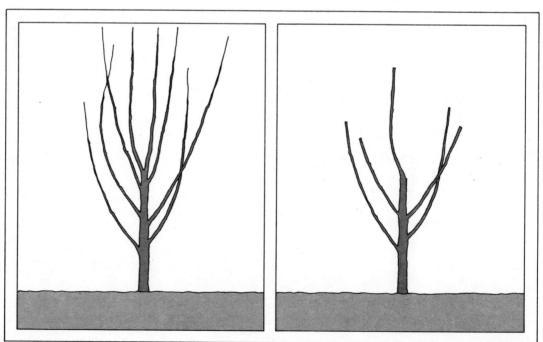

things you can do to insure good growth and early crops.

Trees enclosed in a ball of soil or growing in a pot will not need any cutback. However, bare-rooted trees have probably been dug recently, and chances are good that some of the roots have been seriously damaged in the process. Most mail-order plants are sold bare-rooted, and unless the directions you receive with the tree indicate that it has already been done, you should prune both the roots and top at planting time.

First, cut off any jagged edges on broken roots so they will heal smoothly. Then cut back the top to make it equivalent in size to the root surface. Cut back fruit trees that are whips — those with no side branches — by at least a third: if your tree is six feet tall, for example, cut it back at least two feet, and make the cut on a slant just above a bud.

If your fruit tree has branches, cut off those that are weak, dead-looking, broken, or too close to the ground. Then cut back the top by a third and each strong, healthy limb by at least a third also. Cut each limb back to an outside bud so that the next branch will form toward the outside and the tree will spread outward rather than inward toward the trunk.

Training young apple and pear trees. Top row, opposite page: First year, as planted (left) and pruned just after planting (right). Bottom row, opposite page: Second year, before and after pruning. Above: Third year, before and after pruning. Tree is now growing with a strong central leader and no extra tops.

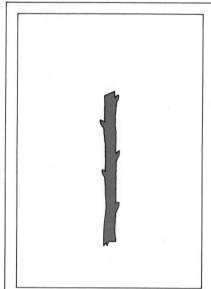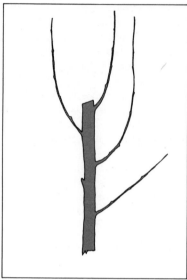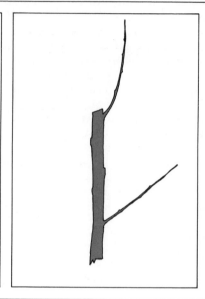

A tree pruned back at planting time (left) may grow several tops the first year (center). Prune back to a single top (right). The remaining side branch may be removed later as the top grows taller.

Keep in mind that these directions are only for pruning new trees. Don't neglect the other ingredients for proper planting, like soaking bare-rooted trees for several hours after arrival, using lots of good soil and water while planting, and planting to the right depth. Most fruit tree failures are due to the lack of proper planting as well as the failure to prune the tree properly at planting time.

Prune lightly to shape the tree during the first years of its life. The old saying "as the twig is bent, so the tree is inclined," is unquestionably true. A little snipping and pinching here and there while the tree is young will save you a lot of heavy pruning later on.

If you have trained your tree properly early in its life, all subsequent pruning will come easier. Whenever you clip or snip off the buds or tiny twigs, try to keep in mind an image of the mature tree. Prune in accordance with the tree's natural growth habit and for the purpose of developing a strong tree with a branch structure sturdy enough to hold up the crop. Keep the branches sparse enough to allow the sunshine in to ripen the fruit.

You should prune very little during the tree's first years — just enough to help shape the tree. Although it's good to prune heavily at planting time, this process may cause it to grow too many branches close to the ground. By pinching or clipping off all these undesirable new sprouts during the first years, you will be training the new tree to grow upright. You'll also avoid the heavier pruning which would delay the tree's first crop.

Some trees need more shaping than others. Many varieties of apples, such as Wealthy and McIntosh, seem to grow into a good shape quite naturally. Other varieties, like the Delicious and Yellow Transparent, tend to grow very upright, forming lots of tops with bad crotches. If left uncorrected, these weak crotches and the limbs coming from them are very likely to break under a heavy load of fruit.

Fruit-loads on plums and cherries are not as heavy as those on pears and apples. Since they are apt to grow into a bushy shape no matter what you do, early shaping is important mainly to keep them from getting too wide or to prevent the branches from growing too close to the ground.

Some trees grow twiggy naturally, and certain apple varieties such as Jonathan, as well as many varieties of cherries, plums, peaches, and apricots, need additional thinning of their bearing wood to let in sunshine to ripen the fruit.

Direct all of your early pruning to guiding the tree into the desired shape. Fruit trees are usually trained in one of three forms: central leader, modified leader, or open center.

113

This tree will be greatly improved by cutting out the two extra tops on the outside, leaving the central leader.

CENTRAL LEADER

Trees that bear heavy crops of large fruit, including apples and pears, are usually best pruned to grow with a central leader, or trunk, at least in their younger days. With only one strong trunk in the center of the tree, branches come strongly out from it at fairly wide angles and can safely bear abundant loads of fruit.

Thin out the branches growing from the central leader as necessary to allow open space between the limbs. Thin also the branches that come from these limbs, and so on to the outermost branches. Sunlight produces colorful, flavorful, vitamin-enriched fruit. Sunlight and circulating air also help to prevent scab, mildew, and a host of other diseases that thrive in shade and high humidity.

Eventually you will have to remove the top of the central leader because this high-growing leader will gradually sag under a load of heavy fruit, forming a canopy over part of the tree that will shut out the light. Cutting back the top helps prevent a canopy from occurring while also keeping the tree from growing too tall.

The top branch of a tree with a strong central leader may bend down under a heavy fruit load, closing up the top of the tree and darkening the interior. This canopy branch should be sawed off.

Three systems of pruning: Central leader (left), modified leader (center), and open center (right).

115

MODIFIED LEADER

The modified leader method is initially the same as the central leader method, but eventually you let the central trunk branch off to form several tops. This training ensures that the loads of fruit at the top of the tree are never as heavy as those at the bottom where limbs are larger. Cut back the tops of larger trees from time to time to shorten the tree or to let in more light. Although the central leader method is preferred by most orchardists for growing apples and pears, the modified leader method is easier to maintain simply because most fruit trees grow that way naturally.

OPEN CENTER

The open center method, also known as the open top or vase method, is an excellent way to let more light into the shady interior of a tree. Since this method produces a tree with a weaker branch structure than if it had a strong central leader, the lightweight fruits are the best subjects: quinces, crab apples, plums, cherries, peaches, nectarines, and apricots.

Prune so that the limbs forming the vase effect do not all come out of the main trunk close to each other, or they will form a cluster of weak crotches. Even with the whole center of the tree open, you'll have to thin the branches and remove the older limbs eventually, just as you would with a tree pruned in the central leader method.

116

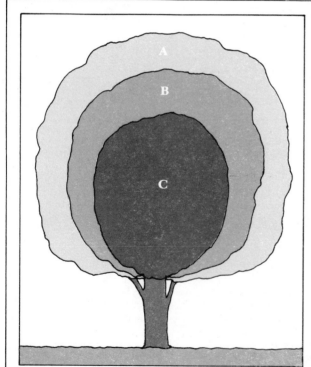
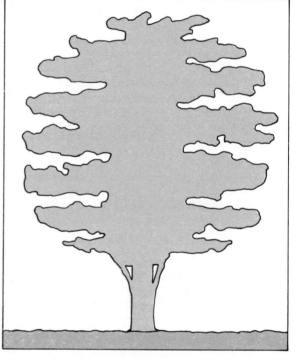

Pruning admits light to fruit-tree branches (right) that would otherwise remain unproductive in the shade. On the unpruned tree (left), area A gets enough light to ripen good fruit, area B gets a fair amount, and C almost none.

Thin clusters of small fruits to a single fruit. Fruits should be 6 inches or more apart.

117

Prune for good crops of quality fruit. Good fruit needs plenty of sunshine, and a fruit tree fortunately has a potentially large area to produce fruit: a full-size, standard tree can be well over 30 feet wide and 20 feet high. However, only 30 percent of an unpruned tree, because of its tight branch structure, gets enough light, while another 40 percent gets only a fair amount of light. As these percentages indicate, when only the top exterior of the tree produces good fruit, you are getting the use of but a third of your tree, and all that fruit is grown where it is most difficult to pick. Even the most careful pruning won't bring the light efficiency to a full 100 percent, but you can greatly increase it.

The drawings on page 116 illustrate the theory of pruning to let the light in. Since a fruit tree is three-dimensional, your tree won't look just like the drawings. They are an exaggerated way of showing why the pruning should be done and how it lets more light into the tree.

Another way to improve the quality of your fruit is to remove the surplus fruit whenever your tree sets too many. Although regular pruning will cut down the number of fruits produced, a tree may still bear a greater number than it can develop to a large size. The production of too many seeds seems to tax a tree's strength, and certain varieties of fruits, unless you give them a helping hand, seem bent on bearing themselves to death. When a tree bears too many fruits in any one year, it usually bears few, if any, fruits the following year. If at any time your tree, regardless of its size or age, appears to be setting too many fruits, thin out extras when they are small. Most trees, as well as their fruits, benefit if you leave only one fruit remaining in each cluster. Make sure that each fruit is at least six inches from its neighbors on either side.

Prune to keep your trees from getting too large. Since standard-size fruit trees can grow to 25 feet or more, they are often pruned to keep them at a more manageable height. A tall tree is difficult and dangerous to work in. And, because so much of the tree is shaded, it often produces poor fruit.

Sometimes trees grow excessively high because farmers let their cattle or horses chew off all the lower branches, forcing the growth upward. Pigs, however, can be allowed to clean up the unused fruit at harvest time.

Trees deprived of sunlight on their lower, outside branches, either by buildings, high or tight fences, or by other trees, will grow too tall and require a lot of drastic pruning later on. Cutting down healthy trees, just because you or someone else planted too many, is a traumatic experience. But crowded

118

Crossed branches spoil an otherwise nicely formed young tree. Only a little pruning is needed to get it into shape.

trees are forced to grow more upright, and thinning them out is often the only answer to a good orchard.

Of course it's best to prune regularly so that your tree won't get too tall in the first place, but if this advice comes too late, consider shortening it. The tree should be healthy enough to stand major surgery. Make sure that there will be enough lower branches left on the tree to sustain it after its upper level has been removed: the leaf surface remaining must be adequate to supply nutrients to the tree.

If these conditions can be met, begin to prune back the top in late summer or early fall. Make the cuts in small stages, cutting off only small pieces of limbs at one time, so that the limb weight will be lightened before you begin the heavy cutting. These small cuts lessen the danger of splitting limbs, and also help insure that you won't drop heavy pieces of wood onto the lower branches. If possible, have a helper handy to catch the limbs as they fall or to guide them away from the tree. Follow the directions for cutting off heavy limbs detailed in Chapter 4.

Don't cut off more than one large limb in any one year. Make sure that some regrowth has started on the lower branches before you make any further cuts. Like an obese person, the tree got into its overgrown condition over a period of many years, so don't try to correct all its problems at once.

Prune to keep your tree healthy. Even young fruit trees occasionally need to be pruned because of some mishap: limbs get broken, tent caterpillars build nests, and as the tree gets older, rot and winter injury often take their toll on the branches.

As soon as you notice any damage, clip or saw off the injured part back to a live limb or the trunk. Even one deteriorating limb is not good for the tree's health, and the accumulation of several sick limbs will rapidly speed up the decline of the tree.

Rejuvenation is vital to a tree's health, especially when your goal is to produce good crops of high-quality fruit over a number of years. Many trees that produce handsome specimens while they are young or middle-aged often bear only small, poor fruit as they grow older. By replacing and renewing the old bearing wood, you encourage the tree to continue bringing forth large red apples, or big crops of juicy plums, or peaches.

Thin out and open up old trees to permit sunshine to enter and ripen the fruit. Air will circulate to discourage disease, and it will be easier for birds to spot and pick up preying insects.

As with every other kind of pruning, you'll get the best results from rejuvenation pruning when you do it on an annual basis rather than as an occasional event. If you remove a few of the older limbs each year to open up the tree to sunlight and air, the whole bearing surface can be renewed every six or eight years, which is like getting a whole new tree. In addition, because you will seldom need to do any drastic pruning of large, heavy limbs, the tree will suffer less.

Large limbs should grow only as an extension of the tree trunk itself, and as a unit from which the smaller limbs grow. These overlarge limbs are a

119

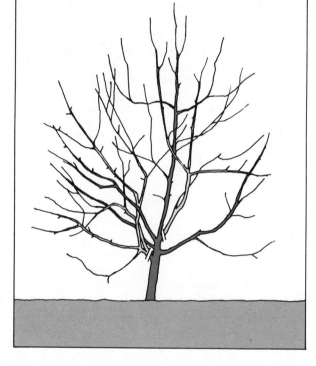

120

The problem here is too many branches growing from one spot on the trunk, forming extra tops. Cut as shown to develop a strong central leader and encourage good branch development.

tremendous strain on the tree, so the fewer, the better. Because fruit trees are pruned more heavily than most other plant life, heavy limb growth is much more likely to result than when a tree is left unpruned or lightly pruned. Cut off crossed branches or branches that might rub to cause wounds in the bark.

Water sprouts are those upright branches that grow in clumps, often from a large pruning wound. They are usually unproductive, and they can weaken the tree by causing additional, unwanted shade. You should remove water sprouts promptly.

Suckers are the branches that grow on the lower part of the tree trunk or from the roots of the tree. Usually they grow from below the graft, so if you don't remove them, they'll grow into a wild tree or bush that will crowd out the good part of the tree within a few years. A lot of sucker growth results on fruit trees when a slower-growing variety is grafted on a vigorous-growing rootstock. Usually the suckers appear as a cluster of branches close to the base of the tree trunk, but sometimes (especially on plum trees) they may pop up out of the roots anywhere under the tree, even a distance away from the trunk. Mow or clip them off at ground level as soon as they appear.

Sometimes gardeners ask if the suckers that look like new, young trees can be transplanted to form new fruit trees of the same variety. As I have mentioned, such trees will usually produce fruit of inferior quality. They can be used for grafting stock, however, if you'd like to experiment. You can produce new trees that are of good quality by cutting a small, pencil-thin limb or bud from a named variety of fruit tree such as Delicious or Rome Beauty, grafting it onto one of your wild sucker trees, and planting it where you'd like a new tree to grow.

In some unmowed orchards, trees sprout and grow from seeds of unused fruit that fall on the ground. These seedling trees should be treated like suckers and removed as soon as they begin to grow. Like any weed, they sap the energy of the orchard by depleting the water and fertility of the soil, and

Water sprouts (from branches) and root suckers (from ground).

Trees with bad crotches (left) collect water, begin to rot, and eventually break off at the crotches. One central leader stem (right) is better.

eventually they crowd out the good trees. Although they often resemble the named varieties, their appearance is deceitful, and almost always the fruit is of inferior quality. Don't allow them or any other weed or bushy growth to compete with the vast root system your tree needs to support the large crop of fruit you're anticipating.

Fruit trees are not often recommended as ornamentals, because there are many other flowering trees that need less care and have fewer disease and insect problems. But many people feel a fruit tree doesn't need much special attention when grown for its appearance rather than for its produce. (Keep in mind that fruit trees need pruning occasionally to keep them healthy, even if you never eat their produce.) And some people enjoy encouraging a good crop on lawns that otherwise would offer no food.

When to Prune

There is an ever-continuing argument among pomologists about the best time to prune fruit trees. Magazines often run articles supporting one time of year or another, and each professional orchardist and experienced home grower has a favorite time. Meanwhile, beginners can get completely confused listening to the controversy.

Perhaps the best way to help answer the question is to describe what happens when you prune at different seasons. Seasonal conditions vary greatly throughout the country, so your location is an important factor in determining when you should prune.

Spring. Most people agree that pruning a fruit tree when it is just beginning to make its most active growth is one of the worst times. The tree will probably bleed heavily, and it may have trouble recovering from the loss of so much sap. Also, infections such as fire blight are most active and easily spread around in the spring. If a book suggests pruning in early spring, the author often means late winter — before any sign of growth begins.

The only pruning you should do in the spring is to remove any branches that have been broken by winter storms or injured by the cold. Immediately tack bark that has split from the trunk back onto the wood, and seal the wound with tree paint to prevent air from drying the bare wood.

123

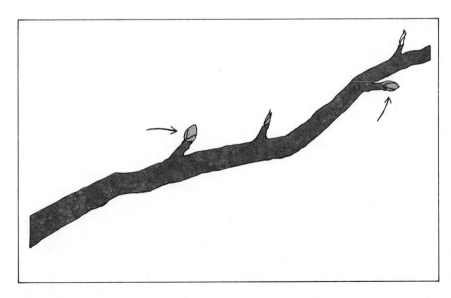

Fruit buds (indicated by arrows) are plumper than leaf buds.

Early summer. Although I don't recommend major pruning in early summer, this is a good time to pinch off buds and snip off small branches that are growing in the wrong direction or in the wrong place. Remove suckers, water sprouts, and branches that have formed too low on the stem as soon as you notice them.

Fruit trees grown in planters or tubs, espaliered trees, and other artistically shaped trees should be clipped regularly to keep them looking their best. Clip or pinch back new growth on tight hedges, "bean poles," or fences as soon as they begin to grow, and continue throughout the summer to keep them in the intended size and shape.

LORETTE PRUNING

Developed in Europe by M. Lorette, this is an excellent method for intensive fruit growing. It is especially useful on dwarf fruit trees and on trees grown as espaliers, cordons, hedges, and fences. (See Chapter 9.)

To prevent useless limb growth, begin pruning in early summer and continue until early fall. No dormant pruning is done at all. By frequent clipping and pinching, you direct the tree's energy into producing fruit buds near the trunk or on a few short limbs, rather than out at the ends of long branches. This is somewhat like shearing a hedge, and results in small, easy-to-care-for trees that bear fruit at an early age. Each part of the tree is in full sunlight because there is so little leaf area. Therefore, the fruit is of superior quality.

In cold regions, the Lorette method is risky, since trees pruned in summer tend to keep growing later in the season, and this growth may be injured in the winter. For the same reason, even in areas where the growing season is long, vigorous-growing trees such as the peach and apricot are often difficult to grow by the Lorette method.

Late summer. Late summer is a favorite time for many people to prune their fruit trees. By pruning after the tree has completed its yearly growth and hardened its wood, and before it has lost its leaves, you stimulate less regrowth. You still have to take care of any frost injury in late winter, but this late summer-early fall pruning works well if extensive winter damage is not likely.

Wherever growing seasons are short and the extreme cold or heavy snow and ice loads may cause injury to the trees, late-winter pruning is best. Don't cut back the tree in late summer if there's a good chance that the remaining branches will be winter-killed. You'll have to prune away too much of the tree.

Late fall and winter. Late fall or winter is a favorite time to prune in the warmer parts of the country. Orchardists have more spare time then, and the

A young apple tree well started in a modified leader form.

trees are bare, so it is easier to see what needs to be done. You should choose days when the temperature is above freezing, however, to avoid injury to the wood. Because frozen wood is very brittle, it breaks easily when hit by a ladder or pruning tool.

However, if you live in a cold part of the country, or if you are growing tree varieties that are inclined to have winter injury, wait until the coldest weather is over before pruning.

Late winter. This season is probably the most popular time for northern gardeners to prune. As in late fall and winter, the tree is completely dormant, and since the leaves are off, it is easy to see where to make the cuts. You can repair any winter injury, the weather is usually warm enough during the day, and most orchardists are not too busy during this season.

If you prune your trees regularly each year, late winter is a satisfactory time to prune because you don't have to remove large amounts of wood. However, if the trees have been neglected for a few years and are badly in need of a cutback, late winter is not the best time to prune. Excessive pruning in late winter usually stimulates a great deal of growth the following spring and summer, because the tree tries to replace its lost wood. Branches, suckers, and water sprouts are likely to grow in great abundance. If a major pruning job is necessary, do all or at least a large part of it in late summer or early fall so that you won't cause a great amount of regrowth.

Winter Injury and Sunscald

When I first started growing fruit trees, I was puzzled to find that the tree bark sometimes looked blistered and was splitting open. Finally someone told me that it was the sun's fault. The common name for it is sunscald, and it may take place in any climate when the warm sun shines directly on the tree's bark. It often occurs in the North on late winter days when the bright sun warms the bark to temperatures far above the surrounding air. The damage occurs when a cloud suddenly covers the sun, or the sun drops behind a hill, or perhaps a quick, cold breeze comes up. The sudden cooling of the tree's surface, and the subsequent tightening of the bark and freezing of the cells, often causes either small cracks in the bark or large slits that run up and down the tree.

If you don't repair sunscald damage at once, the wood and loose bark separate and the wood around the wound dies, sometimes necessitating a major pruning job in the spring. However, when the damage is spotted early, you can stick the loose bark back onto the limb with large thumb tacks or small nails with large heads. After tacking, cover the whole area with tree dressing.

We like to spray a thinned white latex paint on our trees every two or three years. We try to cover the trunk and lower branches on the southern and eastern exposures where the sun shines brightest in late winter. This helps keep the tree sap cool and prevents sunscald and other winter injury caused by sudden temperature changes. This whitewashing of the tree stems is useful in the South too, where excessive sun often blisters the bark during hot summers.

In addition to sunscald, several other situations can cause winter injury. Sometimes a tree doesn't stop growing early enough in the summer to harden up its wood properly, and it isn't able to withstand the first cold spell or the extreme cold in winter. Untimely warm spells in late winter may stimulate bud activity, and the trees lose moisture that the frozen roots can't replace. Occasionally, extreme cold or chilling winds during cold periods can cause cell damage. Also, during a cold, windy time or a prolonged cold spell, the insulating bark may be penetrated by the low temperatures, causing damage to the interior of the tree and the roots.

By choosing varieties that are suitable for growing in your region, and by pruning carefully and at the right time, you will have a head start on preventing winter injury. Another preventative step is to fertilize only early in the season so that you don't stimulate late growth. Also, cover the roots of the tree with a heavy mulch of hay, shredded bark, or leaves so that the ground doesn't freeze deep or warm up suddenly. The mulch will help to prevent root injury and will also keep the tree from running out of moisture.

During years when winter damage is severe, a heavy pruning of damaged wood will probably be all that the tree can stand, so don't do any other pruning that year. When this happens, avoid fertilizing for a year or so to prevent overstimulation of growth on an already weak tree.

PRUNING IN SNOW COUNTRY

You may need to prune differently if your fruit trees are growing in an area where snows are heavy and the average accumulation is three feet or more, or if the snow drifts that high around the trees.

Although in most regions it's best to allow a fruit tree to grow its branches close to the ground, this isn't the thing to do in deep snow country. Heavy, icy crusts sometimes settle as the snow underneath melts, breaking lower limbs in the process. This causes ugly wounds in the tree's trunk. Since the branches of dwarf fruit trees are practically all low-growing, they are a poor choice in heavy snow country.

A cautionary note: Make sure that the wood is really dead before you start pruning. Sometimes it is difficult to tell which limbs are really dead and which are merely slow about leafing out. Whenever you're in doubt, postpone the pruning for a few weeks, just to be sure.

Pruning Dwarf Trees

Many of the fruit trees being sold today are the dwarf or semidwarf type rather than full-size or standard trees. Although the tops of these small trees are the same variety and produce the same size fruit as ordinary trees, their special rootstocks keep them from getting large. Dwarf and semidwarf trees vary from about 5 to 12 feet high when fully grown, depending on their kind of rootstock.

Dwarf trees require some pruning just as full-size trees do, but their height needs no control, and, since they grow more slowly, the pruning is needed less often. You may also, just as on standard trees, need to do some thinning of the fruit to produce the best quality. Miniature fruit trees grown in tubs or planters for ornamental purposes will also need some shearing or snipping back during the summer to keep them in an attractive shape.

Dwarfing a Full-Size Tree

In some areas, the regular dwarf fruit trees are not entirely satisfactory because of their lack of hardiness, a tendency to break in high winds or heavy snows, and their susceptibility to insect and disease damage. Full-size trees can be dwarfed by surgery without much trouble, even for an amateur.

The purpose of the surgery is to slow down the tree's growth. Although the operation is easy, precision cutting is important because a careless cut with a sharp knife could kill the tree.

In early summer, cut a strip of bark about ¾-inch wide completely around the tree by making two rings. Cut to, but not into, the wood. Next, remove the bark, turn it upside down, and replace it, with the green side still inward. Then cover the whole thing with grafting wax, tree dressing, or rubber electrical tape (not plastic) to seal out the air. Let the covering wear away by itself.

Dwarfing a fruit tree by surgery is interesting and effective, even if it isn't a common practice. Because it slows down the growth of the tree, the process usually makes it bear at a younger age, too. The surgery will be effective for many years, but eventually all the inverted bark cells will be replaced by those that are headed in the right direction, and the tree will grow at its normal rate until it reaches full size.

Pruning to Make Trees Bear

The time required by a young fruit tree to begin bearing is generally from 2 to 12 years, depending on the kind of fruit, the variety, and the growing conditions. You should not allow your tree to bear fruit while it is still small, or it will be weakened and won't bear again for many years. It's difficult to say exactly when the tree is strong enough to bear its first crop, but you can make that judgment by evaluating the strength of the limbs, the height, and the general health of the tree. If you feel that your tree is still too small to mature fruit, pick off its first blooms or small fruits.

Sometimes, instead of bearing early in life, a tree will do just the opposite. Some varieties naturally take a long time to produce, such as the Baldwin apple and certain pears; others, in spite of your careful pruning, will grow too luxuriously and are so comfortable just growing away that they forget to settle down and bear fruit. Delayed bearing may be the result of overly rich soil. Whatever the reason, enterprising gardeners have figured out how to slow down overactive growth and thereby get the tree to produce. Some old-timers used unconventional methods, like putting a good-size rock in the first crotch of branches. Others bent branches toward the ground and fastened them, like pegging down a tent, to make the tree produce faster. Not long ago, a gardening friend of mine who believes strongly in the secret life of plants told me he had excellent results from showing his delinquent tree a chain saw and voicing loud threats.

If you're skeptical of these methods, you could try the one described under "Dwarfing a Full-Size Tree." (See page 127.) If you don't want to dwarf the entire tree, it's possible to reverse the bark on only a limb or two. Root pruning (page 31) is another often-used method to slow down tree growth without injuring the tree.

An easier way to slow growth is called ringing. Cut a single slit three-quarters of the way around one or two limbs of the tree in early summer. Use a sharp knife and don't scar the bark any more than necessary. Cut through the bark, but not into the wood.

Ringing is a harsh operation and although you may force the tree to bear, it isn't likely to do the tree any good, so do it only as a last resort. Occasionally we hear of healthy, rugged trees, a dozen or more years old, that have yet to produce a single bloom. On them, it's worth a try.

The Old Orchard

Not long ago, a newlywed couple we were visiting asked me to look at the old orchard they wanted to rejuvenate. It was an interesting experience. Walking through a decrepit old orchard that provided bountifully for a family three or four generations ago is a bit like wandering through a ghost town. They wanted to know if they could salvage it. Many people ask the same question when they're faced with an old tree or orchard. Sometimes, unfortunately, it is much better to clear the land, stack up a big woodpile, and start over — but not always.

Before you decide, ask yourself some objective questions. First: Are the trees too far gone to save? If their trunks are full of rot and large holes, or if they are half-dead and splitting apart, they're probably on their last legs, and any pruning might finish them off.

Next, the most important question: Is the fruit the trees produce any good? If it is green, hard, sour, and small, the trees are probably of a poor variety. Perhaps they grew as suckers from the roots of other trees now gone,

An apple tree well over a century old can still produce in spite of poor branch structure and no pruning. Fruits are small, however, and the tree likely will bear only every other year.

This old apple tree needs pruning. Because of a bad fork, open center pruning is called for. The top can be cut back somewhat, and heavy limb growth should be gradually thinned out.

or from seed that grew out of fallen, unused fruit. Unless they are worth cooking or making into cider, it's just as well to get rid of the trees.

However, if they are in sound condition, and the fruit looks as if it could be improved by thinning, fertilizing, and pruning, clean up the orchard and prune the trees. It will certainly be time well spent. Although it may never look like a model orchard, you should reap lots of good fruit and enjoy the happy feeling that you have taken a sad, old fruit grove and made it into something worthwhile.

In the first year, with your saw and scythe, remove all the brush and weeds, all trees other than fruit trees, and any fruit trees that look decrepit or produce worthless fruit. Knock off all the loose bark on the remaining good trees, being careful not to open new wounds. Then cut off the dead limbs and all broken branches, making sure to cut each one back to a live branch or to the trunk without leaving a stub. Follow the directions for cutting large branches (see Chapter 4) so that the wood doesn't split back into the trunk. Cut out any limbs with woodpecker holes, and those that have suffered weather damage or have signs of insect or disease infestation. Haul away the wood, bark, and brush, so that insects and disease won't reproduce in them. Then paint over the cut areas with a good tree paint.

PRUNING FRUIT TREES

This may be all the pruning you'll want to do the first year on those trees that needed severe pruning. On trees that required little surgery, however, you can begin some light removal of the smaller limbs around the top of the tree to let in more light. Don't cut out too many live limbs in any one year though, unless their weight seems to be threatening the tree.

In the second year begin a light pruning at the top of the tree so that more sunlight can reach the interior. Cut out the older, medium-size, weak, and unproductive branches.

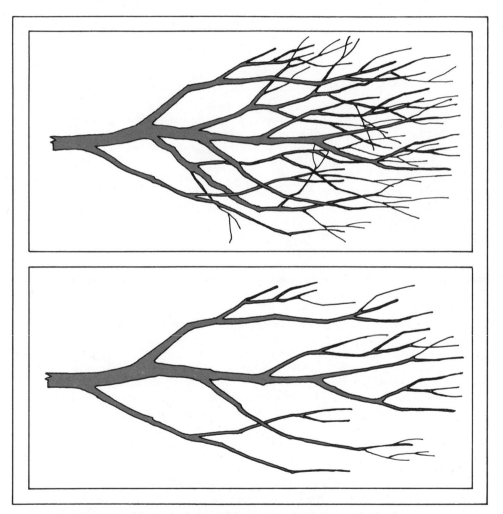

Horizontal branches should be trimmed of some side limbs to reduce the fruit-producing surface and to permit more light to enter the tree.

In the third year thin out the branches even more. You can begin to remove a few of the larger branches, if you think it's necessary.

From then on, prune in a normal way, but unless the tree appears to be in good physical condition with lots of lower limbs and adequate new growth, avoid any major cosmetic surgery such as removing the top of a large tree to make it lower.

There is usually no way to get a sprawling, crotchy old tree back to growing with a model central leader without serious shock to the tree, and you can't top tall trees safely if they are past their prime. Usually, opening up the tree's center and thinning the wood is all the pruning you can hope to do for an elderly tree. In addition to pruning, however, you can help to rejuvenate it by fertilizing the soil generously and thinning the fruit during the years when it sets too big a crop.

Pruning Sanitation

As I mentioned before, some of the most serious diseases are carried by pruning tools. Fire blight, for example, a bacteria-caused disease that's lethal to fruit trees, has spread around many orchards this way.

132

If you suspect disease, think of yourself as a tree doctor as you prune. You wouldn't expect a surgeon to take out your gallbladder with the same dirty instruments he had used to remove his last patient's appendix. Your prized Bartlett pear deserves careful treatment, with tools that have been disinfected.

If you feel that there might be disease in your orchard, disinfect your gloves and tools after pruning each tree. Professional orchardists often use a mixture of bichloride of mercury and cyanide of mercury for this purpose, but both of these chemicals are very poisonous and are not recommended for home use. For the home orchardist, it is safer and quite effective to soak the tools in a pail containing full-strength Clorox or similar home bleach as you go between branches or trees. With these germ-free tools, you can approach your patients with a clear conscience and not feel they are drawing their limbs about them in fear and trembling.

Disease also spreads around the orchard via the wind and insects. A good way to keep fungus, germs, and insects out of a tree is to seal up all cuts and open wounds with an antiseptic paint. Most tree infections are especially active in the spring, so do your painting and sealing early in the season before they get started. Remove all of the pruning debris from the area, and either burn it or take it to a dump or landfill.

Cutting Grafting Wood

In recent years, there has been a renewed interest in home-grafting of fruit trees. Just as our ancestors did a century ago, gardeners are growing their own trees, creating varieties that nurseries don't sell. It's fun to propagate choice old varieties that are nearly obsolete.

Grafting is not a mysterious operation, and nearly any good fruit-growing book or encyclopedia will show you how it is done. Basically, you take a branch from a tree that bears good fruit and surgically transplant it to the root of a wild or unimproved tree. Bud grafting is similar except that you use a single dormant bud.

For regular grafting, cut these branches — called scions — very early in the spring before any growth starts. Look for a branch about a foot long that grew the previous year, preferably one that is filled with nice, fat buds. You can cut this into shorter pieces when you get ready to use it. Meanwhile, wrap it in a plastic bag and store it in a cool place. Just as with any pruning, cut your scions on a slant close to an outside bud, don't leave a stub, and don't cut off more limbs than the tree can safely spare.

Some people, including myself, are trying to rescue old varieties of fruit trees by grafting, but we often run into difficulty finding any young growth when trying to get a branch from an aging tree. Elderly trees that have never been pruned often make such a small amount of new growth each year that you may have to go to the top of the tree to find any. I've found that I can encourage a limited amount of new growth by moderately pruning a few limbs in late winter.

There is usually no shortage of scions available on young trees and on mature trees that have been kept pruned. Make sure that your method of cutting the scions fits into your pruning program for that tree.

133

Pruning Spur-Type Fruit Trees

Trees bear their fruit either on the limbs or on short, stubby spurs between the branches. Pears, plums, and cherries grow mostly on spurs, peaches grow on one-year-old limb growth, and most varieties of apples are produced both on spurs and on limbs.

Because spur-type fruit trees make less limb growth, they need less pruning. Since this means considerably less labor for the orchardist, scientists have worked on breeding trees that produce mostly on spurs, and there are now many varieties of this type of fruit tree available.

When too many fruit spurs develop along a branch, cut out some of them to encourage bigger and better fruits on the rest. After a few years of experience, you'll be able to judge about how many spurs are right for the tree. Each spur will usually produce for several years, but then you should cut it off to allow a replacement to grow. You'll be able to spot the older spurs by their aging appearance.

Pruning a Five-in-One Fruit Tree

As a novelty, some nurseries sell three-in-one or five-in-one apple trees, and some even feature trees with plums, cherries, peaches, nectarines, and apricots all growing on the same tree. Some people like to graft several varieties of fruit on their own single tree too, either for the fun of it, or because they have a small growing area.

These multiple-variety fruit trees are difficult to prune. However, if you have one or feel you must buy or graft your own, you can prune them if you take some precautions. You will have to remember each year where the different varieties are located or else you're likely to cut off the only limb bearing a certain kind of fruit. If you don't have a good memory, you can tie ribbons of various colors to identify each variety. Multiple-fruit trees usually must be grown with an open center, since there will be three or more strong limbs. Each different kind of limb will grow at its own rate and in a different manner, so corrective pruning will be necessary to produce a well-balanced tree. It's a big job, but if you keep at it, you can avoid bad crotches, water sprouts, and lopsided growth.

We used to have a tree growing in our backyard with red, yellow, and green apples. Each year I grafted some new varieties on it, but unfortunately, I also mistakenly pruned a few others off, so the tree never became the masterpiece I had hoped it would be. Still, I had fun, and someday intend to do another.

Commercial Orchards

Pruning large orchards is similar to pruning a home planting, except that commercial growers are often able to take advantage of pneumatic pruners and other power equipment. They also usually have the advantage of years of experience at their craft.

In recent years, commercial orchardists have exhibited a great interest in high-density planting. They are pruning fruit trees into dense hedges or cordons, or pruning in other ways to increase production and also to lower the costs of pruning, disease and insect control, and harvesting.

You'd probably enjoy a visit to a commercial orchard at pruning time. Most amateurs are surprised at how much wood orchardists remove from a mature tree each season. Perhaps you should go more than once, since many of us need to be reminded occasionally that we should prune boldly and vigorously rather than timidly and apologetically.

Apple

When pruning apple trees *(Malus)*, follow the general directions for pruning fruit trees. Try to keep the tree growing with a central leader, if possible, and correct any bad growth habits that your variety of tree might have naturally.

Since apples are the most commonly grown fruit in home gardens, I am listing the most popular varieties with their growth characteristics to help you with your pruning.

Cortland. This tree has a spreading, somewhat drooping habit of growth, so don't allow it to branch too close to the ground. Prune and thin it to encourage large fruit. Open the top for good color, and brace the limbs if they droop too low.

Delicious. A dense grower, this tree will form many weak crotches if left to itself, so it needs careful pruning. Without overpruning, allow in lots of sunlight. Thin it heavily for giant-size fruit.

Duchess of Oldenberg. This is a rugged, semiupright, medium-size tree. It bears on limbs and on short spurs, and will yield heavy crops annually for a long time if you keep it pruned and thinned.

Early McIntosh. This is a semiupright, large tree. It needs careful pruning and thinning to correct its natural habit of forming bad crotches. It tends to bear biennially, producing small- to medium-size fruit.

Empire. A semiupright growing tree, producing small- to medium-size, high-colored fruit of excellent quality. Although an annual bearer, it will benefit from regular pruning and some thinning. It bears mostly on short spurs.

Grannie Smith. This high-quality apple tree can be grown only in the warmer areas offering a long growing season. It is an annual bearer, and requires ordinary pruning.

Holly. A semiupright, medium-size tree. Expect good crops annually. The fruit is of excellent quality and color. This tree requires ordinary pruning.

Honeygold. A semiupright tree, bearing medium-size apples that taste much like the Yellow Delicious. Thinning and pruning will increase the size of the fruit. Although this is a hardy tree, it's not a good choice in the areas that have very short growing seasons.

Jersey Mac. This is an early-ripening McIntosh. It's a large tree with a spreading habit, and is an annual bearer of good-quality fruit. The fruit tends to drop early, but heavy thinning helps.

Jonagold. This is a large, semiupright tree. You will have to prune it heavily to correct its twiggy habit of growth. It bears large and excellent-quality fruit when cared for properly.

Jonamac. This is a semiupright tree, less twiggy than Jonagold, and it produces larger fruit than do many Jonathan-type trees. The apples are of excellent quality, and they stay on the tree well.

Jonathan. This tree tends to produce lots of small branches that need regular pruning out. Also, you must thin out growing fruit heavily, or the naturally small apples will be even smaller.

Lobo. A large, semispreading, McIntosh-type tree, bearing good-quality fruit that ripens somewhat earlier than regular McIntosh. For annual bearing, prune and thin it if necessary.

Lodi. This tree produces an apple similar to a Yellow Transparent, but with somewhat firmer fruit. Prune it to correct its upright growth habit, and thin to prevent an overlarge crop every other year.

Sometimes it is advisable to prune a bare-rooted, 2-year-old, branched apple tree quite heavily at planting time. More than half of the twig surface of this tree has been removed to compensate for the damage inflicted on the roots when it was dug.

McIntosh. This is nearly the ideal tree. If you prune it adequately, the fruit will need little thinning. Although a strong, spreading tree, its limbs may need bracing to support heavy crops.

Macoun. The high quality of its apple makes this tree very popular, yet pruning its long, lanky branches is so demanding that many commercial growers have given up planting it. However, it's an excellent choice for a conscientious home gardener. This upright-growing tree tends to bear its small- to medium-size fruit biennially.

Melba. The high-quality McIntosh fruit of this early-bearing tree tends to ripen over a long season and is good for home use. Prune and thin it to discourage biennial bearing.

Melrose. This large, semiupright tree is a heavy bearer of excellent-quality fruits that stay on the tree well. It tends to bear biennially, so thin it heavily.

Milton. This tree bears an excellent, medium-size, McIntosh-Yellow Transparent cross. It's ideal for home use. The fruit ripens over a long season, but the tree tends to bear biennially unless it's pruned and thinned.

Mutsu. A semiupright variety from Japan that grows large fruit. It's a heavy producer, yet it seldom weakens itself by overbearing. Thin it heavily for large fruit.

Northern Spy. This tree produces long-keeping, superior fruit, but it is difficult to prune. It tends to grow very upright, and needs heavy pruning, but

137

Pruning a 3-year-old tree. Cut branches that compete with each other and those that stray too far from the rest of the tree. Weak and dead branches are removed as well.

unless you do it carefully, you will affect the crop. Thin it to get the largest fruit and to insure annual bearing.

Prima. A vigorous, spreading tree that is resistant to scab and other fruit diseases. The fruit is good, and the tree requires ordinary pruning.

Priscilla. This is a semispreading tree, resistant to mildew, fire blight, and scab and is an excellent tree for organic gardeners, because it doesn't require much spraying. This tree produces good fruit, and requires ordinary pruning.

Quinte. A semispreading tree, producing an excellent early apple with beautiful color. The tree is not always a heavy bearer, but pruning and thinning will increase the apple size and promote regular bearing.

Red Astrachan. This semispreading tree produces an excellent, early, old-time apple. It will need regular pruning and heavy thinning, or it will bear biennially.

Red Duchess. Its semispreading shape will benefit from pruning and thinning. It usually needs topping, or it will grow too tall.

Regent. This semiupright tree has fruit that usually grows singly instead of in clusters, so it needs less thinning. The high-quality fruit hangs on well. The tree usually bears annually and requires ordinary pruning.

Rhode Island Greening. The limbs of this very spreading tree will probably need bracing, as fruit loads get heavy. Prune it heavily, and thin the apples to encourage annual bearing.

Rome Beauty. Because Rome Beauty is very upright-growing and rather difficult to prune to a central leader, careful early pruning is necessary to develop a strong tree.

Spartan. This is a large tree with a somewhat semispreading habit of growth. It bears heavily, and needs careful pruning. The tree tends to bear biennially, and the fruit often drops early, and while thinning helps these conditions, the fruit still tends to be small. The quality of the apple, however, is excellent.

Spijon. This spreading, drooping tree is an annual bearer. The quality of the fruit is only fair. You can grow the tree with an open center.

Stayman's Winesap. Prune back this variety, as it tends to produce long, leggy branches. Be sure to correct any bad growing habits early.

Twenty Ounce. A large, upright-growing tree, best pruned to a central leader and allowed to spread.

138

Viking. This semiupright, hardy tree produces an excellent early apple. Prune and thin it to be an annual bearer. The apple is good for home use.

Wealthy. This tree tends to overbear its high-quality fruit on alternate years. Prune and thin it regularly to correct this habit and to prevent the fruit from getting smaller as the tree grows older.

Winesap. Like the Delicious, Winesap needs careful pruning to prevent it from forming weak crotches. Thin it to allow in sunlight and to increase the size of the fruit.

Yellow or Golden Delicious. The Delicious tends to grow upright and crotchy, with long, leggy branches. Prune it to correct bad crotches and to prevent the limbs from breaking under a heavy load of fruit. Thin heavily for giant-size fruit.

Yellow Transparent. This upright grower bears while still young and tends to bear too heavily. Careful pruning and thinning is necessary, or the tree will produce an abundance of small apples and will be short-lived. Be sure to correct bad crotches early so that the branches won't split under the weight of the fruit. This tree is unusually susceptible to sunscald, so whitewashing may be necessary to prevent bark injury.

York Imperial. Because this tree tends to bear a large crop every other year, you should prune the fruit spurs heavily in the late winter preceding the bearing year. Thin out small fruits to help even-out yields. Prune to keep the top of the tree open.

Apricot

Pruning apricots *(Prunus Armeniaca)* is similar to pruning peaches. (See page 141.) Heavy pruning is necessary to produce good fruit. The open center method is best, and in addition to cutting back the limbs, you may need to thin out the bearing spurs. Root pruning is beneficial to help prevent excessive growth and subsequent winter injury where the growing season is short.

Cherry

Cherry trees *(Prunus Cerasus, P. avium)* need less pruning than other fruit trees. Start pruning to a central leader when your tree is young to encourage a strong tree, especially if it is one of the larger-growing types. Because of the tree's natural habit of growth, you probably will have to change to a modified leader or open center as the tree gets older.

You'll need to do some pruning to let in the sun to color the fruit, and to thin the bearing wood, but beware of overpruning, a cause of winter injury and premature aging.

Citrus Fruit

Since oranges, grapefruits, lemons, and limes *(Citrus)* grow in the hottest parts of the United States, they usually need less pruning than fruit grown in the North, where we need to let sunshine into the trees. However, bare-rooted trees need a severe cutback at planting time, and you should train young trees early to grow in the shape you want. As the tree grows, you'll want to continue the shaping.

Since many citrus varieties tend to grow unevenly, some pruning back of overlong limbs is usually necessary. You can do this at any time of year, but in areas where frost is likely, wait until all danger is over in the spring. The dwarf citrus tree is becoming very popular now for backyard planting, and just like other dwarf fruits, it needs a lot less pruning than the standard tree.

Both dwarf and full-size citrus trees often lose their vigor as they get older, so a rejuvenation pruning may be necessary to help them bear well again. Citrus trees can stand a more rigorous cutback than peaches or apples because winter injury is rarely a problem.

If you cut back a tree severely, you will need to do some clipping and training of the new branches to make sure that the tree grows back into a good shape. It will probably take at least two years before beginning to bear well again. Since the hot summer can blister tender citrus bark very easily, be sure to cover with white paint any bark that you suddenly expose to the sun through heavy pruning. Also, paint any bark that has become exposed because of winter injury.

You can prune all citrus trees into fancy shapes, such as espaliers, cordons, and fences, if you do it with care. As with the cool-weather fruits, the dwarf varieties are usually more suitable, and they can also be grown in large pots or planters.

Citrus trees grown for fruit production in commercial orchards are usually allowed to branch quite close to the ground. This makes the fruit easier to pick, and the heavier shading helps fight grass and weed competition. Trees grown in the backyard are basal-pruned higher for better appearance and easier lawn care. Basal-prune higher than it seems necessary while the tree is still young, because just as with apple and peach trees, the weight of the fruit will cause the branches to hang lower to the ground as the tree grows.

Usually orange and grapefruit trees need less pruning than do lemons. Lemon trees tend to produce an abundance of upright-growing suckers that you'll have to cut away frequently. They also grow quite unevenly, and some of the limbs will need cutting back to keep the tree symmetrical.

Fig

Since fig trees *(Ficus carica)* bleed badly, it is important to prune them only during their dormant season. White and brown figs bloom and bear only on new wood, so the usual practice is to cut these back severely each year for better production. Prune black figs more like other fruits, by cutting back the wood that is over one year old.

140

Figs grow from 25 to 40 feet tall. They can stand heavy pruning and make good espaliered trees. When you're growing them for an attractive landscape effect, keep them in balance by snipping and pinching. Don't allow them to branch as close to the ground as they would if being grown for their fruit. Root pruning is sometimes necessary to promote fruiting if they are growing in overfertile soil. In fact, fig trees do better when the soil isn't too rich.

Peach and Nectarine

The peach *(Prunus Persica)* has always represented a real challenge to dedicated gardeners. It is fussy about soils and climate, sensitive to spring frosts, and grows so vigorously that much pruning is needed. Yet the juicy, tasty peach is so enticing that even northerners keep trying to grow it.

Pruning a 5-year-old peach tree.

Those fortunate enough to live where it grows well naturally want to grow it to perfection. Proper pruning plays an important part in peach culture, and an unpruned tree is a sad sight, bearing fruit only at the ends of its branches. Usually both the peach and the nectarine should be grown with an open center. The trees tend to grow fast and late in the season, and pruning makes them grow even faster. In areas where winter damage often kills improperly hardened wood, root pruning may be the only effective way to check excessive limb growth late in the season.

Don't allow peach and nectarine trees to branch closely to the ground, or you won't be able to keep trunk borers under control. Inspect the trunks of the trees frequently, and if you spot a borer's hole, take a wire and dispense with the fat grub at once. Then seal up the hole with either tree sealer, caulking compound, or plastic wood.

Peach, nectarine, and apricot trees are likely to grow tall, and since the best fruit often grows at the top of the tree, keep the tops low and accessible. The best method is to cut back the tall-growing limbs each year, but if you haven't done this, you can remove the top of the tree during the dormant season with no damage to the tree. However, the fruit crop may be less the following year as the tree recovers from its loss.

The best time to prune is in late winter so that you can cut away wood injured by low temperatures. In years when winter damage is heavy, that pruning may be all the tree can stand. Don't feed the tree after you've had heavy winter damage or after you have pruned it severely, because you don't want to stimulate a rapid regrowth.

Like all fruit trees, peaches often set far too many little fruits, even if you have pruned the tree carefully. As a result, the tree produces a large crop of small peaches. To get large, luscious peaches, thin them when they are about the size of marbles. This may involve a lot of work, because you should space the ones you leave on the tree about seven inches apart, but the results will be well worth your effort.

Even if you faithfully do your pruning and thinning, peach trees have a tendency to set such a heavy crop that broken branches may be a real danger. If this looks likely, you can save your tree by propping up the weighty limbs with wide planks.

Pear

Pears (*Pyrus communis*) are not as difficult to grow as peaches, but in past years fire blight has killed off many of the trees. Now, thanks to more resistant varieties and a better understanding of the disease, this fruit is coming back in both large orchards and backyard gardens. Like most fruits, pears need a partner for pollination purposes, so always plant your trees in pairs.

Pruning back bare-rooted pear trees at planting time is important, and the rules are the same as for any other fruit. Usually, two-year-old, branched trees are the best kind to plant.

The training of pears in their early life is quite similar to that of apples. Prune the tree to a central leader for the first few years. After that, you can grow it with a modified leader, if you wish. The growth of most varieties tends

A young pear tree that is ready for pruning. It has borne its first crop, and bad crotches need to be corrected to get the tree back to a strong central leader.

143

to be upright, so direct your early pruning toward thinning excess branches and encouraging a spreading tree. An annual light pruning is preferable to an infrequent heavy one for two important reasons: heavy pruning delays bearing, and it encourages fire blight.

Pears bloom and bear their fruit on the short, sharp spurs that grow between the branches. Spurs need regular thinning, and occasionally you should remove older spurs so they may be replaced by more vigorous ones. Thin out the small fruits too, if too many are set in any year.

Always be on guard for signs of fire blight. You'll be able to spot it easily, because the limbs, leaves, and twigs look as if they have been held over a fire. If you see any infection, cut off the diseased limbs completely back into good, healthy wood. Remove them to a safe distance, and burn, bury, or otherwise destroy them, so that the disease won't spread. As when pruning any diseased trees, sterilize your gloves and all tools in a strong Clorox solution after pruning each tree to prevent spreading bacterial disease.

Early detection of fire blight is important so that you can bring it quickly under control. Fortunately for us pear lovers, quite a few varieties of blight-resistant pears have been introduced in recent years, and you may want to consider these if you are making a new planting. Magness, Moonglow, Morgan, and Starking Delicious are a few of these.

Plum

The plum *(Prunus)* is one of my favorite fruits. It comes in reds, blues, purples, yellows, and greens, and is available in a wide range of sizes and flavors. The trees produce abundantly and though I eat them by the bushel and drink gallons of their juice, I never tire of them. The years when the blossoms freeze and the crop is poor are sad indeed, so I always hope for warm nights while they are in bloom.

144

A plum with dense limb growth. If this were a European plum, it would be ready for heavy pruning. Being an American hybrid, it needs only a light thinning.

Prune plums carefully to help them produce well and to allow the sun to ripen the fruit before the first frost hits. Due to their straggly habit of growth, plums are almost always grown to an open center.

Follow the usual directions for pruning when planting. One-year-old whips, from four to seven feet tall, are the best choice if you're planting European and American plums, and two-year-old, slightly branched trees are preferable if you are planting the Japanese varieties. Cut back the whips about a third, to a fat bud, and cut off any side branches until you've removed from a third to a half of the total wood area.

Japanese plums require a lot of pruning, and you should do this annually in late winter. European plums, on the other hand, need very little, and an occasional thinning of the older wood is usually all that is necessary. Most American plums and hybrids of American plums need only moderate pruning to keep them bearing well; however, some varieties, including some of the cherry-plum hybrids, grow very long branches that hang on the ground and should be shortened. Prune the tree to keep it in balance. Many plum roots sucker badly, so periodically cut off the small trees growing from the tree's roots unless you keep the area under the tree well-mowed.

If your plum trees have a habit of bearing a large crop every other year, you may want to thin out some of the fruit to limit the large crop, to increase fruit size, and to encourage annual bearing. Trees producing large plums especially benefit from thinning. Pick off the extra fruits when they are still tiny in early summer so that the plums are five inches apart.

Some varieties of plums, especially the European kinds, are quite susceptible to a disease called black knot. Thick excrescences form along the twigs and are especially noticeable in winter. As there is no spray available to control this problem, pruning is necessary. Attack it with your pruning shears whenever the infection appears during the summer. Disinfect the tools as you work, and burn or dispose of the diseased parts promptly to prevent any spreading of the trouble. It is also a good idea to remove any infected wild plums or cherries growing nearby.

145

Quince

Quinces *(Cydonia oblonga)* are one of the few fruit-tree varieties that need almost no pruning, although you should remove any broken, dead, or crossed branches as a matter of course. Do any necessary basal pruning to get the tree growing into a good tree-like shape. Thin out the limbs only if they get so thick that harvesting of the fruit is difficult.

Like pears, quince trees are extremely susceptible to fire blight, and you should follow all the precautions recommended for pears should this disease strike your quince tree.

Tropical and Semitropical Fruit

Avocados. This plant needs only light pruning. In tropical climates, any opening up of the trees will cause sunburn on the tender bark. When your primary purpose for growing the trees is for fruit, allow the trees to grow naturally. If you grow them primarily for beauty, pinch and clip them back lightly to keep them looking good.

Mangos. These trees need no special pruning care when grown as an outdoor plant in the South, but they do need more attention when grown as a pot plant in the North. Their beautiful, shiny foliage makes them most attractive, and you can grow them easily from seed.

Pinching back and occasional root pruning (see Chapter 4) will prevent the plants from getting too large, but even so, you may have to repot them from time to time. Use ordinary good garden soil, and keep it moist but not soaking wet.

Olives. Olives need more pruning than most other tropical plants, and through centuries of cultivation, the art has become well developed. Although they are usually grown as trees, it's possible to prune them to grow as shrubs or even as tall, thick, hedge plants. When grown as trees, olives must frequently be pruned of their basal suckers and an occasional older branch. Often you'll want to thin the fruit by removing some of the blooms. If you prune them carefully, the trees can be very productive to a ripe, old age.

146

Papayas. These can grow where frosts are unlikely. In cooler climates, the melonlike fruits are sometimes grown in greenhouses. Papayas resemble a large plant or perennial more than a tree, and they tend to grow tall with no lower branches. Cutting back the top in early spring will encourage branching and greater production. Its old brown and yellow leaves often hang on the tree during the winter, and should be pruned for appearance' sake.

Pomegranates. These ornamental trees grow to an attractive shape with little care. If you want to grow one in an artistic form, you can prune it as a Japanese tree, tall screen, bonsai, or espalier. (See Chapters 9 and 15.) For food production, however, it is best grown in a tree form. Removal of the suckers is about all the pruning that's necessary.

Chapter 11

Pruning Small Fruits

Much of our family's best winter eating comes from the berry patch. Each year we fill up a large portion of the freezer with dozens of packages of strawberries, raspberries, blueberries, currants, gooseberries, and elderberries. By late fall, jars filled with preserves and colorful juices line our pantry shelves, standing by to help us struggle through the winter blizzards. Small fruits come in a wide assortment of colors, flavors, shapes, and sizes. There are red, pink, and green varieties of gooseberries, black, purple, red, and pink raspberries, and many different kinds of grapes, blueberries, blackberries, and currants.

Small fruits are not only colorful, tasty, and full of healthy vitamins, but most of the plants are easy to grow, as well. They are very productive, most bear a year or two after planting, they take very little room in the garden, they're usually inexpensive, and they need surprisingly little care.

You prune small-fruit plants for the same reasons that you prune the tree fruits — for larger fruit, better crops, and plants that are more disease-resistant. You can pick the berries more easily from well-pruned bushes too. Another bonus is that, just as with other trees and shrubs, proper pruning will extend the useful life of a small fruit patch for many years. The method of pruning small fruits is somewhat different from that of the tree fruits, however, and different terminology is used.

The word "cane" is often used when referring to the bush and bramble fruits. A cane is a stem or stalk of the raspberry, blackberry, dewberry, elderberry, and sometimes of the grape.

Grapes

The grape (*Vitis*) is one of the oldest fruits in cultivation. Early Greek, Roman, and biblical writings refer often to "the vine" and the wine that was made from it. Many centuries before orange juice and apple pie, horticulturists were busy trying to figure out how to prune this remarkable plant so that it would produce bountifully. When you prune a grape vine, you are following in an ancient tradition and using a skill developed milleniums ago.

Over the years, many varieties of grapes have been introduced, and we are growing thousands of old and new varieties today. You may choose to develop your own little vineyard for delicious, fresh grapes, grapes for wine, unfermented juice, or perhaps for grape jelly. You may even decide to grow them simply for their beauty.

Since many varieties of grapes are rank growers, an unpruned vine can spread quickly all over a large area, forcing the plant's energy into the vine, rather than into the production of grapes. To get good crops of this superb fruit, you must prune the vine.

Grapes grow mostly on one-year-old wood. As an unpruned vine matures, it carries more and more wood that is much older than one year, and thus becomes unproductive. Your goal should be to allow the canes to grow one year and bear fruit the next, and then you should remove them. This means that each summer your plant should have canes at two stages of growth: canes that grew last year and are now bearing, and new canes that will bear next year. Besides pruning any canes that are older than a year, you should prune to keep the vine in a manageable size, to direct the energy of the vine into producing fruit rather than vines and leaves, and to keep the crop growing close to the main stem so that the sap doesn't have to travel far to produce grapes. Also you must allow the sun to get in and ripen the fruit. Grapes must ripen on the vine because, unlike most fruits, grapes do not continue to ripen after they are picked.

There are many methods of accomplishing the results you want, and the method you use to prune will depend on a lot of things, including where you decide to grow your grapes — on a fence, an arbor, trellis, or as a free-standing plant.

Pruning at planting time. Because pruning at planting time is so important to the grape vine's future success, most nurseries prune the vines before they sell them. If they haven't done this for you, you should do it yourself, unless the vine is potted with its roots intact.

Although it seems drastic, cut off three-quarters or more of the top. Prune off all the side branches, and cut back the stem so that it is no more than five inches tall. This heavy pruning encourages the roots to grow faster than the top, and insures the beginnings of a strong vine that will start to bear heavy crops in two or three years.

Do any future pruning when the vine is dormant — after the time that the leaves drop off in the fall and before the buds begin to swell in the spring, provided the temperature is above freezing. Most northern gardeners choose early spring pruning so that any winter injury can be cut off at the same time.

Some people grow their grapes on an arbor so they can enjoy the beauty of the vines and watch the ripening grapes hang down from overhead. Others prefer a trellis, where they can espalier the vines against a wall or a building.

Whether you choose to use an arbor or trellis, your pruning may be as elaborate or as minimal as you wish. If you want a thick, shady vine with a few grapes hanging on it for effect, you'll need to prune it only from becoming too

148

overgrown. If you want grapes as well as beauty, however, you'll need to prune annually to get rid of all the wood over a year old. Cut back part of the year-old wood, too, leaving only enough to cover the arbor and produce grapes the following year.

The Kniffen system. Many of us are more practical and less artistic, preferring to grow our grapes simply on a wire fence the way most commercial growers do. One of the easiest and best ways to care for grapes is through the Kniffen system. Your fence should consist of two strands of smooth 9- or 10-gauge wire stapled on two posts set solidly in the ground and spaced about eight feet apart.

Space the lower wire about two feet above the ground and the second about one foot higher. It's important to brace each end so that the wires won't sag as they get loaded with fruit and vines. Plant each grape vine midway between the two posts. Your chances for growing a thrifty specimen will be improved if you plant and water the vine carefully. Make sure that your vines

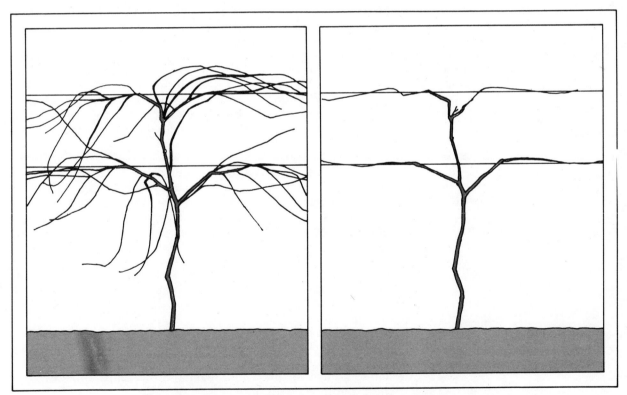

A large grape vine, trained to the Kniffen system, before and after pruning.

will get as much sun as possible, and as little of the chilling north wind as possible.

During the first summer, allow the vine to grow naturally, with only a bit of minor pinching of side buds. Remove these buds so that the vine will grow upward toward the wires with a minimum of side growth.

The following year, in late winter while the vine is still dormant, prune it back to a single stem with no branches. This cutback will encourage even more vigorous growth during the coming summer when fruit buds will be formed for the next year. During the summer, by pinching and pruning, allow only two vines to grow along the wires in each direction (four in all). If the vines grow well, they should cover the wires by the end of the summer. If they grow more than this, cut back any extra growth and any side branches right after the first hard frost.

The tendrils on the grapes should wrap around the wires and hold the vines securely. If any vines fall off the wires and need to be tied back on, be sure to use a material like narrow plastic ribbon (not tape) that won't cut into the grape's tender bark.

In the third year, allow four more new vines to grow paralleling the first four that grew the previous season. These newcomers are your replacements for the ones that grew the second year. Let these droop on the ground until you have cut off the old vines and are ready to fasten them to the wires. The year-old vines should bloom and set grapes all along the wires this summer. Don't allow too many bunches to form this first bearing year, because over-bearing will weaken the plant and jeopardize future crops. If you're like I was, you'll be so thrilled with your first crop that you'll hate to part with any. But brace yourself and snip off a few of the clusters of the tiny grapes if more than three or four bunches are forming. Throughout the growing season, continue to pinch back any new growth that is headed in the wrong direction. Four new canes are all you'll need.

In late winter or very early spring of the fourth year, cut off the four canes that bore fruit the previous year, and make sure that you secure the four new canes to the wires. These will replace last year's bearing vines and will produce this year's crop. Cut off all extra growth, and during the summer, pinch the new canes occasionally in order to train four more canes that will replace the ones presently bearing. Repeat this process every year.

Each year, thin fruit clusters whenever too many appear. Usually a healthy, vigorous vine should produce from 30 to 60 bunches a year, with an average of 8 to 15 per branch. Don't allow the plant to produce a greater number, because overproduction is likely to weaken the vine, and you'll get quantity rather than quality.

There are many other ways of growing grapes in addition to the Kniffen method. Some gardeners, especially wine growers, like to prune their vines so that they have a long, tall trunk, like a cordon. Each year after fruiting, they cut back all the canes almost to this trunk, leaving a few short stubs to bear fruit and from which the new canes appear.

Grape-pruning methods also vary because different varieties of grapes grow at different rates, so the pruning must be adjusted accordingly. Pruning also varies with different soils and climates; look over your neighbor's shoulder when he is pruning his vines, especially if he seems to be having exceptionally good luck.

Pruning an old, neglected grape vine. If it becomes your duty to take over a grape vine that has been neglected for years, you very likely have a difficult job cut out for you. But it can be done. For the vine's sake, spread your pruning job over several years with the idea firmly in mind that you will eventually get the vine back to a single trunk with only four strong, well-spaced branches. Then you can train it into a Kniffen or other manageable system. Have a truck standing by to haul away the prunings, or plan a brisk bonfire in a safe place, because you'll have to get rid of lots of deadwood.

It's difficult to specify exactly how much wood you can take off in any one year. Your own good judgment is the best guide. There is always a temptation to get the messy job done as soon as possible, but this would be hard on the plant. Instead, spread the pruning over a period of time — from two to four years, depending on how overgrown the vine has become.

Vines that have trailed over the ground for many years often root and form many new plants. If you want to, you can salvage these new plants. In early spring, cut them back to about a foot. Then dig them up with a ball of soil, and replant them where you please. If you decide not to use the new plants that have formed, cut off all rooted vines at ground level, and don't allow them to grow back. Mowing, or spreading a heavy mulch over the area, will help to prevent any regrowth.

The Bush Fruits

Each year, our family discovers new ways to use the produce of the currant, elderberry, gooseberry, blueberry, and cranberry bushes. Last year, for the first time, we fried the flowers of the elderberry in batter for tasty fritters, and used the highbush cranberries to decorate our Christmas wreaths. But the bulk of our crop — the part we don't eat fresh, that is — goes into delicious juices, sauces, conserves, jellies, pies, and other desserts.

Pruning the bush fruits is not nearly as demanding as pruning either the tree fruits, brambles, or grape vines. I know of old farmsteads with currant and gooseberry bushes that still produce large crops of excellent fruit after decades of neglect. This is partly because the bush fruits are comparative newcomers to the garden, and they still have many of the good qualities of wild plants. In addition to the fact that they need very little pruning, they are also highly resistant to disease and insects and, with the exception of blueberries, they are not at all fussy about soil. However, each bush can be encouraged to do much better with a little care, and this care includes some pruning.

Unless you have bought a potted plant, or one growing with a well-wrapped and undisturbed, solid ball of earth, you'll need to prune it when you set it out. Treat a bare-rooted bush fruit just as you would any low-growing shrub. Cut back each branch about halfway, to a bud or to another branch.

Even though you'll be eager to eat the produce of the bush, encourage it to grow lots of sturdy roots and new branches the first year, instead of wasting its energy in producing fruit. In spite of your heavy pruning, it still may have

151

a few blooms the first year. If this happens, pinch the flowers off as soon as they appear.

Usually the initial pruning will be all the bush needs for several years. Of course, cut off any twigs or branches that have been broken by weather or resting birds. Otherwise, just speak to it kindly and let it grow.

After the bush has borne several large crops of fruit, you may notice that it looks a bit overgrown and that the fruit is getting smaller. This would be a good time to thin it out. Select a few of the oldest and woodiest branches and cut them right to the ground, either in late fall or early spring. If you do this faithfully every few years, the bush should be productive and thrive for at least your lifetime.

Blueberry. Compared with other small fruits, the blueberry *(Vaccinium)* is a slow grower, taking as many as ten years to come into full production. So that you won't delay bearing, prune the bush, especially a small one, sparingly

152

At 3 years, blueberries will need their first pruning. Cut out dead wood and short, weak branches.

Highbush blueberries are likely to grow twiggy with age. Cut off part of this thick end-growth and thin out branches to encourage better fruiting.

during its first years. Clip only to shape it or to remove injured or broken limbs.

Blueberries tend to grow in a bushy manner with lots of small twigs, and as the plant gets older, the twigs get thicker and bear less fruit. Should this happen, thin out the bush by cutting two or three of the older main stems right back to the ground. Then thin out about half of the end twigs from the remaining branches to stimulate the plant to bear more heavily.

As with many other fruits, blueberries grown in the South should be pruned more heavily than those suffering a short growing season and a cold winter. If your garden is in the more wintry regions, prune lightly each year, experimenting until you find what amount seems most beneficial to the plant. Fertilize the plants only when they're making poor growth. Both overfeeding and overpruning may induce winter injury and severely limit your crop.

In areas where the winters are mild, you can prune your bushes anytime from when the leaves come off in the fall to the time that growth starts in very early spring. Be careful never to prune frozen wood, because your cuts won't heal over easily, resulting in additional winter injury to the plant.

In colder sections of the country it's best to prune in very early spring so that you can cut away any wood that has been injured during the winter.

Cranberry, bog. You probably won't want to tackle the bog cranberry *(Vaccinium macrocarpon)* unless you happen to have a swamp in your backyard, because it is very fussy about climate, soil, and moisture. It needs an abundance of water and an acid soil, and it is so particular that there are only a few places in North America where it grows well. Usually you can cultivate it only where an abundance of water is readily available, since water protects the plants from spring and fall frosts, and controls insects and weeds. You must regulate the water carefully so that the fields can be flooded or drained whenever necessary. Ordinary watering isn't a satisfactory substitute. Commercial growers who have tried to grow cranberries under irrigation rather than in bogs have run into many problems.

Though the initial grading and planting are expensive, a well-managed cranberry bog can go on producing practically forever. Pruning is simple. When the plants get overgrown, mow or cut off the tops close to the ground. Then allow them to grow back, thereby creating a whole new plant. So if you can get a bog started, you are set for life, but most of us will have to be content with buying our cranberries in bags or cans at the supermarket.

Cranberry, highbush. I've noticed that new, improved strains of the native American cranberry are appearing in the seed catalogs, so this attractive and useful plant may soon be a part of more home fruit gardens. Although few people consider the quality of the fruit as good as that of its cousin, the bog cranberry, the berries do make superb jelly after a few hard frosts. They're beloved by the birds, as well.

The native highbush cranberry grows a bit large (12 to 15 feet) for small backyard plantings, but many of the new, improved kinds are smaller and more manageable. If you want cranberries for eating, plant the American *(Viburnum trilobum)* rather than the European cranberry *(V. Opulus).* Although the latter is readily available in nurseries as an ornamental plant, the berries are too bitter for the human palate — birds don't care for them either.

Highbush cranberries need very little pruning. Probably you'll just need to thin out some of the old wood once in several years, and you may want to top your bushes if they start growing too tall. Sometimes bushes get into the habit of bearing heavily every other year, producing only a few berries during the alternate years. If this happens to yours, you can return them to an annual bearing pattern if, during the heavy-producing years, you prune off about a third of the blossom clusters as soon as the buds appear. The subsequent reduction in fruit will usually conserve the production energy of the bush enough so that it will produce a good crop the following year.

Currants and gooseberries. Currants and gooseberries *(Ribes)* are cool-weather plants in every sense, grown strictly in the northern areas. Although new varieties are being developed for the South, these fine bush fruits grow

154

best where summers are cool and winters are cold. Even the large-fruiting hybrids are closely related to their wild cousins and, like them, will grow with little care. Badly neglected plants often continue to produce good crops for decades, even though the fruit is small.

For the best yields of the biggest fruit, begin to thin out your bush when it is about three years old. Stems that are older than that bear poorly and should be cut off at ground level or as close to the soil as possible. New, vigorous growth will quickly replace them. To produce well, a currant or gooseberry bush should have some wood that is one to three years old, but practically none that is any older.

If you have a neglected bush, you can give it a new lease on life by cutting it off at ground level and letting a new bush grow back. Doing all this in one year would be hard on even a vigorous plant, so spread the job over at least a couple of years. In very early spring, before any green shows, cut off about half of the old stems at ground level, leaving any young, lively ones. That year, you should see a lot of new growth. The next year, cut off the remaining old stems to the ground. These, too, will regrow, and you will have a completely new plant that you'll be proud to show the garden club and one that you can prune and care for in the usual manner.

You can force giant-size gooseberry varieties to grow even larger fruit by heavier pruning and by thinning out the berries as soon as they form. If you decide to thin them, do it when the berries are very small. Pick off the tiniest ones, and leave the remaining berries about an inch apart on the branch. Some varieties of gooseberries may grow as large as grapes and small plums, but this thinning process may not be an entirely pleasant task or worth the trouble, especially with the thorny varieties.

Currants are seldom thinned, since their berry size is not often greatly improved by picking off part of the clusters of blooms. Like gooseberries, they'll need only an occasional pruning out of old wood and a heavy annual feeding of manure to keep them producing large crops annually almost forever.

Elderberries. Both wild and garden elderberries *(Sorbus)* are a fine addition to anyone's backyard berry patch. They are such extremely vigorous growers that you should plant them where you can keep them safely under control by mowing around them regularly. I'd never plant them near my vegetable garden, flower bed, or other berries or plants.

Because they are so productive and robust, and since all the improved varieties have only recently emerged from the wild, they need very little pruning to keep them productive. Pinching off the top of the young plant during the first summer will encourage side branching and earlier bearing, and, unlike the other bush fruits, early bearing won't hurt an elderberry plant at all. Cut out any wood that was broken during the winter, and remove old, corky stalks that no longer produce well. Mow or prune off the sucker plants that continually try to grow outside the row. You can prune elderberries anytime, since they are such vigorous growers. It's a wonderful fruit and I'd hate to be without it.

155

The Bramble Fruits

Raspberry and blackberry plants, and their dozens of cousins — including the boysenberry, dewberry, and youngberry — are usually referred to as the brambles (*Rubus*). Unlike the bush fruits that are really small trees, the brambles are woody biennials. The *canes* are woody biennials, that is. The roots are perennial, and under the right conditions, brambles will live for decades, perhaps even for centuries. Each cane sprouts from the roots and will grow to its full height in a season. The following year it blooms, produces fruit, and then dies that same season. At the same time, other canes are growing that will produce their fruit the following year. And so the patch marches on.

Cutting out the old canes after fruiting is the most important part of bramble-fruit culture. A fellow Yankee neighbor of ours who was quite frugal once told me he "warn't goin' to cut nothing" out of his patch, because there was always a chance the dead canes might bear something another year. In about three years, he had a jungle of dead canes and almost no fruit — his patch had killed itself by overpopulation. All of us who enjoy wild-berry picking have seen this happen to a wild raspberry or blackberry patch — in a

156

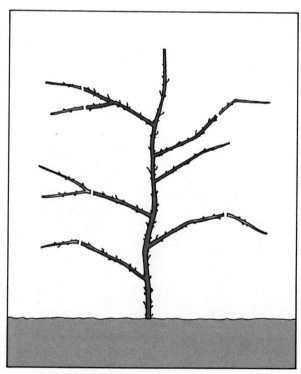

This blackberry plant is properly thinned, but should be cut back as shown next spring.

few years, there are no plants left. Nature has arranged it so that the brambles are an interim crop, holding their own only until the trees can get a foothold.

Pruning makes a difference, however. We started a small patch of raspberries in our backyard over 20 years ago, and it is producing even better crops today.

Pruning while planting. Cut back your new berry plants, unless they're potted, to about two inches above the ground after planting to give the roots time to get established before the top outdistances them.

Set the plants 24 to 36 inches apart in a straight row, and if you plant more than one row, keep the rows at least six feet apart. While this may seem like wasted space, the berry plants are such virile growers that they will soon make a wide row. Unless you leave adequate space, you'll have no room to walk between the rows. By spacing them correctly, you won't have to cut out a lot of thorny plants.

You'll still have to prune out the unwanted suckers that all red and yellow raspberries and upright-growing blackberries send up from their large root systems. Sometimes these even come up several feet away from the row. You can spread a heavy mulch to cut down on the spreading of the suckers and thereby avoid future pruning. Mowing or cultivating is frequently necessary to confine the plants to their row. Since they love to travel, don't plant the brambles anywhere near your vegetable garden or flower bed, or they will soon sneak into it.

Purple and black raspberries and trailing blackberries form new plants by a process known as tipping. In late summer their long canes bend over until the tips touch the soil; roots then grow at these tips, and a new plant is born. Don't allow these tips to spread outside the row. Keep them under constant control, just as with suckers.

When enough canes have tipped, and the row is well filled with plants, you can prevent any more plants from forming by cutting back the tall canes in late summer so that they can't bend over. The following spring, the shortened canes will branch heavily and set lots of fruit.

Pruning bearing plants. Cutting out the old canes as soon as they finish bearing each summer is an extremely important part of bramble-fruit culture. As I said before, this process contributes to your patch's health, longevity, and, most important, productivity. So be sure to do it every year.

You'll be able to identify the old canes by their appearance — they'll look dead, and they'll be branched, unlike the new canes. Any leaves hanging on them will be yellow and sick-looking.

Wearing heavy gloves, use hand clippers to snip out the brittle canes close to the ground. Then burn them, or get them out of the neighborhood as fast as possible. Never use the canes as a mulch or put them in the compost pile, because they rot slowly, and they may be harboring harmful insects or disease.

While you're clipping off the old canes, it is a good time to thin out the new ones, as well. First, cut out all the weak, small, short, or spindly canes. Then thin all the healthy, large ones so that the canes are about six inches apart. This thinning will allow better air circulation and will cut down on the

157

158

Black raspberry, before and after pruning.

chances of mildew, spur blight, and other diseases. It will also result in larger berries.

Finally, at some point before winter begins, cut the tops off all the remaining plants of the red and yellow raspberries and blackberries. (You've probably already cut back the black and purple raspberries so that they won't tip.) You can cut back the tall-growing brambles, such as Viking raspberries, two feet or more, but short-growing varieties, like the Newburgh raspberries, need to have only a few inches snipped off. By snipping off any flimsy top that has a few old leaves still attached, you leave only the stiff canes that will produce the fruit the following summer. Also, by being cut back, the canes should manage to stand winter winds and snows without breaking. The stiff stems will be better able to hold up the following year's fruit without flopping to the ground.

Even with their tops cut back, raspberries and upright blackberries may still need a strand of wire supported by posts to hold them up. Always grow trailing blackberries (dewberries) on a fence to keep them off the ground during the summer.

Check the patch often throughout the summer to see that disease and insects haven't launched an assault. Spur blight, a condition that causes the whole cane to wilt and die, is one common disease. Prune out and cart away all the dying canes as soon as you notice them.

Another pest is the cane borer. In early summer you may notice that some of the top leaves on the new canes have wilted and that the tops are drooping over. This means that the cane borer has laid an egg right between the two circles around the cane. Cut off the top of the cane just below the lower circle, and burn it, egg and all. If you don't, the resulting grub will live up to its name by boring down the cane and wrecking it. Then, down near the roots, the grub will develop into a clear-winged moth that will fly about your berry patch some night spreading more eggs and mischief.

Pruning everbearing raspberries. Several varieties of red and yellow raspberry plants are now being sold in catalogs as "everbearers." They do not produce constantly throughout the summer, as the name implies, but they do bear a crop in midsummer on the year-old canes as do most raspberries, and

159

This raspberry should be pruned back to those branches shown here as darkly shaded.

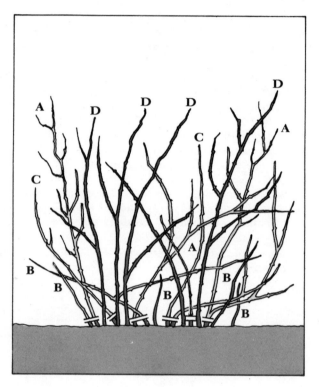

Pruning raspberries and upright blackberries. Old, dying canes (A) that produced fruit this year should be removed by cutting to the ground. Small, weak canes (B) should be cut out at the ground level to divert the plant's energy into the main stems. Thin plants coming up between the rows (C). Thin strong canes (D) so that they are at least 5 or 6 inches apart. Those remaining should be cut back a few inches to produce strong, husky canes that can support a heavy crop.

160

another, usually smaller crop, in the fall on the new canes that have just finished growing.

If you have only one kind of raspberry and it is an everbearer, you can treat it just as you do the regular bearers. Cut out the old canes just after they finish bearing their summer crop, and then harvest a fall crop off the new canes, leaving them to produce again the following summer.

However, many gardeners who have both the regular-bearing and the everbearing varieties prefer to skip the summer crop on the latter to harvest a bigger fall crop. They do this by treating the raspberry canes as annuals, cutting them to the ground right after they harvest the fall crop. Since there are never any one-year-old canes, there is never any summer crop the following year. The fall harvest is not only larger, but earlier as well, since all the plant's energy is going into it. There's only one thing as tasty as a fresh raspberry in season, and that's a fresh raspberry *out* of season.

Strawberries

When your strawberry *(Fragaria)* plants arrive, you'll notice that they have long, stringy roots. The directions you receive will tell you, no doubt, to snip off an inch or two of these root tips. Be sure to do this, even if cutting off valuable roots doesn't make much sense to you — pruning will make it easier for you to spread the roots when setting out your plants, and even more important, you will stimulate them to grow lots of new little roots. The resulting lush plants will be able to bear heavy crops the following year.

Since husky plant growth is what you want most the first season, pick off all the blossoms that try to form during the first month after planting. Bearing fruit so soon after it is set out will weaken the plant, and it will diminish the following year's crop.

If you are growing everbearing strawberries, you can allow them to bear a light crop in late summer of this first year. However, you should pick off the spring blooms the first year.

Strawberries are grown by two main methods: the hill system and the matted-row or runner system. One makes use of runners, and one does not.

Strawberry plants reproduce by forming new plants from runners. These small, vinelike sprouts come from the main plant, form a whole new plant, and, if unchecked, go on to form another and another. If set early and growing well, the plants will grow runners and new plants early enough in the season so that these new plants will bear the following summer.

In the hill system, you set your strawberry plants 12 to 18 inches apart, pruning off all of the runners. Since none of the plant's strength goes into producing new plants, a good number of extra-large berries is produced, and the plant will live and produce for several years, getting larger and huskier each year. By pruning off the runners, and by doing the necessary mulching or cultivating, the plants will last for several years longer than strawberry plants with runners, and you'll avoid having to buy new plants and preparing new soil.

The more common matted-row method involves allowing each plant to form two or more runners in each direction along the row. These runners form small plants until, by midsummer, the row is filled with well-spaced plants. As soon as the row is full, you prune off all extra runners and the plants that they are forming. It is time-consuming, but it's worth the trouble and nets you a large crop of berries.

Though the matted-row method is usually more productive and better suited to commercial growing than the hill method, you do have to start new plants each year, since usually the bed bears really well only one time — the year after planting. You can sometimes extend the life of your home bed a year or more if you prune off all runners from the matted-row plants the second season so that the beds do not become overgrown. In addition, you have to be especially careful to control weeds and grass growth in a matted-row patch.

A third and less-used method is a compromise between the hill and the matted-row methods. Set the plants two feet apart in the row, and allow them to set four runners — two headed in each direction along the row. Allow each runner to make only one plant. Keep cutting off all other plants and runners. Some growers feel that this method combines the best of both the hill and the matted-row system, and it does require fewer initial plants than the hill method.

161

Chapter 12

Pruning Nut Trees

Many thousands of years ago, before men became hunters and herdsmen, nuts were one of the main sources of protein. They had the added advantage of being able to keep fresh for years in their water-tight shells. Even after they were not needed as an essential staple in the diet, nuts were prized as a dessert.

Most older people in our area remember foraging with their families in the back country each fall, bringing back bags of nuts for winter treats. Now, with the interest in natural foods and vegetarianism, nuts are once again becoming a protein staple in the diet of some people. Each fall, more people are racing the squirrels to the nut trees, and trying to find ways to keep their attics and garages squirrel-proof so that they can store their valued caches of nuts safely.

Since the great wild nut forests of early America have been cut for their beautiful lumber, destroyed to make way for civilization, or killed by disease, you'll probably have to grow your own. Most nut trees grow far too large for a small backyard, but some of them make satisfactory shade trees and are often planted along country roads. The demand for homegrown nuts has spurred a search for better strains, and nut growers are now developing new varieties of bigger, better-flavored, and easier-to-crack nuts.

Naturally, those nuts that have been grown commercially for centuries, like the walnut, filbert, pecan, and almond, have the most named varieties. Most of these were the result of careful scientific crossbreeding of outstanding trees rather than accidents of nature.

The wild native trees, on the other hand, have been rather neglected, and only in recent years has there been a serious attempt to find superior trees. Growers are crossing these trees with related European and Asiatic

This young nut tree has good branch structure, but competing brush at the base should be clipped off.

varieties. As a result, we are beginning to see improved black walnut, butternut, hickory, and chestnut trees. Beech trees have been developed that produce larger nuts, and oak trees that yield edible acorns. This research has also resulted in trees that are more disease-resistant and some that are well suited for growing in areas where nuts could not be grown previously.

Though some grafted, named varieties are available, many of the nut trees sold by nurseries are seedling trees. One of the easiest ways for you to get a nut tree is to plant the seed (nut) where you want a tree to grow, and thus avoid the transplanting and early pruning. You can grow nut trees easily this way. In fact, the great American nut forests were probably planted by squirrels who buried the nuts and forgot to dig them up.

Although seedling trees may grow as fast, or faster, than grafted trees, they take a long time to bear — usually from 6 to 12 years. If grafted trees are available and are hardy where you live, they are probably a much better choice. Not only are the nuts larger and easier to crack, but the trees usually bear earlier and more regularly and produce heavier crops than trees grown from seed.

A distinctive feature of most nut trees is a central taproot that goes straight down. This makes it tricky to dig up and transplant a tree, because the taproot should not be broken or cut off at digging time, nor should it be bent over when planted. Moving nut trees that are over six feet tall is risky, whether from a nursery or from the wild.

Pruning at Planting Time

If you buy a nut tree, it will probably be bare-rooted and wrapped in some packing material. Follow the directions for planting, and don't neglect the pruning. You have a choice of several pruning methods, all of which are designed to accomplish the same thing — keeping the top of the tree from growing faster than the roots' ability to supply it with the necessary nutrients.

If your tree is lightly branched, cut back all the branches to the main stem, leaving the top intact, and plant the tree as a whip. If you prefer, you can cut back all the branches to the first bud from the end, and cut the top back to the second bud from the top, following the directions in Chapter 4.

If your tree has no branches, you should prune it when planting by cutting off about a third of the total length of the tree. Cut on a slant to just above the bud, as usual.

Many nut growers prefer not to prune a small tree at all at planting time. Instead, they pinch off any new sprouts as they form on the side branches. They want to retain all the leaves possible to help feed the young tree, yet they don't want any new growth to start that will demand energy that the roots cannot yet supply. Although effective, this method is more time-demanding than pruning off part of the tree, since you must pinch frequently during the first few weeks of the growth.

Early Training

Nut trees growing in a forest tend to grow straight and tall, while their lower limbs gradually die as the trees reach higher for the sun. On the other hand, many varieties of large nut trees living in the open spread out, and their limbs grow huge and in weird shapes. Sometimes the limbs grow straight up, forming a second top, or they may grow straight out.

If your young nut tree is a large-growing variety, try to train it to grow to a strong central leader. (See page 114.) Sooner or later, you will have to give up and allow the tree to grow crotchy and limby just as it wants to, but for as long as you can, keep the limbs from reaching out at angles that will weaken the tree. Long, heavy, horizontal limbs put a great strain on any tree and will probably split off eventually. Crotches that form in a 45-degree angle are always weak also, so prune to avoid them.

Prune smaller nut trees, such as the almond, much like fruit trees. (See Chapter 10.) The filbert is an exception, as easterners prune it into a large bush, while on the West Coast, they prune it as a small tree.

Nut trees that are grown in commercial orchards must be planted and pruned according to whatever cultural and harvesting methods are planned for them. Because some nuts are harvested with a gigantic mechanical vibrator that shakes the nuts off the trees, the trees must be the right size and shape for it to work well.

Pruning Mature Trees

Prune large-growing nut trees for the same reasons that you would prune a shade tree — to remove dead or injured limbs and to lighten the load on weak crotches. Although home growers don't usually prune to increase nut yields, commercial orchardists do prune their trees more intensively to boost production by cutting out old wood and thinning out the branches to allow in more light.

If you need to cut off heavy limbs for any reason, be sure to do it in stages, as shown in Chapter 4. Be sure to paint the scar left after any large cut, and clean and seal any cavities.

Almond

The almond *(Prunus dulcis)* is a member of the rose family, as are the plum, peach, and other stone-fruit trees, and it closely resembles them in its growth habits. It grows 20 to 25 feet high — about the same size as a standard apple tree. Also, like fruit trees, the almond is pollinated by bees rather than by wind, so you don't need to plant them as close together as other nut trees.

While the tree is still young, early pruning should consist of training the tree into a good modified leader system. (See page 115.) Avoid any unnecessary pruning as it will stimulate extra leaf growth and delay bearing.

Almond trees bear nuts on short, stubby spurs, so as the tree grows older, begin to thin out the bearing spurs by cutting them off flush to the tree. Open up the branch area to keep the interior of the tree from becoming too dense and dark, just as you would prune a fruit tree. Do all pruning when the tree is dormant.

Different varieties of almond trees grow in different shapes — some are low and bushy and others more upright. Your pruning should conform to the habit of growth of your tree. If you care for your tree properly, it should produce for 50 years or more.

Black Walnut and Butternut

Both of these members of the walnut family are valued for their nuts and lumber. They look so much alike when they are young that it's difficult to tell them apart. The butternut *(Juglans cinerea)* is hardier than the walnut *(J. nigra)* and grows well throughout the northern United States and southern Canada.

If you are growing the trees for nuts, space them 30 to 40 feet away from any other tree. Although it's not easy, try to get them to grow with a strong central leader for the first few years. The terminal bud is easily damaged by weather, and if this happens, two or three sprouts will grow. To prevent the tree from growing into a bush, keep pinching and snipping it into one main trunk for as long as possible. Do all pruning in early fall, after the nuts have dropped off.

Both butternut and black walnut trees have very strong wood, so the unusual crotches that insist on growing are less hazardous to the tree's health than they would be on many weaker trees.

If you are growing your trees for lumber, space them about 15 feet apart. It is especially important to grow them with a strong central leader so that you'll have a log or two that is straight and free from large limbs. As the trees grow taller, prune off a few of the lower branches each fall, always leaving at least twice as much branched area as you have limb-free trunk. Don't wait until the tree is full-grown to start cutting off the bottom limbs. The resulting wounds will never heal over, and the trunk will be permanently scarred.

Both butternuts and black walnuts are subject to Juglans dieback *(Melanconis juglandis)*, a disease that apparently came into the country with Oriental nut trees. Afflicted trees have a shortened life span and an unhealthy appearance. Most wild trees are now infected, and little can be done except to cut off any limbs that look sick. Vigorous, healthy trees seldom show these symptoms, so keep your trees in excellent condition. Make sure that they have an adequate supply of fertilizer, and give them plenty of water during dry seasons.

Chestnut

If you remember the classic Early American poem by Longfellow, you know that the chestnut *(Castanea)* is a naturally spreading tree: "Under the spreading chestnut tree/the village smithy stands." In the woods, however, they grow tall and straight, and produce beautiful lumber. Unfortunately, both forests and smithies lost most of their trees in the great chestnut blight that swept the country in the early 1900s. The few trees that survived the disaster have been propagated and crossed with imported, blight-resistant varieties, so now there is a variety of chestnut trees available from nurseries. None are entirely blight-proof, but many are quite resistant.

The wood is very brittle, so your early pruning should guide the tree to a strong central leader with a balanced branch formation. Early in the life of the tree, prevent bad crotches that will break easily later on. Prune when the tree is dormant.

The Japanese chestnut *(Castanea crenata)* grows usually as a small tree or large bush. Although some strains become good-size trees, most seldom grow much over 30 feet tall, in contrast to the large American chestnut. You can prune both the Japanese and the widely planted Chinese chestnut *(C. mollissima)* to grow low. The Chinese is probably the most blight-resistant of those that are commonly grown, and it also produces the best-flavored nuts. Because its wood is especially brittle, prune back long branches to prevent breakage.

Filbert

Filberts *(Corylus)* range from the small native American hazelnut to the improved and named varieties of the European filbert, the only member of the specie cultivated to any extent. Because the tree stays small, it suits the home garden better than most other nut trees.

The filbert is one of the few nut trees that has no deep-growing taproot, so it is much easier to transplant than most nut trees. Because it has a fibrous root system, you can also root-prune it, if necessary. (See page 31.)

As I mentioned before, filberts are usually grown as shrubs or large bushes, except in the West where they are pruned into a tree form with a single main stem. You can grow your own filbert tree from either seeds or layers — that is, by bending over a low branch and covering the middle section with soil so that it can root. Because filberts are easily propagated in this way, they are seldom grafted. If you do have a grafted tree, however, be especially careful to prune away all the little wild trees growing around the bottom of the main stem so that they won't crowd out the good part of the tree. You should prune most of the suckers growing from the roots of non-grafted trees too, to keep the tree from getting too bushy.

Usually, mature filberts need to be pruned mostly to keep them in shape and to let more light into the tree. Cut out some of the old branches while they are dormant, so that new ones will replace them. If you are growing your filbert in a clump, keep it pruned to only five or six main stems so that the bush won't become too wide and unmanageable.

Hickory

Although premium meats are often smoked with its bark, the hickory *(Carya)* is practically unknown in most of the country, and its nuts are seldom found in stores. However, the wood of the hickory has long been valued for its strength, and is widely used for tool handles, baseball bats, and skis.

There are several strains of this rugged tree, ranging from the practically inedible bitternut, which is hardy even in Ontario, to the pecan, grown mostly in the South and in California. The hickory family is native only to the central part of North America, and includes the shagbark, the water hickory, the mockernut, the pignut, and the shellbark, as well as the pecan and the bitter-nut. In addition, natural hybrids have originated and others have been developed by man. Some are chiefly ornamental, but others produce high-quality nuts and nuts that are easier to crack.

You should basal-prune your trees as they grow so that by the time they are 15 feet tall, none of the lower limbs will be closer than 6 to 8 feet to the ground. If you are growing your trees for lumber, you should, of course, prune higher as the tree continues to grow. Prune in early fall, after the nuts drop off.

Pruning the mature trees is not usually necessary or practical because of their height. They tend to grow upright, and have a naturally strong central leader. They also grow very tall, sometimes over 100 feet in height. To anchor a tree of this size, nature has equipped the hickory with a long taproot that develops early in life, so planting or moving even a small tree is not easy. When starting a new tree, unless you want to try one of the hybrids, you had better plant a nut where you want the tree to grow so that you won't have to move it.

Pecan

Pecans *(Carya illinoinensis)*, one of the best-known edible hickories, are grown mostly in the southern and southwestern areas of the United States. Although they are primarily a commercial nut, they are also grown extensively on farms and in backyard gardens.

Pecans have long, deep taproots, and they need the same care you'd give any of the hickories when you're digging and planting the small trees. Never cut or bend the taproot during the moving process.

Give the tree some snipping during the growing season for its first years so that it will grow with a strong central leader. Also, prune away a few bottom limbs each year during the dormant season, until it has six to eight feet of branch-free lower trunk. This is probably all the pruning a backyard tree will ever need.

Some of the newer varieties of pecans have growth habits different from the native kinds. Many of these are more suitable for the home gardener, since they are smaller and have a growth habit that is less upright.

Walnut

The Persian walnut *(Juglans regia)* is the true name of the English walnut. We call it the English walnut because it arrived in the colonies on English ships. Actually, the cool climate of the British Isles is not at all suitable for the culture of the Persian walnut, since it needs a very warm climate to grow well.

Since the introduction of the Carpathian strain of Persian walnut from Poland, walnut trees grow in home gardens all over the country, and they are no longer restricted to the West Coast. Careful breeding and seed selection are slowly extending the growing region even into the northern states and southern Canada.

Most walnuts in commercial groves, and even some of those growing in backyard gardens, are grafted, often onto black walnut seedlings. It's easy to see a difference in the bark below and above the graft on these trees, and you should prune any suckers growing from the base of the tree. Because its wood is rather brittle, you should stake a newly planted tree to prevent it from breaking off at the graft.

Some of the walnut hybrids bear such heavy crops of nuts that you should prune them to grow with a strong central leader for the first years. After that, you can allow them to develop into a tree with a modified leader system. Some varieties — Mayette, for instance — tend to be of such spreading growth that an open center method of pruning is best. (See page 116.) It may be necessary to shorten the limb growth on some varieties, since they bear so heavily that the branches sag, and eventually they develop a droopy habit of growth. When you buy a tree, ask about its growth and bearing habits, and prune accordingly.

It's important to basal-prune walnuts. Remove all branches to about six feet above the ground as soon as the tree is tall enough to permit this safely. Do all the pruning in early fall, after the nuts are harvested, since walnuts tend to bleed badly when pruned in the spring.

The bark of a young walnut tree sunburns so easily that you'd do well to whitewash the trunk of your newly planted tree, or to cover it with tree wrap for its first few years.

Mature walnuts need occasional pruning to let more light into the interior of the tree. Also, cut out some of the older, unproductive wood so that it will be replaced by new, young branches. Although the commercial growers who grow walnuts in large orchards prune them so that they can harvest the nuts with a mechanical shaker, most home owners shake the tree themselves, so the shape isn't as important.

Chapter 13

Pruning Vines and Ground Covers

Every gardener's idea of heaven is a place filled with heavily laden fruit trees, gardens brimming with exquisite flowers, and, in the midst of it all, a vine-covered cottage.

There is nothing wrong with daydreams. We must have high ideals if we are to be good gardeners. The danger lies in believing that such perfection will come about without careful planning and some hard work.

We have to accept the fact that vines will not quickly grow to just the right height, then stop growing and look nice ever after. And, in spite of our dreams, we must live with the knowledge that no ground cover exists that will spread over our lawn within a few weeks, stay just the right height, and stop growing right at the edge of flower beds, vegetable gardens, and the neighbor's putting green — unless we install artificial football turf.

Both vines and ground covers are useful additions to home landscaping, however, and you can keep most of them looking good and under control with very little care. Because the care and pruning of both are similar, I'm including them in the same chapter. Occasionally one plant can be used for both purposes. Many vines, such as the ivies, woodbine, and honeysuckle, make useful ground covers.

Some small, woody bushes, such as the creeping junipers, or herbacious plants like thyme, make good ground covers. They spread by various methods. A number have vigorous root systems that sprout new plants as they spread — goutweed, for example. Myrtle sends out running vines that root and form new plants, while others, like tickseed and crown vetch, scatter seeds that grow easily.

The term "vines" encompasses many different types of plants with trailing growth habits. These may be annuals grown from seed each year, such as sweet peas and morning glory, or perennials like wisteria and bittersweet. A few vines have roots that are perennial and tops that are annual; many tender vines, such as kudzu, grow this way in the North but are entirely perennial in the South.

Some vines have huge leaves like the Dutchman's-pipe, and others have very small ones. Some, such as the grape, may develop large trunks when very old, but others, like the ivy, have small, wiry stems and can trail over acres of brick walls. Vines come in such a wide variety that there is at least one suitable for every need in nearly every climate.

Pruning at Planting Time

Potted plants need no pruning when you plant them, but if you have a bare-rooted, woody vine — that is, a vine with a hard, woody stem — you should cut the top back about half, to a bud, before planting. This pruning will prevent the top growth from beginning until new roots can supply enough energy to support that growth. As with all plants, when you allow the roots to get well established before the top starts growing, the plant will become a much more vigorous specimen. Carefully follow all the other proper planting procedures regarding location, watering, fertilizer, and soil, as well.

171

Renewing an old vine by cutting it down to a stump, leaving several 1-year-old spurs.

Early Training

To get your vine off to a good start, you should know how it grows and especially how it climbs. Some so-called vines, like the climbing and rambler roses (Chapter 5), produce long canes that usually have to be tied or interlaced with a trellis for support. A true vine, however, has a natural climbing habit, with its own way of holding onto whatever it shinnies up — fence, arbor, or brick wall.

Many vines, such as honeysuckle or morning glory, will twine around a post or wire, winding their way upward.

A few vines are clinging, and they hold on in several different ways. Some attach themselves by springlike tendrils. Both grapes and clematis grow in this fashion. However, vines with tendrils need something to wrap around, and are not too adept at climbing up stone and brick walls. The ivy family is better at that. The Boston ivy hangs on with small sucker discs that become attached firmly to hard surfaces. The climbing hydrangea and English ivy can also cling to smooth surfaces, but instead of the sucker discs, they use many small rootlets to grip onto walls.

Ivies and similar vines grow well with little training, support, or other care, on brick and stone structures in climates where they are perennial. Their method of growth, however, is not suitable on wooden buildings, because the vines hold moisture and are likely to rot the wood. Ivies also make painting difficult.

Some early pinching and snipping will add considerably to the general appearance of most vines. Form a mental image of the way you want them to look in their prime, and prune them accordingly. Although not a true vine, climbing roses will look better if you allow a few tall, narrow branches to climb to the top of a trellis, where they can grow thickly and bloom heavily. To encourage this kind of growth, cut off most of the weak vines near the ground so that the plant's strength goes into the few remaining ones.

Morning glory and clematis, on the other hand, look their best if they grow thickly and bloom heavily all the way up the trellis. Thus, when the new vine is about a foot tall, pinch the top buds off the few long vines to encourage side branching. A week or two later you should again pinch the terminal buds of the new side shoots. Continue this practice until the vines have filled your trellis.

In addition to understanding your vine's climbing habit, you'll also want to know its blossoming habit, since it will make a difference in how you prune. Most flowering vines bloom on wood that grew the previous year, though a few, like some kinds of clematis, can bloom on wood that grew the same year.

When you're pruning vines that bloom on year-old wood, you must be careful not to cut back the vine too severely. Thin out the old wood when necessary, but avoid any heavy cutback of last year's growth, if possible.

Pruning the Mature Vine

After the vine has reached the height and width you want, most of your pruning will consist of snipping back any growth that goes beyond those limits. Occasionally, you may have to thin out some deadwood to keep the vine from choking itself. Also, prune out any part of the vine that has been hurt by winter damage or eaten by insects, or that shows signs of disease.

Although you can do light pruning during the growing season, do any severe pruning only when the vine is dormant. Even vines that make the rankest growth and can withstand the hardest cutback should be pruned only when the vine is not growing.

Cutting out the deadwood from an overgrown, twining vine is a major job. Fortunately, most species of vines are extremely resilient, and you can safely cut them back to the ground. The best time to do this is in very early spring while the vine is still dormant so that regrowth can start soon after. Leave a few young stalks, if there are any, growing near the main stem.

When the vine begins to send up new shoots, clip most of them off, leaving only three or four of the most vigorous. These will grow rapidly, and you will soon have a full-size, healthy new vine.

It may become necessary to cut back a vine to the ground before you begin a remodeling or painting job. If so, plan your project for early spring or late fall, when the pruning will be least harmful to the plant.

If you must do the job in midsummer, keep the cutting to the barest possible minimum to prevent a lot of late summer regrowth. Unless the vine is very stiff and brittle, cut off just enough to loosen it from its support, and lay it down carefully on the ground. Protect it from being trampled while the work is going on, and don't allow any materials to be piled on top of it. Return it to its upright position as soon as the job is finished, and tie it to its support until it anchors itself.

173

VINES AS BLINDS

Some people grow their vines especially to cover a rainspout, television mast, or some other unsightly object. Twining vines, such as bittersweet and fleece vine, are ideal for this because they are vigorous growers. If you plant vines to hide a specific object, remember to prune them to keep them within bounds. A well-groomed, vine-covered cottage may be a delight, but vines climbing telephone poles or shade trees and drooping over windows are not especially attractive.

VINES FOR HEDGES

In areas where a hedge would take too much valuable space, vines make a good substitute. Build a woven-wire fence with well-spaced and well-braced posts, and plant tight-growing vines all along it. In a few years, you'll have an effective barrier. Just shear them occasionally to keep them confined to the fence.

VINES FOR FOOD AND DRINK

Vines that produce food are being planted more and more to replace the purely ornamental vines. Grapes are an obvious choice, but you can also plant dewberries, climbing strawberries, climbing garden cucumbers, pole and flowering beans, and hops.

You must prune more precisely when your vines are growing food. Most food plants need a lot of sun, so never allow the vines to become thick and overgrown. Because grapes and berries produce best only on year-old wood, you should cut away all wood older than that every year if fruit is your primary interest. (See Chapter 11.)

The Twining Vines

174

The twining vines can wind their way up wires, trellises, or waterspouts. They are not good for planting on walls or brick buildings, but they make ideal screens on porches and fences.

Some vines twine from left to right, that is, counterclockwise as you look down at them. Bittersweet and Kentucky wisteria grow in this manner. Others, such as honeysuckle and Japanese wisteria, twine from right to left (clockwise). Here are some of the common twining vines.

Actinidia. The bower *(A. arguta)* is hardier and more widely planted than the Chinese variety *(A. chinensis)*, but it's less attractive. Do your heavy pruning in early spring, but leave some old wood on the plant, as it flowers on wood that is at least a year old. Thin it out and cut it back during the summer for best appearance.

Akebia quinata (Fiber-leaf akebia). This vine is of Oriental origin, and it is a nice vine when planted where there is room for it to grow. You can easily control it by cutting it back regularly during the winter. Every ten or twelve years, cut it to the ground in early spring and it will renew itself.

Aristolochia durior (Dutchman's-pipe). This popular vine grows slowly when first planted. Its large, heavy leaves are too coarse for some locations, but are ideal in others. Prune to keep it under control and to remove any dangling vines. Cut off any old wood and signs of winter injury.

Celastrus (bittersweet). Although only the female plants produce berries, you'll need both male and female plants in each planting for pollination. Besides keeping suckers cut off, pruning is necessary only to keep it under control. Prune while it's dormant.

Humulus Lupulus (hops). The male and female flowers grow on separate plants. This is a long-lived perennial, and you can easily grow it from seed or cuttings. Hops can be a rank grower and may need pruning back.

Kadsura japonica. This evergreen is suitable only for the warmer parts of the country. It produces red berries and has a nice reddish fall color. You need to invest only ordinary training and pruning to control it.

Lonicera (**honeysuckle**). The honeysuckle vine is ideal in the right location. It covers old fences, stumps, and eyesores quickly, but it can become weedy if left unchecked. Prune heavily during the summer to keep it from growing wild. Thin out the vine and remove suckers after blooming.

Polygonum Aubertii (**silver lace vine**). This is one of the fastest growing vines and will cover a large trellis in a single season. It blooms in late summer, but the thick foliage is lovelier than the flowers. Prune, if necessary, while it is dormant.

Pueraria lobata (**kudzu vine**). This southern vine is another fast grower, one that often becomes a vicious weed. Although usually recommended for the warmer parts of the country, it may be safer to grow it in the central states where it dies to the ground each winter. You must prune it ruthlessly to keep it under control.

Schisandra propinqua (**magnolia vine**). Here's another vine with separate sexes on different plants, so if you want red berries, you must plant both male and female plants. Prune it only lightly.

Trachelospermum jasminoides (**star jasmine**). Another southern evergreen vine, this one has fragrant white flowers, and the new growth is an attractive bronze. It seldom needs pruning.

Wisteria. This is a well-known, attractive, and useful vine, and there are so many varieties that one can be found for nearly every purpose. Some varieties are delightfully fragrant. The Japanese wisteria (*floribunda*) is hardy enough to grow in central New York State. Prune it heavily in early spring and, if necessary, in summer. Do not allow suckers to grow from the root because many varieties of wisteria are grafted and suckers will crowd out the good plant. You can renew varieties that are not grafted by cutting them back nearly to the ground.

Wisteria vines can grow as an attractive large bush if you cut and pinch back all the vinelike tendrils as they grow. These plants usually need staking, at least for the first ten years.

175

The Clinging Vines

Clinging vines come in several types. Some grow with small tendrils that grab and cling on wires, trellises, or other plants — for example, the bignonia, clematis, passiflora, and vitex (grapes). Others such as campsis, hedera (English ivy), climbing hydrangea, and parthenocissus (Boston ivy), have small sucker discs or rootlets, known as holdfasts, that clamp onto brick, stone, or concrete.

Some clinging vines have vigorous tendrils and can support great weights. Others need to have some extra growth pruned off from time to time, or the weight of the vine will become too much for the tendrils to hold. You should always snip away large masses of dangling green, in any case, for appearance' sake.

Bignonia (**cross vine**). This is an evergreen that climbs by means of tendrils and is excellent for screening. Prune it in early spring to control it and to remove weak shoots.

Campsis (**trumpet creeper**). This woody vine uses holdfasts to cling to stone or brick. Prune to keep it from becoming too heavy, as this is a husky grower. Cut off fading flowers, and prune back dangling and trailing vines.

Clematis. The beautiful clematis is not as widely grown as it should be, possibly because it is fussy about soil, sun, and temperature. It's easy to grow, as long as it's planted in "sweet" soil (pH 7), and has a cool, deep mulch of lawn clippings or similar material over its roots. Also, plant the vine where the hot afternoon sun won't shine on the roots and lower part of the vine. Clematis seems to do best if planted on the east or northeast side of the house where it gets only morning sun.

Pruning is rarely necessary at planting time, since you usually plant a vine that is potted. As soon as it gets a foot or so tall, however, pinch off the top buds on the growing sprouts to encourage them to branch up into more vines and thus make a bushier plant.

In the North, clematis vines are often taken off the trellis, laid on the ground, and covered up for the winter. You'll have to do some pruning to get them off the trellis. Do this carefully so you can salvage as much of the vine as possible. In the spring, prune off any winter injury that may have occurred.

Besides pinching for bushiness or pruning in northern climates for winter damage, the vines are likely to need only an occasional thinning out of old unsightly and thick vines.

If you ever have to move a fragile clematis vine, pruning will make the job easier and the results more likely to be successful. In early spring, cut the

176

BLOOMING HABITS OF CLEMATIS

On Year-Old Wood	On Current Year's Growth
Belle of Woking	Comtesse de Bouchard
Duchess of Edinburgh	Crimson King
Enchantress	Duchess of Albany
Guiding Star	Elsa Spath
Miss Baleman	Ernest Markham
Nelly Moser	Fairy Queen
President	Gipsy Queen
	Lady Betty Balfour
	Lord Neville
	Mme. Andre'
	Ramona
	Ville de Lyon

vine to within a foot or two of the ground. Dig all around the plant roots, and move the entire root ball, soil and all, disturbing the roots as little as possible. On an older plant, the root ball may be nearly the size of a bushel basket, but it will be considerably smaller on younger plants. If you save most of the roots, and if the vine has been cut back, survival is practically assured.

The named varieties of hybrid clematis bloom in two different ways. As I mentioned, some bloom on wood grown the previous year, and some on wood grown the same year. If you live in the North, choose a kind that blooms on the current season's growth, because even if it is covered, a hard winter may kill the vine to the ground. If you plant the right variety, however, a whole new vine will grow each spring from the roots and will bloom lavishly the same season.

Distictis buccinatoria (**blood trumpet**). This warm-weather vine can bloom year-round in its native Mexico. A fast grower with excellent screening qualities, it clings tightly by disc tendrils. Prune it like an ivy.

Euonymus Fortunei. Many named varieties are available that are suitable for either vines or ground covers. It clings by tiny roots to rocks and even tree trunks, rooting easily wherever the vine touches the ground. Prune to keep it within bounds during spring and early summer.

Hedera (**ivy**). Ivies are the old standbys for covering brick and stone buildings, and they are sometimes used for covering the concrete foundations of wooden buildings too. The different varieties vary widely in hardiness, appearance, and fruiting habits. All make good ground covers as well as climbing vines. Prune mostly to control it. Cut off dangling or torn pieces, as well as those vines that are creeping over doors and windows. Ivies are so vigorous that they seem to be able to stand pruning in almost any amount at any time of the year.

Hydrangea anomala (**climbing hydrangea**). This will grow on a brick building, clinging with small holdfasts. It is one of the best clinging vines, and looks good even in the winter. Prune in early spring to keep it under control and to remove loose, hanging parts.

Macfadyena (**cat's claw creeper**). Pruning is necessary to keep this attractive vine from growing too fast and becoming thin at the base. Pruning will encourage a bushy growth habit, and should be done just after it has finished blooming.

Parthenocissus tricuspidata (**Boston ivy**), *P. quinque folia* (**Virginia creeper**). The Boston ivy is hardier than the English ivy and is famous for covering the brick buildings of the eastern Ivy League colleges. The Virginia creeper, or woodbine, is not as clinging, but is hardy in the far North. As a vigorous-growing vine or ground cover, it is useful for covering ugly banks, old dumps, and unsightly rock piles, and can even shinny up the trunks of large trees. Prune it anytime.

Vitis (**grape**). The wild grapes and the many named varieties of garden grapes are so well known that no description is necessary. If you are growing them to cover fences, bowers, or trellises, you'll need to prune them only to keep them under control. If you're growing them for fruit, follow the directions in Chapter 11.

177

Annual Vines

Annual vines, those that you can grow from seed to their full height in one season, have certain advantages: they are out of the way during the winter, they give you quick results, and many are especially attractive with colorful blooms or fruit. They usually need little or no pruning, although a little pinching of the terminal buds helps keep them thick, and most need a bit of training to start them growing up their supports.

Wherever the growing season is short, you can give them a head start by planting the seeds inside in February or March. Set them outside only after danger of frost is over. This procedure will make early blooming possible for morning glories, sweet peas, and others. Some, such as the wild cucumber, usually self-seed so that the plants grow back each year without replanting. Various climbing beans can be used as annual vines, such as scarlet runner beans that produce edible seed, and Kentucky wonder beans that can be eaten green or dried.

Most annual vines are the twining type. A few, like gourds, produce colorful fruit. These are some of the most common.

Cardiospermum (balloon vine)
Cobaea (cup-and-saucer vine)
Echinocystis (wild or mock cucumber)
Gourds
Humulus japonicus (Japanese hop)
Ipomoea (morning glory)
Lathyrus (sweet pea)
Momordica (balsam apple)
Phaseolus (scarlet runner bean)
Tropaeolum (nasturtium)

Pruning Ground Covers

Ground covers usually need very little care, which is one of the main reasons we plant them — to avoid mowing steep or unsightly places. Occasionally, though, it's necessary to remove competing weed and brush growth or to cut out dead or damaged plants, so they are not entirely care-free.

Those plants that grow along paths, terraces, steps, and borders may need frequent shearing to keep them within bounds. You can often accomplish this by pinching, on a small scale, or with grass shears, an edger, lawn mower, or pruning shears. Do it anytime it seems necessary. If you make wise use of metal or plastic edgings, bricks, or stones at planting time, you can often save a great deal of pruning.

You should chop back large masses of woody ground covers such as bittersweet and Virginia creeper when they get badly overgrown. When you remove the old wood, the vine will renew itself in short order.

Some ground covers are rock garden plants grown for their beauty, and are not at all competitive against weeds. Others are planted mainly because they are rank growers, competing well against weeds, and will quickly and thickly cover an area.

Here are some of the most frequently planted ground covers.

Aegopodium (goutweed, bishop's weed). These are good ground covers for difficult places, but can become vicious weeds if planted where they can escape into lawns, flower beds, or gardens.

Ajuga (bugleweed). This is a good ground cover for sunny places, and can stand light traffic. Some varieties have colored foliage.

Akebia quinata (five-leaf akebia). Akebia is a rank-growing vine that needs tight control if it is to remain attractive and not smother shrubs and even trees.

Arctostaphylos Uva-ursi (bearberry). This evergreen vine turns bronze in the fall. It grows well in full sun in poor soil and is a well-behaved ground cover.

Armeria (thrift). Thrift grows up to a tall 8 or 12 inches. There are several varieties worth considering.

Asarum (wild ginger). Both the native and the European varieties make good ground covers in shade, but the attractive European is better, growing dense with no care.

Calluna vulgaris (Scotch heather). Heather provides color on terraces or rockeries. Prune it to remove deadwood and flowers, and to keep it in groups for an attractive bed.

Cerastium tomentosum (snow-in-summer). This plant has gray foliage and white flowers. It's good for small areas as it's not too competitive. Plant it in rock gardens, on terraces, or as an edging for paths.

Convallaria majalis (lily-of-the-valley). This does best in shady places with somewhat acid soil. Its flowers are fragrant. The plant is quite competitive with grass and weeds.

Coreopsis (tickseed). In some areas this is a good ground cover that you can grow from seed. Plant it in full sunlight. Its bright yellow flowers bloom in early summer.

Coronilla varia (crown vetch). Plant this vigorous vine on large banks, away from lawns and gardens. It spreads rapidly.

Cotoneaster. These are woody plants of various heights. Many varieties have colorful blossoms and fruit. The creeping kinds grow well on banks, but all may need hand weeding. Prune off deadwood, broken branches, and winter-injured limbs when necessary.

Dicentra eximia (wild bleeding-heart). Creeping roots spread this everblooming perennial. It is good for rockeries and borders, but it doesn't compete well with weeds. Cut it back to keep it in control.

Epimedium grandiflorum. This is an excellent low-maintenance ground cover for shady spots. It's very competitive and thick-growing.

Erica carnea (spring heath). You'll find several varieties of these colorful, heatherlike plants. Provide sun, a sheltered spot if in the North, and well-drained acid soil that is not too rich. It's an ideal vine for rockeries, but some need heavy pruning of winter injury.

179

Euonymus Fortunei 'Colorata' (**purple winter creeper**). Euonymus vines are good either as upright vines or ground covers. Colorata is especially good as a ground cover and has a good fall color, too. Prune to keep it within bounds.

Euphorbia Cyparissias (**cypress euphorbia**). This fast-growing ground cover needs pruning to keep it under control. It may become a weed unless you restrain it.

Fragaria (**strawberry**). Strawberries are good rockery plants and can be an effective ground cover where weed and grass competition is not too great.

Galium mollugo (**white bedstraw**). At a height of one to three feet, it's a bit tall for a ground cover, but creates a tight mat. It's easy to grow in sun or light shade.

Hedera helix 'Baltica' (**English ivy**). The ivies are good ground covers wherever they are hardy. They grow fast once they are well established. Prune off parts that are growing too high and irregular.

Hosta (**plantain lily**). This large-leafed perennial is suitable for massive plantings in shady areas. It's very competitive, but spreads slowly.

Hydrangea anomala subsp. *petiolaris* (**climbing hydrangea**). A magnificent vine, this hydrangea can also be used as a ground cover. When well established, the heavy leaves shade out weed competition. Prune it when necessary for appearance and control.

180

Hypericum calycinum (**Aaron's beard, creeping St.-John's-wort**). This perennial with colorful yellow flowers grows well in rockeries, where weed growth is not too threatening.

Juniperus (**juniper**). The juniper is a woody evergreen plant of many low-growing varieties suitable for ground covers. The cost of these plants limits their use, but some of the spreading low-growers layer their branches to form new plants and cover an area in time. Junipers are not very competitive with weed growth, so they need some care. You must clip out dead branches often, as they are susceptible to disease and winter injury.

Lonicera (**honeysuckle**). The honeysuckle vine is a fine ground cover, especially when large areas need to be covered at small expense. It's very competitive and needs to be pruned to keep under control.

Pachysandra terminalis (**Japanese pachysandra**). This is one of the best ground covers where it will grow well. It's attractive, grows rapidly, is well behaved, and you can keep under control by mowing around it.

Parthenocissus quinquefolia (**Virginia creeper**). Woodbine, as it is sometimes called, is a good ground cover for northern areas, covering unsightly banks, rocks, fences, even buildings in a short time. It needs pruning to keep it under control.

Pelargonium peltatum (**ivy geranium**). This is grown as a ground cover only in the warmest parts of the United States. It's colorful and is suitable for rock gardens, hillsides, and along paths.

Phlox subulata (**creeping phlox**). This plant is good on banks or in rock gardens where you can keep weeds and grass away from it. It comes in many colors.

Polygonum (**fleece flower**). Several varieties of this ground cover are available, but the Reynoutria fleece flower (*P. Reynoutria*) is one of the best.

Pueraria lobata (**kudzu vine**). One of the rankest and fastest growing vines, this is much too overpowering to use unless there is a sure way to control it. It has become a serious pest in many parts of the South.

Rosa Wichuraiana (**memorial rose**). This rose does well on steep banks. Its long stems root to start new plants easily. Prune it only if necessary.

Rosmarinus officinalis '**Prostratus**' (**dwarf rosemary**). This fragrant plant grows well only in the warmest parts of the country. It grows well on banks and in rock gardens where it can trail over stones.

Sedum spurium (**sedum**). Sedum is a good ground cover for poor soil. Check the variety carefully, because some are better than others for certain applications, and some can become very weedy.

Sempervivum tectorum (**hen-and-chickens**). This is a poor ground cover except in rockeries and other spots that you can weed by hand. It's a colorful plant, but you must keep the fading blooms cut off.

Thymus (**thyme**). This excellent rock garden plant works well between flagstones in terraces and garden paths. It's fragrant and can stand light traffic.

Vaccinium angustifolium (**lowbush blueberry**). Use this plant for dry banks with acid soil. It needs little care and will live for years. Cut out deadwood when necessary.

Veronica filiformis (**veronica**). Although this creeping weed is the scourge of lawns and golf courses, it's fine in its place. Beware of introducing it where it might later haunt you.

Vinca minor (**myrtle, common periwinkle**). This is a good ground cover for shady areas. Keep it away from flower beds, lawns, and gardens, because it is a difficult plant to control. It bears lovely blue flowers.

Viola (**violet**). This plant grows well on banks, especially under deciduous trees. It blooms heavily and spreads by seed. You can walk on it, and even mow it by setting your mower up high. It needs little care.

Chapter 14

Pruning Garden Plants and Houseplants

The competition among gardeners in my hometown was keen while I was growing up, and the residents along our one main street were anxious to have the best flower garden in town. As an apprentice to several of them, I

Pinching a chrysanthemum.

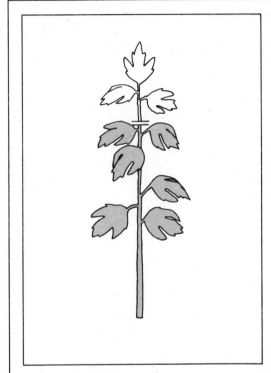

Pinching mums, early (left) and later (right) in development.

had a wonderful opportunity to see how they managed their grounds. After a time, it became easy for me to separate the real gardeners from the nongardeners.

The real gardeners not only planted carefully, fertilized religiously, and watered often, but they were always snipping away at something. The nongardeners usually found any kind of pruning difficult and, for the most part, didn't do any. Their flowers went to seed, and every few years their gardens became overgrown. Finally, when the rank-growing perennials had crowded out the more delicate ones, the garden had to be made over, a job I detested.

Although garden flowers don't need pruning in the same way that evergreens and fruit trees do, some of them benefit greatly by an occasional cutback.

There are six main reasons for pruning perennials:

Prune to encourage bushy plants. Certain plants, such as dahlias and chrysanthemums, will often grow one or two tall stems with only a few flowers on them unless you pinch them back several times. When chrysanthemums are about three inches tall, for example, you should pinch off the growing end of the stems. Continue to pinch them off several times during the early part of the growing season, so they will grow into a bushy, symmetrical plant that will bear a lot of blossoms. In milder climates, all pinching should be done before July 15. In northern areas with short growing seasons, however, move the deadline back to June 21, so the plants will bloom early in the fall. Of course this isn't done if you're trying to grow a tall plant with only a few giant-size flowers.

You can also pinch back tall-growing plants such as delphiniums and hollyhocks. The result is a different-looking, branched-out plant that is less likely to need staking in high wind, although you may find it less attractive than one allowed to grow to its full height.

Prune to increase the size of blooms. By disbudding, cutting off, or pinching off most of the small, weak buds on certain plants, you can grow the remaining blooms with longer stems, and they'll be larger, too. You can force

184

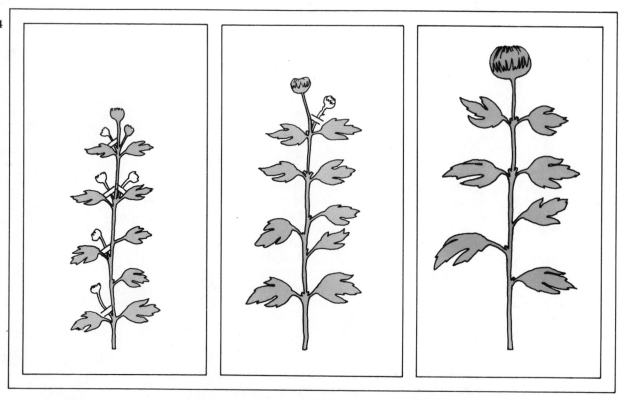

In disbudding mums, take off all but 2 buds (left). Later, remove the smaller of the 2 buds (center) to produce the plant on the right.

peonies, roses, chrysanthemums, asters, zinnias, and dahlias to produce giant-size blooms in this manner.

Prune to remove old blooms. Although it seems like an obvious thing for a neat housekeeper or gardener to do, not everybody is careful about picking off the faded blossoms. Biennials and annuals, as well as perennials, benefit from having the old blooms removed from the plant as soon as they fade. This pruning greatly improves appearance and encourages more blooming. Faded flowers that are not removed will go to seed quickly, and when plants go to seed, they often stop blooming.

Frequent picking will keep pansies, petunias, asters, marigolds, fuchsias, and many other flowers in bloom until frost. Delphiniums will often bloom a second time the same summer if you cut them back immediately after blooming, and they are likely to live much longer, as well.

Of course there are always exceptions. Some biennials and short-lived perennials keep on going year after year in the garden only by reseeding themselves. Allow Canterbury bells, foxglove, and sweet William to let a few of their best blooms go to seed so they will continue to grow in your garden, unless you set new plants each year.

Prune to prevent the plant from reverting. Some produce seeds that grow into plants that closely resemble their wild ancestors. A large percentage of phlox seedlings, for instance, are likely to be the wild magenta color, so your planting will quickly deteriorate if you allow the young, vigorous, poorly colored seedlings to crowd out the colorful, attractive, named varieties. If you prune back the flower heads immediately after they have faded, you will prevent this from happening to your phlox, lupines, and others.

Prune to get plants ready for winter. You may have noticed that the well-kept gardens in your neighborhood are always "put to bed" for the winter. For the sake of neatness and to aid in disease control, remove your annuals and cut back your perennials to a height of two or three inches after a hard autumn frost. Make sure you don't cut the tops off until they have begun to lose their green color. Food produced in the tops must move back into the roots before the leaves are removed, or the plants will be considerably weakened. You can recycle the tops in the compost pile. Finally, fertilize your flower beds with manure or compost, and mulch them for the winter.

Prune to keep the plants growing in attractive clumps. Plants sometimes need to be disciplined, and you must prevent the ranker varieties from crowding the others out. Sometimes you can control this by simply pulling up the encroaching new sprouts. Other times, however, you'll have to divide perennial clumps to keep them in their place. Divide them in early spring, soon after they've come up, so that the plants won't wilt. Often you can find a new home for the plants you've divided, so your friends will benefit, as well as your garden.

The Perennial Food Garden

Gardeners are sometimes puzzled about how to handle an asparagus bed and other kinds of food plants that die down each fall and come back the next year.

185

When you harvest asparagus in the spring, cut it with a sharp knife just under ground level, to keep the plants producing throughout the season. Even after you stop cutting asparagus for food, you can snip small amounts from the top of your fernlike asparagus plants for an occasional bouquet filler. Don't overdo it, because the plant needs considerable greenery to supply nourishment for the roots.

In the fall, cut the stalks down to the ground with clippers as soon as they turn yellow. Take the tops to the compost pile, or use them as a mulch on your berries or fruit trees. If you don't cut the tops off, the little red asparagus berries will mature and scatter seed all over, starting new plants that will soon crowd the established ones into unproductivity.

Rhubarb, the perennial spring tonic, doesn't need any special care. We occasionally meet people who try to harvest it by cutting off the stalks, a practice that isn't good for the plant. Twist each stalk and pull it up gently from the root so that you don't leave a stub. Healthy rhubarb plants should be divided every seven or eight years to keep them from getting too ingrown. Take a sharp spade and slice off parts of the huge root of the plant, and either transplant them or give them away. Pull off any dead leaves that still show in late summer.

186

Jerusalem artichokes and horseradish should have their roots harvested in adequate amounts in early spring or late fall every year so that you keep the plants from spreading all over the place. Cut their tops off in the fall if they don't die back by themselves.

Many perennial herb plants, like the mints and thyme, need a frequent cutback to prevent them from taking over the garden. It's best to keep them away from the vegetable garden, in a place where you can mow around their bed to keep them under control.

Houseplants

Because of the wide variety of houseplants, it would be impossible to list here the precise pruning directions for each. Instead, the general directions that follow apply to most plants, and I'll have a few specific suggestions for the most commonly grown.

Just as with woody outdoor plants, you should always cut or pinch houseplants back to a bud or live branch when pruning so that you don't leave a stub that will die and rot. Do likewise if you are snipping off slips or cuttings to propagate new plants.

Pruning is almost always necessary for shaping houseplants. If your plant is growing straggly, pinch it to stop its leggy growth and encourage some side branches to form. Although blossoming will be delayed a bit, the product is a much better shaped plant. Many window box plants, as well as those that are potted, never look their best because they never get the pinching they need. Coleus, petunias, geraniums, and begonias are just a few of the plants that benefit greatly from regular pinching.

Remember to take off the fading blooms, too. Potted plants, window-box plants, and those in hanging baskets all need to have their old blossoms removed, just as much as the garden flowers do. Removing the old flowers is important to the plant's appearance, and most plants will stop blooming if you allow their blossoms to go to seed.

We also prune our houseplants to rejuvenate them. Many plants benefit from an occasional trimming so that a new, healthy top can replace an aging, less energetic one. The best time to cut back a plant severely is right after the plant finishes blooming. Although your plant may look like a fugitive from the compost pile after the pruning, it will grow into a better shape during the following seasons, and the blooms will be considerably better and more abundant.

Drastic pruning, while beneficial to a Christmas cactus or a geranium, might prove fatal to one of the slower-growing plants. Generally the rule is, the more vigorous-growing a plant is, the more you can cut it back without damage.

Some houseplants, like the rubber plants, jade plants, and certain cacti, grow slowly and can live for many years — sometimes for centuries. Others, like the artillery plant, are short-lived and should be replaced every few years with a new plant. If you know the life expectancy of your plant, you'll be better able to prune it.

Always prune with an eye to your plant's health. Cut off any leaves and stems that are diseased or discolored, whenever they appear. Watch closely for damage and prune off or tape back any part of the plant that is accidentally broken.

You'll find that a sharp knife and small pruning shears are handy tools for cutting those plant parts that are too tough for pinching. When using tools, guard against letting them spread disease among your plants. If you use clippers or a knife on any plant that you suspect might be harboring a disease, sterilize the tool in alcohol, boiling water, or Clorox before using it on another plant. Many diseases, such as botrytis on geraniums, have been spread far and wide by someone who has taken cuttings with a knife carrying infection.

187

Heavy Pruning

Frequent pinching and light pruning will usually eliminate the need for any heavy pruning. Sometimes, however, in spite of our best intentions, a plant will get away from us and grow out of proportion. Houseplants left outside for the summer often do this. So do poinsettias, azaleas, and other woody plants.

Cut back overgrown plants while they are resting, usually in late winter, just before their growing season begins. Then, when they start to grow, the new shoots will quickly cover the cut areas. Most houseplants of the branching variety, like geraniums or ivies, can stand a lot of pruning at that time and recover very quickly, but most heavily pruned plants will look rather sick for a time. Again, always cut back to a live branch or bud, leaving no stubs that could possibly infect the plant. Give newly pruned plants a chance to begin growing before putting on fertilizer, and pinch them to keep them bushy as they grow.

Hanging Baskets

Cascade petunias, ivy geraniums, hanging begonias, hanging fuchsias, and other trailing plants in baskets or sitting on pedestals need a frequent pruning to keep them in shape. Pinch off the ends of runners that are getting too long, snip off parts that are getting too woody, and move around the trailing parts so that the plant doesn't grow lopsided. The accomplished gardener realizes that frequent shearings are as important to the plant as moisture, the right pot size, fertilizer, and light conditions that suit it best. As with other plants, keep the faded flowers picked off so they will bloom for the longest possible time.

Root Pruning

Many plants cannot be top-pruned successfully. The succulents — aloe, echeveria, semperviviums, cactus, sedum, gasteria, and agave, for example — do not heal over properly when cut. Ferns that come directly from the soil cannot be successfully pruned either, nor can palms, dracaena, and many tropical plants. Since you can't allow many of these to grow to their full size if you have limited growing space, you can control their size for many years by cutting back the roots occasionally in much the same way as you would treat a bonsai. Early spring is the best time to root-prune, because the cut ends heal over well, and new growth begins more quickly then.

When you root-prune, first make sure that your plant is just a little damp, since wet soil is messy and dry soil is likely to fall off the roots. Then pop the plant out of its container, and chop off the small roots on the outside just as if you were starting to sharpen a pencil with a jackknife. In fact, a long, sharp kitchen knife is about the best tool for this operation, because clippers tend to crush the root ends too much.

Take off about an inch of roots and soil all around the root ball, being careful not to cut into the thick, fleshy roots. Then repot the plant into good soil, and water it.

Keep any newly potted plant in a sheltered spot for a few days, out of the sun and drafts, while it recovers from the surgery. If it has lost a lot of roots, the remaining ones may not be able to supply enough moisture to the top. Some plant experts feel that it's a good idea to cover the entire plant with a large, transparent plastic bag to retain the moisture while it is recovering. As soon as you see a few new shoots beginning to grow, you'll know that your plant has made it. You can take it out of the "recovery room" and begin to treat it as before.

Pruning for Winter Storage

Many of us like to grow large numbers of begonias, geraniums, chrysanthemums, fuchsias, or similar plants in window boxes or on terraces during the summer. When fall comes, naturally we don't want to throw them away but have no room indoors to use them as houseplants, so we store them in a cool basement or the root cellar for the winter. New gardeners sometimes wonder how to treat their plants in winter storage.

You can leave the plants in their pots, but before you take them into their basement home, allow the soil to get moderately dry. Then prune back the tops to a height of two or three inches, and be sure that the storage room will be cool but not too damp. Check them at least once a month, and when necessary, water them lightly so that they don't ever dry out completely. Don't overwater them, though, since this may cause the plants to rot or mold.

In the spring, when danger of frost is over, you can bring the plants outside again, exposing them gradually to the sun and wind. Prune off any sickly branches, and in a short time they should be thriving again. Best of all, your salvaged plants will have cost you nothing but a little extra care.

Chapter 15

Pruning Bonsai

It takes patience and skill to make a tree that is only a few years old and several inches tall look like a miniature copy of gnarled, 100-year-old specimens growing on a windy, rocky hillside. It is difficult to imagine a more advanced form of pruning than that required by bonsai, the Japanese art of dwarfing shrubs and trees. Bonsai demands precise thinning, pinching, clipping, and root-pruning skills. In fact, many finished bonsai sell for hundreds of dollars a piece, although you can buy started bonsai plants at a much lower price.

Buying a bonsai will save you a lot of time and work, of course, but growing your own can be fun and a most satisfying hobby. Like any form of gardening, however, you never completely finish it. It demands so much patience and attention that you can get a great feeling of achievement from the creation and care of only a few plants. In fact, bonsai plants often become very much the center of attention in the household. We know people who cannot take a vacation without continual concern for the welfare of their green pets.

Although the art of growing large trees in miniature form in outdoor gardens has been cultivated for centuries in Japan and elsewhere, growing tiny bonsai in pots is a more recent practice. Many of the techniques now used for training these specimens have been developed within this past century. The art has spawned many different methods, and a short chapter on the subject is sure to upset any of you who are experts. The guidelines here are simply an introduction to the subject for a beginning grower. A serious fancier should read some books devoted entirely to this complex and fascinating subject.

Choosing Your Specimen

Although working with a skilled bonsai gardener would give anyone a tremendous advantage, the best insurance for good results is to start with a good plant. In theory, any variety of tree can be grown successfully as a bonsai, though some, such as weeping willows and mountain ash, would be very difficult to train. Traditionally, bonsai plants are grown from Japanese or other Oriental species of trees. Although a native Oriental specimen is ideal if the weather conditions are right, this kind of plant may not be the best choice for northern gardeners. Luckily, there are many native varieties of plant life that are well suited for dwarfing.

There is a distinct advantage, especially for a beginning grower, in choosing a variety that is naturally dwarf and slow-growing, and one that is likely to grow well in poor, rocky soil. The height of a mature bonsai should range from a few inches to about three feet. You can use either deciduous or evergreen trees, but choose one with small leaves or short needles, as they will look better proportioned (although the dwarfing process accomplishes this to some degree). Some of the varieties of trees and shrubs most often used for bonsai are: apple, arborvitae, azalea, beech, birch, boxwood, cedar, cherry, cotoneaster, cypress, daphne, elm, flowering cherry, flowering quince, ginkgo, hawthorn, hemlock, Japanese holly, juniper, maple (especially Amur and Japanese maple), dwarf-growing pine (especially mugho and bristlecone), plum, pyracantha, spruce, wisteria, and yew.

Most growers like to start with a tree that is already a bit misshapen, distorted, or stunted, and will search through nursery rows for hours looking for a wierdly shaped transplant or seedling. One-sided growth and a thick trunk at the base are particularly desirable.

Other gardeners put on their hiking shoes and climb up to high elevations near the timberline to search for a plant that has been dwarfed by years of exposure to harsh wind and weather. The best plant you can choose often hides in a small pocket of soil among the rocky crevices because this growing media most closely resembles the small dish of soil in which it will reside in the future.

If you decide to hunt down your own bonsai prospect, you must realize that moving plants from a rocky mountaintop can be a tricky process. You can't just pull up a tree, stuff it in a bag, and take it home expecting it to survive. Although the tree may be only a few inches high, it may have already lived there for several decades, and may not take kindly to being uprooted and transferred to your back porch. Bonsai growers who work with this kind of plant usually try to spread the moving process over a year or more. They know that even though the soil is limited, the plant may have a fairly large root system. Early in the spring, without digging up the plant, they take a sharp knife and carefully prune off a major part of these roots by cutting straight down in the soil around the plant. The following spring, after the tree has grown a few new feeder roots close to its main stem and has become adjusted to its more compact root structure, you can safely move it.

If you don't have the opportunity to search rows of nursery trees or make visits to mountain ranges, you can still grow a bonsai that is exclusively yours. It just may take a little longer. Simply start with a small tree that is 8 to 15 inches tall, because trees larger than that often prove too difficult to work with. Since some plants are sure to grow into a better shape than others, if

191

you're growing your own it's a good idea to start several so that you can choose the best ones for bonsai training.

Containers

The container is as important as the plant in bonsai culture and should be chosen just as carefully. The Japanese seldom use ornate pots for their bonsai because they believe that the plant itself should be the center of attention.

The best kind are shallow, unglazed, and one or more inches deep, and they may be square, round, or oval — whichever shape compliments the plant. Above all, they must have perfect drainage. Although there are a lot of attractive pots on the market, many do not have the necessary large holes in them. It is important that you choose a pot with good drainage, since a plant cannot tolerate sitting in water for even a short time. Place small pieces of wire screen over the holes to prevent the soil from falling out.

Equipment

You can prune the small limbs and delicate roots of bonsai best with special small pruning shears, so owning a pair is advisable if you're serious about bonsai culture. You'll also need some 18- to 20-gauge copper or aluminum wire, a short wooden chopstick or dowel (1/4- to 1/2-inch in diameter) for packing the soil when transplanting, and a pair of large tweezers.

Many garden stores and mail-order houses offer bonsai tools and kits at prices ranging from a few dollars up to expensive assortments that look like a brain surgeon's instrument tray. Start with a simple, but sturdy, basic set of tools.

Soil Mixture

An excellent soil mixture is important for any potted plant, and for bonsai plants it is even more vital because the soil is shallow, and the roots cannot go searching for soil that they prefer. Avoid heavy soil, as it both inhibits the fine hair-root growth that is important for proper feeding of the plant and creates a drainage problem that could cause disease, poor growth, or even drowning.

Although the experts vary the texture of their soil, many beginning bonsai growers use a soil mixture of the following ingredients. (Measures are by volume and not by weight.)

1/3 good, dry garden soil

1/3 sharp sand

1/3 peat moss, composted bark, or well-rotted leaf mold

Add 1 tablespoon dried cow, sheep, or poultry manure per quart of mixture.

Add 1 tablespoon lime, unless you are working with acid-loving plants such as azalea, hemlock, or pine.

Mix the ingredients thoroughly, since you'll be using small amounts and

Trees grown according to the Japanese aesthetic are pruned to look old and weathered.

193

each pot must have a balanced mixture. Sift it all through a screen to strain out stones, weeds, worms, plant roots, and big lumps.

Planting

Early spring is the best time of year to pot your plant, because it can best stand the shock of being root-pruned at that time. The wounds heal more quickly, and new root growth will soon begin.

First, remove most of the soil from the root ball so that you can better see where to prune. It will probably be necessary to cut off a lot of the root system before you can fit the root ball into the container. Try to leave as many fibrous hair roots as possible, because they are most essential to the plant. Whenever you can, cut the fleshy taproots instead, taking some out entirely and shortening the others until the root ball fills about half of the pot. Don't allow the roots to dry out. Dip them in water occasionally while you're working on them.

Cover the bottom of the pot with the sifted soil, and carefully spread out the roots. Gently place the soil among them, tamping it with the dowel so there will be no air pockets left. Continue to fill the pot with soil, but leave about a 3/8-inch space at the top so that future waterings won't overflow the pot.

Pruning

Before you start to prune a new plant, decide on the way in which you want it to grow. A good bonsai designer has a mental picture of the finished tree when he starts the training, just as a good artist envisions his finished painting before the first stroke. If you are not familiar with the range of possibilities, it's a good idea to study photographs of bonsai or attend a flower show to grasp a feeling for the way the professional growers do it.

Begin the top pruning by first thinning out part of the branches to make the plant look old. Then cut back the remaining limbs according to your bonsai plan. Make all cuts close to the trunk, and if large cuts are necessary, concave them into the trunk slightly so that the depressed wound will heal over more quickly. Treat all the wounds with a tree paint or sealer, so they will heal better.

Finally, after you finish the top pruning, water the plant heavily, and cover the entire plant with a clear plastic bag. Set it in a cool place where it will get plenty of light but no direct sun, and leave it there for two or three weeks while it recoups.

Training

Some bonsai fanciers like to begin their training soon after planting, while others prefer to wait several months or even a year to first let it get well established in the pot. Train evergreens in the fall or winter during their dormant season and deciduous trees in early summer when the sap is flowing and they are flexible. If you shape them in the spring before they begin to grow, the tender, dormant buds are too likely to be damaged; wait until the buds begin to grow so that you can wire around them without danger.

For shaping trees with fairly heavy trunks you will need 8- or 9-gauge wire. Stick it through the holes in the bottom of the pot to anchor it and then wrap it around the tree, spiraling it upward at about a 45-degree twist. Place bits of paper under the wire to protect trees with especially tender bark. As you wire, bend the tree to the desired shape. The wire will hold it.

You can use a lighter wire, of either 18- or 20-gauge, for trees with smaller trunks and for shaping the branches and tops of larger trees. Bend down the branches to create the aging look, but don't distort the plant too much as you shape it. A century ago, the more grotesque the bonsai, the more prized it was, but today most growers prefer to create more natural-looking plants.

After the plant has grown accustomed to growing in its new shape, remove the wires. On deciduous trees this can usually be done about three or four months after wiring. Leave the wires on evergreens much longer, sometimes as long as a year. Don't leave the wire on any longer than is necessary,

194

however, or the tree may begin to grow around it, permanently disfiguring the trunk.

As the plant starts to grow, pinch off sprouts growing in the wrong places, and trim back branches that are growing too long. You might like to choose one side of your bonsai as the front, and make this the old-looking, thinned-out side. In this way you can allow the back side of the tree to have a slightly denser growth to give body to the plant, and to produce additional leaf surface for healthy growth.

Some growers like to allow one limb near the bottom of the plant to grow freely while they are in the process of training the rest of the plant. This limb uses most of the plant's energy and makes the shaping of the remainder of the tree easier. After the training is complete, the untrained limb can be carefully clipped off and the resulting wound kept sealed or painted until it has healed.

A fleshy, old, weathered trunk is often a feature of bonsai. One way to develop this is to plant your potential bonsai in a deep pot for a year or so. Bury the fibrous roots in good soil in the bottom of the pot, but allow the upper part of the root and the lower section of the trunk to grow in shredded sphagnum moss. Keep both soil and moss moist. After a year, pull away the moss and check the stem. If it is developing the right appearance, gradually begin to remove the moss. This root will now be a part of the trunk, and it will soon weather into an ancient look. You can also use this method to grow bonsai with long, rootlike stems that trail over rocks.

You can plant a short-growing moss around your tree for a woodland effect. It's better not to apply a mulch or allow leaves to accumulate on the soil, as this makes it difficult to see when the plant needs water and also provides a place for harmful insects to breed.

Care

Whether you buy a bonsai plant or develop a specimen entirely by yourself, you should be aware that even after the training period is over, bonsai need far more care than other plants. Because of their small containers and the tiny amount of soil available to them, it's necessary to water them daily, and perhaps even more often if the plants are exposed to hot, dry air. Perhaps you can convince a neighbor to join you in the hobby so you'll have a backup if you decide to take a holiday away from home.

Watering must always be done sparingly, since overwatering can ruin a bonsai in short order. Check the drainage holes frequently to see that root growth or hardening soil has not sealed them shut.

An occasional light feeding of fish emulsion, or a tiny amount of dried cow manure added to the water will be all the fertilizer they need. Fast growth may be desirable in your corn patch, but it is definitely not your goal in a bonsai.

Keep an eye out for possible insect damage, as you'd do with any planting, and give the foliage a light dusting of rotenone should potential pests appear.

Repotting

Every few years your bonsai will become root-bound. You can check to see by gently tipping the tree out of its container and inspecting the roots. If the bottom of the soil ball is a thick, tight mass of roots, it's time to repot the tree. Ordinarily, deciduous trees need to be repotted every year or two, and evergreens need repotting every four or five years.

After you have carefully taken the tree out of the pot, wash most of the soil off the roots by swishing them gently in a tub of water. Clip off about a third of the roots growing at the outside of the root ball. Then, reach in and cut out part of the large, fleshy roots, making sure first that they are not attached to large masses of fibrous roots.

Replant the tree in the same pot in the same method as for the original planting, using a fresh batch of the same mixture described earlier. Then water the tree thoroughly, and cover it with a clear plastic bag. Keep it in a cool place out of direct sun for two or three weeks, just as before.

Special Considerations

Keep in mind that just because your bonsai is alive and growing in a pot, it isn't an ordinary houseplant. Most plants grown as bonsai are trees that are found outside in a temperate climate, and do best on a sunny, open, yet protected porch. You can take it inside the house for short periods and even grow it in a sunny window in spring and early summer, but by middle or late summer, depending upon where you live, it should go outside to get ready for its dormant season.

Most bonsai need a cool spot to spend the winter, and their dormancy shouldn't be interrupted by taking the plant into a warm room for Christmas. Choose the winter quarters with care. Since the roots must always be able to reach moisture, the plant should not freeze hard for extended periods. Some growers bury the pots in moist peat moss in a cold frame where the plants will be cool but won't freeze. Others store them in a cool greenhouse or even in a garage that does not get too cold.

In milder climates they can be kept outdoors all winter, but they still must never be allowed to dry out.

A bonsai plant is really more pet than plant, and just like a puppy, cat, or hamster, it needs daily attention. Unless you are sure you can give the time and attention a bonsai requires, you would be better off with a philodendron.

Chapter 16

Pruning Forest Trees

If you live in a rural area, you may be lucky enough to own a few acres of land that you don't want to cultivate or use as a pasture. Years ago, when land was cheap, nobody minded having a little wasted land, but today's prices for real estate and the resulting taxes thereon, make us all feel that we should be getting a little extra income out of those back forty, or four, acres.

As the price of land has risen, the price of forest products has gone up too. Many homesteaders are now spending part of their spare time cashing in on the demand for firewood, pulpwood, lumber, posts, poles, railroad ties, fence rails, Christmas trees, evergreen boughs, or maple syrup. Sometimes there are even tax advantages in harvesting your forest products, since some of that income can be treated as capital gains. You might want to investigate this possibility if you plan to harvest a lot of Christmas trees at one time, or sell all of your lumber at once.

Forests are one of our few renewable resources. A carefully managed forest can yield a crop forever. Tree roots get part of their nourishment from far down in the subsoil, and if you harvest the trees properly and don't allow the cut areas to erode, tree farming won't deplete the topsoil at all. This is quite different from most agricultural projects. You should never feel guilty about cutting down a tree if you allow another good tree to grow in its place. This is what good forestry is all about.

Good forest management is something new in this country. Although our predecessors carefully tended their herds and pruned their orchards, they cut down the good trees and left the poor ones, leaving the woods to regrow naturally. Unfortunately, good woodlands often grew up to poor, worthless trees.

Now, fortunately, that policy is changing. People realize that it is usually better to harvest a light crop of lumber, pulp, or wood every few years than to clear-cut off one big crop every 70 or 80 years. The woods are much healthier too, if the old, leaning, and diseased trees are removed regularly.

Pruning Christmas Trees

Natural Christmas trees are again popular, as the public has grown less enchanted with a plastic and tinsel world. Growing these trees is becoming an important farming operation in many parts of the country, and some plantations cover thousands of acres. Scotch pine, balsam fir, white spruce, Norway spruce, and blue spruce are all widely grown for Christmas trees in the East, while Douglas fir is more popular in the West.

A few years ago, a cry went up that it was not ecologically sound to cut a tree for the holidays. However, Christmas trees, like forest trees, are a renewable crop, and no one should feel guilty about using a natural tree. It is often pointed out that producing an artificial tree takes far more of nature's unrenewable resources and more energy than growing many real ones. Furthermore, Christmas trees can be grown on worn-out land that is quite unsuitable for other crops, and the trees aid in keeping the land semiopen. They also prevent erosion and provide cover for wildlife and birds.

Christmas trees are also a good source of income for small farm owners and homesteaders, offering a quick return for a modest investment. Compared to the harvesting of timber, growing and cutting Christmas trees takes little capital in terms of equipment. Seedling trees are cheap to buy, though many growers prefer to use four-year-old transplants, planting them five feet apart. Many of these can be cut within seven years.

All Christmas trees need some pruning and shearing to grow into premium trees. Begin to shear them as soon as they are about two feet high, and making their fastest growth — usually in May or June in the North. Follow the directions for shearing evergreens given in Chapter 7.

As with ornamentals, the purpose of your shearing is to get every tree to grow into a tight, bushy shape. Some fast-growing pines will probably need an annual shearing to accomplish this, although the slower-growing firs and spruces usually require it only once every two or three years. This means that you may have to shear them only three times before they are harvested. Either shearing knives, clippers, or hedge shears can be used for the job. Commercial tree growers often use power equipment, since all the shearing should be finished before the trees stop growing and the new terminal buds form on the ends of the branches.

As the trees grow taller, the lowest branches should be pruned off to a height of about a foot from the ground, or up to the first good circle of branches. This basal pruning makes cutting and handling much easier, and leaves a good, smooth trunk suited for a tree stand. Sometimes, tall, spindly, wild trees are basal-pruned up to a third of their height in order to force additional growth into their upper branches. This thickens them up and they soon become salable trees.

Pruning for Greens Production

Just as the use of natural Christmas trees has grown, so has the use of natural evergreen boughs. Greens are used in great amounts at Christmas, of course, and also are popular in Memorial Day wreaths, grave blankets, and for general floral work.

Not long ago, greens were often collected by cutting down large trees. Now, most of the boughs are clipped from small and medium-size living trees grown especially for the purpose, just as orchards are planted for producing fruit or nuts.

Balsam fir is the leading evergreen grown for greens in the Northeast, eastern Canada, and the North Central states. Holly is widely grown in the Pacific Northwest, while pines, spruce, cypress, arborvitae, boxwood, and many broadleafed evergreens are grown in various parts of the country.

The harvesting of greens is not limited to a few big producers. Many small farms and homesteads are using their poorer land to grow greens too. Some small operators sell greens in large bundles or bales to city markets, while others process them into wreaths, roping, sprays, centerpieces, or corsages. They either sell them locally or wholesale them to stores, florist shops, and garden centers. Greens are also marketed in large quantities to distillers who produce oils used in fragrances, medicines, and other products.

If you decide to plant a brush orchard, space the trees eight feet apart or more each way, leaving adequate roads so that trucks can get in. Sometimes

199

Such trees with two or more tops should be turned into firewood, as they occupy valuable space and are of little value.

you can thin out wild trees to approximately the same spacing. When the tree reaches a height of about four feet, prune off the top to encourage the production of many short, bushy, side branches rather than a few long, thin ones. As early as the following year, you can make a light cutting. As the tree fills out, more greens will be ready to harvest. Whenever you cut the brush, always cut back the top of the tree so you can keep it to a height of about five feet for easier harvesting.

We've set up a rotation program in our balsam fir lot so that each tree gets a clipping only once every two or three years. The length of time between cuttings will depend, of course, on the vigor of the species being grown. Do all your harvesting carefully with an eye to future crops, and, as with all pruning, remove no more than a quarter to a third of the tree's green material at any one time.

The timing of the harvest is critical. We never plan a vacation during this season, because the trees must always be cut close to the time when you plan to use them or put them in cold storage. Greens cut too early will soon lose their fresh look. Don't cut at all until the tree has stopped growing completely and all the green material is properly hardened in late fall. It usually takes a few hard frosts before the conifers are ready. Large grain or citrus-pulp bags, boxes, or cardboard barrels make handy containers for moving the greens and for storing them out of the wind and sun until you pack or use them.

Pruning for Maple Syrup Production

It takes nearly half a lifetime, 30 years or more, to grow a maple tree that's large enough to be tapped and its sap collected in the spring. It also takes 35 to 50 gallons of sap to make either 1 gallon of maple syrup or eight pounds of sugar. So you can see that starting a sugaring business from scratch is not at all like getting into the business of raising bees or chickens. But pruning goes a long way toward improving the sap production. It is also important to cut out trees that compete with your sugar maples for light and soil.

Although trees grown for lumber should be as close as 12 to 14 feet apart to encourage tall, straight growth for lumber, sugar maples produce better if they have more branches. Your maple trees shouldn't be permitted to grow in clumps, either. They are not as productive that way, and are much harder to fell after the tree has passed its prime. Space each mature tree about 35 to 45 feet apart. You should always allow a few young trees to grow, so they can eventually replace the older ones, but remove all extra trees to encourage large limb growth. Trees cut out of the sugar bush may be used for firewood, either for your own use or for boiling the sap.

Small sap testers are now available, so a maple producer can test the sugar content of each tree during the sugaring season, and then cut out the less-sweet trees while doing the thinning. If only the sweetest trees are left, much less boiling will be necessary to evaporate water from the sap, and the seedlings that grow from the sweeter trees will also tend to produce sweet sap.

Some woodlot owners like to produce both syrup and high-quality maple lumber from the same lot, so they compromise and grow the trees closer together. The shade of the maple is so dense that trees may be grown 20 feet apart. Much less sap will be produced per tree, of course, but since there will be more trees producing, the difference in total yield will not be tremendous.

Basal pruning is seldom necessary on maples, but you should remove any lower limbs on trees grown in the open if they interfere with gathering the sap. Take out any dying or broken trees so that disease and insects won't incubate in them. Brush and small limbs that are left from the cutting create no difficulty, since they will rot in the damp woods within a year or two, lending fertility to the soil.

Index

A

Acer. See Maples
Actinidia, 174
Adventuresome buds. See
  Dormant buds
Aegopodium, 179
Aesculus. See Horse chestnut
Ajuga, 179
Akebia, 174, 179
Almonds, 164, 165
American elm, 38
American hazelnut, 167
Amur maple. See Maples,
  Amur
Apples, 7, 103
    growth patterns of, 38,
    113
    thinning fruit on, 30
    varieties of, 134–39
Apricots, 103, 139
    thinning fruit on, 30
Arborvitae (Thuja), 7, 16, 38,
  79
      American, 95
      for archway, 92
      for topiary, 101
Archway, making of, 92
Arctostaphylos Uva-ursi, 179
Aristolochia durior, 174
Armeria, 179

Artichokes, Jerusalem, 186
Asarum, 179
Ash (Fraximus), 73
    buds on, 25
    mountain, 48
Asparagus, 186
Asphalt compounds, for filling
    cavity, 71
Asters, 29, 185
Avocados, 145–46
Azaleas, 43, 86, 87

B

Balm of Gilead, 74
Balsam fir, 199
Bamboo, 86
Barberry (Berberis), 90, 96, 97
Bark, colored, 61
Basal pruning, 26–29, 37
      of shade trees, 65–67
Baskets, hanging, 188
Basswood (Tilia), 74
Bay laurel, 86
Bearberries, 179
Beeches, 61, 73
Begonias, 29
Beheading, of tree, 11, 30–31
Berberis. See Barberry
Betula. See Birches
Bignonia, 175

Birches, 37, 38, 61
    varieties of, 72
Bishop's weed, 179
Bitternut, 167
Bittersweet, 174
Blackberries, 30, 156–60
Black knot, 145
Black walnuts, 165–66
Bleeding-heart, wild, 179
Blood trumpet, 177
Blooms, faded, removal of, 54
Blueberries (Vaccinium), 11,
    30, 152–54
      as ground cover, 181
Bonsai, 36, 190–96
      choosing plant, 190–91
      containers for, 192
      soil mixture, 192–93
Borers, 9
Bow saw, for pruning, 15
Boxwood (Buxus), 16, 90, 94
      for topiary, 101
Boysenberries, 156
Bracing, of weak limbs, 70–71
Bramble fruits, 156–60
Bridal wreath, 37
Buckeyes, 72
Buckthorn, 97
Buddleia, 38
Buds, types of, 21

203

Bugleweed, 179
Bush fruits, 11, 151–55
Butternuts, 165
Buxus. See Boxwood

C

Cabbage roses, 58
Calluna vulgaris, 179
Camellias, 87, 88, 105
Campsis, 176
Carnations, 29
Carpenter's saws, for pruning, 15
Carpinus. See Hornbeam
Carya. See Hickories
Castanea. See Chestnuts
Cat's claw creeper, 177
Cavity, filling of, 71
Cedar, white (*Thuja*), 95
204 *Celastrus,* 174
Cerastium tomentosum, 179
Chain saw, for pruning, 16, 19
Cherries, 30, 103, 113, 139
Chestnuts, 166
    horse. *See* Horse chestnut
Chinese chestnut, 166
Chinese elm, 95, 101
Christmas trees, 198
Chrysanthemums, 183–84
    disbudding of, 29
Citrus fruits, 103, 140
Clematis, 10, 38, 172, 176–77
Clippers. *See* Pruners
Compensatory pruning. *See* Pruning, when transplanting
Conifers, 11, 76
Convallaria majalis, 179
Coralberry, 62
Cordons, 105–6
Coreopsis, 179
Cork tree, 74
Cornus. See Dogwood
Coronilla varia, 179
Cortland apples, 134
Corylus. See Filberts
Cotoneaster, 11, 49, 62, 97
    for espalier, 105

for ground cover, 179
for topiary, 101
Crab apple (*Malus*), 4, 30, 48
    as barrier hedge, 96
    for espalier, 105
Cranberries, bog, 154
Cranberries, highbush, 3, 50, 154
Crape myrtle, 38
Crataegus. See Hawthorns
Creosote, 71
Cross vine, 175
Crown vetch, 179
Currants, 11, 154–55
Cuts
    angle of, 24
    large, 25–26
    location of, 23–24
Cydonia oblonga. See Quinces
Cypress, 79, 101

D

Dahlias, 29, 183
Dead wood, removal of, 24
Dehorning. *See* Beheading
Delicious apples, 134, 139
Delphiniums, 184
Deutzia, 62
Dewberries, 156
Dicentra eximia, 179
Disbudding, 29
Disease, controlling by pruning, 9–10, 132
Distictis buccinatoria, 177
Dogwood (*Cornus*), 61–62
    red-twigged, 49, 61
Dormant buds, 21
Dressings, tree, 18
Duchess of Oldenberg apples, 135
Dutchman's-pipe, 174
Dwarfing, of standard trees, 7, 82–83, 127–28

E

Early McIntosh apples, 135
Elderberries, 155

Electric shears, for hedges, 16, 92
    safety tips for, 19
Elm (*Ulmus*)
    American, 38
    Chinese, 95, 101
Empire apples, 135
English fences, 106
Epimedium grandiflorum, 179
Equipment. *See* Tools
Erica carnea, 179
Espalier, 7, 103–5
Euonymus, 49, 61, 177, 180
Euphorbia, 180
Evergreens, 75–88
    broadleafed, 11, 36, 86–88
    classes of, 75–76
    dwarf, 81–83
    growth of, 79–80
    narrow-leafed, 83–84
    shaping of, 80–81
    shearing of, 76–78, 79

F

Fagus. See Beeches
Felling, of tree, 40–42
Ficus carica. See Figs
Figs, 103, 140–41
Filberts, 164, 167
Fire blight, 132, 143, 145
Fire thorn (*Pyracantha*), 49, 97, 101, 105
Firs, 16, 79, 80
Fleece flower, 180
Flower garden, pruning of, 182–85
Forsythia, 105
Fragaria. See Strawberries
Fraximus. See Ash
Fruit trees, 7, 36, 108–46
    for cordons, 105
    disease and, 10, 132
    dwarf, 127
    dwarfing of, 127–28
    for espalier, 103
    grafting of, 132–33

multiple-variety, 133–34
renewal of, 11, 129–32
ringing of, 128
root pruning of, 35, 128
shaping of, 112–16
thinning of fruit on, 29–30, 117–18
winter injury to, 126
Fuchsias, 105, 185

G
Galium mollugo, 180
Gardenias, 88
Gardening, as mental therapy, 12
Geranium, ivy, 180
Ginger, wild, 179
Ginkgo, 73
Girdling, of branch, 9–10
Gleditsia. See Honey locust
Gloves, use of, 19
Gooseberries, 11, 30, 154–55
Goutweed, 179
Grafts, on fruit trees, 108, 132–33
Grannie Smith apples, 135
Grapefruits, 140
Grapes, 38, 103, 147–51, 172, 177
thinning fruit on, 30
Greens production, 198–200
Ground covers, 178–81
Growth patterns, of trees, 38

H
Hard hat, use of, 19
Hawthorns *(Crataegus),* 48, 96, 105
Hazelnut, American, 167
Heath, spring, 179
Heather, Scotch, 179
Hedera. See Ivy
Hedges, 89–99
annual, 99
as barriers, 95–96
flower- and berry-producing, 96–97

formal, 94–95
low-maintenance, 97–99
planting, 90
shapes of, 93
shearing of, 90–93
Hedge shears, 16, 17
Hemlock *(Tsuga),* 7, 16
for archway, 92
creeping, 38
growing season of, 79
for hedge, 95
shape of, 80
for topiary, 101
Hen-and-chickens, 181
Hibiscus, 29, 38, 87
Hickories, 167–68
Hill system, of growing strawberries, 161
Holly *(Ilex),* 86, 87, 94
for greens, 199
for topiary, 101
Holly apples, 135
Hollygrape, 86
Hollyhocks, 184
Honeygold apples, 135
Honey locust, 73, 96
Honeysuckle, 10, 37, 97, 172, 175
as ground cover, 180
Hops, 174
Hornbeam, 73
Horse chestnut, 72
Horseradish, 186
Hosta, 180
Houseplants, 186–89
root pruning of, 35–36, 188
Humulus Lupulus, 174
Hydrangea, 10, 38, 43, 62
climbing, 172, 177, 180
as hedge, 97
pruning of, 53
Hypericum, 97, 180

I
Ilex. See Holly

Internodal buds. *See* Dormant buds
Ivy, 177
Boston, 172
English, 101, 172, 180

J
Japanese chestnut, 166
Japanese gardens, 106–7
Japanese holly, 90, 94
Japanese rose, 61
Jasmine, 62, 86
Jersey Mac apples, 135
Jerusalem artichokes, 186
Jonagold apples, 135
Jonamac apples, 135
Jonathan apples, 135
Juglans. See Walnuts
Juglans dieback, 166
Junipers, 38, 76
creeping, 82, 180
growing season of, 79

K
Kadsura japonica, 174–75
Kerria japonica, 61
Knife, shearing. *See* Machete
Kniffen system, of grape growing, 149–50
Kochia, 99
Kudzu, 175, 181

L
Ladder, use of, 19
Larch, 76
Lateral buds, 21
Laurel, 105
Lavender, 62
Leader, of fruit tree, 114–15
Lemons, 140
Leucothoe, 86
Life stages, of plant, 38–40
Ligustrum. See Privet
Lilacs *(Syringa),* 10, 37, 43, 52–55
as hedge, 97
tree, 48

205

Lily-of-the-valley, 179
Lime, garden, as fertilizer, 54
Limes, 140
Linden, 74
Liquidambar, 62
Liriodendron Tulipifera. See
   Tulip tree
Lobo apples, 135
Lodi apples, 135
Lombardy poplar, 38, 39, 74
Lonicera. See Honeysuckle
Loppers, for pruning, 15, 17
Lorette pruning, 124

M
Macfadyena, 177
Machete, for shearing, 16–18,
   19
McIntosh apples, 136
206 Macoun apples, 136
Magnolias, 88, 105
Magnolia vine, 175
Malus. See Crab apple
Mangos, 146
Manure, as fertilizer, 54
Maples *(Acer),* 37, 61
   Amur, 49, 101
   buds on, 25
   for topiary, 101
   varieties of, 72
Maple syrup production,
   200–201
Marigolds, 185
Matted-row system, of
   growing strawberries, 161
Melba apples, 136
Melrose apples, 137
Mexican firebush *(Kochia),* 99
Mildew, 9
Milton apples, 137
Mockernut, 167
Mock orange, 97
Morning glory, 172
Morus alba, 62
Moss roses, 58
Mountain laurel, 86, 87
Mulberry, 62

Mutsu apples, 137
Myrtle, 181

N
Nectarines, 30, 141–42
Ninebark, 16, 90, 95
   for topiary, 101
Northern Spy apples, 137–38

O
Oak, 74
Oil, on tools, 19–20
Oleander, 86
Olives, 86, 146
Oranges, 140
   mock, 97
Ornamentals. *See* Shrubs,
   flowering; Trees, flowering
Overpruning, dangers of, 42

P
Pachysandra, 180
Paint, tree. *See* Tree paint
Pansies, 185
Papayas, 146
Parthenocissus tricuspidata.
   See Ivy, Boston
Peaches, 103, 141–42
   thinning fruit on, 30
Pears, 30, 103, 113, 142–44
Pecans, 167, 168
Pelargonium peltatum, 180
Peonies, 29
Perennial food garden,
   pruning of, 185–86
Periwinkle, 181
Persian walnuts, 168–69
Petunias, 185
Phellodendron amurense, 74
Philadelphus, 97
Phlox, 180
Photosynthesis, 42
Physocarpus. See Ninebark
Picea. See Spruce
Pignut, 167
Pinching, of branch tips, 29

Pine, 16
   bristlecone, 39
   growing season of, 79
   mugho, 82
   shape of, 80
   white, 7
Pitch, on tools, 20
Plane tree, 74
Plantain lily, 180
Platanus, 74
Plums, 103, 113, 144–45
   flowering, 97
   as hedge, 96
   thinning fruit on, 30
Poinsettia, 88
Pole pruner, 15, 17
Pole saws, for pruning, 15, 17
Polygonum, 175, 180
Pomegranates, 146
Poplar, 74
   Lombardy, 38, 39, 74
Potentilla, 10, 38, 47
Potted trees, 7
Prima apples, 138
Priscilla apples, 138
Privet, 16, 90, 94–95
   for topiary, 101
Pruners, 15, 17
Pruning. *See also* Cuts;
   Shearing
   for appearance, 8–9. *See*
     also Topiary
   artistic, 100–107
   to control size, 7–8, 35,
     82–83, 118–19, 127–28
   for fruit production, 9,
     50, 117–18, 128–29
   for health, 9–12, 50–52,
     85–86, 119–20
   Lorette, 124
   methods of, 21–42
     basal, 26–29, 37, 65–67
     beheading, 30–31
     disbudding, 29
     pinching, 29
     shearing, 22–23, 76–78,
       79, 90–93

over-, 42
reasons for, 3, 7–12, 109–23
root, 31–36, 128, 188
timing of, 36–38, 123–25
tools for, 14–20
to train young tree, 7, 64–67, 112–16, 164–65
when transplanting, 4–6, 45–48, 109–12, 164
by wildlife, 1, 10
Pueraria lobata, 175, 181
Pyracantha. See Fire thorn
Pyrus communis. See Pears

Q

Quercus. See Oak
Quinces, 30, 103, 145
Quinte apples, 138

R

Raspberries, 3, 156–60
everbearing, 159–60
Red Astrachan apples, 138
Red Duchess apples, 138
Regent apples, 138
Rhamnus, 97
Rhode Island Greening apples, 138
Rhododendrons, 43, 86, 87
Rhubarb, 186
Ribes. See Currants; Gooseberries
Ringing, of fruit tree, 128
Rome Beauty apples, 138
Root pruning, 31–36, 128, 188
Oklahoma method, 32
Rose hips, 59
Rosemary, 181
Roses, 36, 47, 55–60, 97
climbing, 59–60, 172
disbudding of, 29
floribundas, 58
hedges, 60, 91, 96
polyanthus, 58
rambler, 59, 172
shrub, 58

tea, 57
tree, 60
Rugosa roses, 58, 59

S

Safety, 18–19
Salix. See Willow
Sanitation, when pruning fruit trees, 132
Saws, for pruning, 15–16, 17
Scale, 9
Schisandra propinqua, 175
Sedum, 181
Seeds, energy needed to produce, 30, 54
Sempervivum tectorum, 181
Sharpening, of tools, 19
Shearing, 22–23
of evergreens, 76–78, 79
of hedges, 90–93
Shears, 16–18
Shoes, for tree climbing, 26
Shrubs, berry-producing, 11, 49, 61
Shrubs, flowering, 7
choosing, 43–45
planting of, 45–48
pruning of, 48–52
Silver lace vine, 175
Size, of plant, controlling by pruning, 7–8, 35, 82–83, 118–19, 127–28
Snips. *See* Pruners
Snowberry, 62
Snow-in-summer, 179
Soaking, of bare-rooted stock, 45
Sorbus. See Elderberries
Spade, nursery, 17, 18
Spartan apples, 138
Spijon apples, 138
Spireas, 37, 47
Spruce, 16, 79, 80
blue, 3–4
for hedge, 95, 96
for topiary, 101

Staking, in artistic pruning, 101
Star jasmine, 175
Stayman's Winesap apples, 138
Strawberries, 30, 34, 160–61, 180
Stump, removal of, 42
Succulents, root pruning of, 188
Suckers, 10, 48, 120–21
Sunscald, of fruit trees, 126
Sweetbriers, 58
Sycamore, 74
Symphoricarpos, 62

T

Tamarisk, 38, 62
Tamarix parviflora, 38, 62
Taxodium, 76
Taxus. See Yews
Terminal buds, 21
Thrift, 179
Thuja. See Arborvitae; Cedar, white
Thyme, 181
Tickseed, 179
Tilia, 74
Tipping, of bramble fruits, 157
Tools, for pruning, 14–20
care of, 19–20
power, 14
pruners, 15, 17
saws, 15–16, 17
shears, 16, 17, 92
Topiary, 101–3
Trachelospermum jasminoides, 175
Training, of young tree, 7, 64–67, 112–16, 164–65
See also Espalier; Topiary
Transplanting
pruning when, 4–6, 45–48, 109–12, 164
root pruning before, 33, 34–35

Tree(s)
    felling of, 40–42
    fruit. *See* Fruit trees
    growth patterns of, 38
    parts of, 5
Tree(s), Christmas, 198
Tree(s), flowering, 45–48
Tree(s), forest, 197–201
Tree(s), nut, 162–69
    taproot, 163
Tree(s), shade, 63–74
    choosing of, 72–74
    mature, 69–70
    shapes of, 67–69
    young, 64–67
Tree paint, 10, 18
Tree surgery, 70–72
Tree-topping. *See* Beheading
Trumpet creeper, 176
208 Trunks, protection of, 10
Tsuga. See Hemlock
Tulip tree, 73
Twenty Ounce apples, 138

U
Ulmus. See Elm

Undercut, when removing
    large branches, 26

V
Vaccinium. See Blueberries
Veronica, 181
Viburnum, 11, 45, 49
    as hedge, 97
Viking apples, 139
Vinca minor, 181
Vines, 170–81
    annual, 178
    clinging, 175–77
    planting, 171
    training, 172
    twining, 174–75
Violet, 181
Virginia creeper, 177, 180
Vitality, of plant, pruning
    method and, 39
Vitis. See Grapes

W
Walnuts, 165–66, 168–69
Water sprouts, 10, 120

Wealthy apples, 139
Weather conditions, pruning
    and, 36
Weigela, 48, 62
White bedstraw, 180
Wildlife, pruning by, 1, 10
Willow, 38, 74
Windbreak, pruning for, 12,
    84–85
Winesap apples, 139
Winter injury, to fruit trees,
    126
Wisteria, 175

Y
Yellow Delicious apples, 139
Yellow Transparent apples,
    139
Yews, 76, 79, 95
    spreading, 82
    for topiary, 101
York Imperial apples, 139
Youngberries, 156

Z
Zinnias, 29